Leadership in Management

LEADERSHIP
IN
MANAGEMENT

Barry Maude

BUSINESS BOOKS ᒲᒧ

COMMUNICA - EUROPA

First published 1978

ISBN 0 220 66361 0

Printed by Thomson Litho Ltd., East Kilbride, Scotland.
Bound by Mansell Bookbinders Limited, Witham, Essex.
For the publishers, Business Books Limited,
24 Highbury Crescent, London N5.

Contents

*Status-stripping — Stages of maturity — Predicting
the leader's performance — Leaders at different
levels — Identifying leaders — Individualistic leaders
the best? — Formidable individuals — New kinds of
leadership — Task determines management style? —
Subtler methods needed — Range of styles — Ten
roles*

*Change-lovers — Lone-wolf leaders — 'Balanced'
management — Leading by example — Most managers
are administrators — Opportunity-seeking — Fitting
in — Avoiding change — Faceless companies — Is
leadership an art? — The group's representative —
Taking personal risks — Opportunism — Non-con-
formists — Trend-setting — Leadership on the board
— Information challenge — Continuous reform —
Stimulating innovation — Losing market-grip —
'Doomed to failure' — Creating a favourable climate
— The innovative organisation — Control over projects
— Marketing arrangements — The cautious approach —
Shortage of investment capital*

*Mistakes allowed — Making leaders feel strong —
Strong new direction — Clear-cut authority —
Structural reforms — Building strong leaders
via decentralisation — Centralisation and
control — Keeping track of the money — Stay-
small strategy — Production cells — Self-control
possible — Vulnerable to stoppages — Flexible
leaders*

*Boosting self-confidence — Checklist — Wrestling
with real problems — General management jobs
— Leaders in leader-development — Ways and
means — Experience-based development —
Executive interchange — New style MBO —
Adaptable leaders — Top-level involvement —
Action-centred leadership — Learning-by-doing —
Leaders are grown — Key factors in a leader's
development — Changing specialists into
generalists — Formal training — New perspectives
— Widespread cynicism — Disadvantages — Useful
courses — Sensitivity training — Role-playing*

*Hard-line hazards — When pressure gets results —
A hard-driving style — When times are lean, get
tough and mean — Leading a new company*

*Social leader — 'Primarily a communicator' —
Top leaders isolated? — Keeping communication
lines open — Shop-floor leader — Bridging the
perception gap — Affable leaders — Employees
prefer communicative leaders — The leader as
therapist — Roaming the plant — First-line
leaders — Useful techniques — Informal networks
— Pumping information downwards — Information
and productivity — Leader's duty — Communicating
the plan of campaign — Going down the chain —
Gauging information needs — How to avoid information distortion — Reliable sources — Presentation methods — Communication is a technique*

*Control of money and materials — Control of pro-
duction costs — Financial nit-picking — Control by
budget — Budgeting — Keeping systems simple —
Forward budgeting — Prompt information for
tighter control — Applying the controls — Technical leaders — Control information — Corrective
actions — Operating reports — Accuracy essential
— Control and coordination of people — Multi-
national companies — Liaison leadership — Controlling from a distance — Control-selective involvement — Control via delegation — Reports on progress
— Control of time — Fragmentation — Creating time
— Delegation*

*'Hard' information — Avoiding indecision — The
four-stage method — Jury-of-executive-opinion —
Inter-related decisions — The 'impact of decisions'
— The time-span of decisions — High-quality in-
formation — How much information is enough? —
Styles of decision-making — Irrational decisions —
Self-interest*

Foreword

by D.A.S. Plastow
Group Managing Director
Rolls-Royce Motors Limited

Leadership is one of those things which is almost impossible to pin down in words but which everyone recognises when they see it. The manager — particularly the senior executive — finds his business and himself subjected to conflicting pressures and influences. Governments interfere more and more; employees — rightly — expect to be more involved in the organisation they work for; products get more complex; consumers are more informed and more demanding. To succeed, a business needs a clear sense of direction and that comes from leaders who show by example that they are committed to success.

In Rolls-Royce Motors we believe in setting our managers challenging targets and rewarding them well for success. We also believe in communication within the company — upwards and downwards — which this book identifies as a crucial aspect of successful leadership.

Barry Maude has drawn on the accumulated experience of many leaders in different fields. Their varied views are valuable precisely because they have one thing in common — they have all been out in front: leading.

Acknowledgements

I should like to thank all those people whose contributions have made this book possible, especially the many managers, from a wide range of organisations, who gave me their time and whose comments and example have supplied me with much of my basic material. I should also like to thank the following magazines for permission to include in the book material that first appeared in article form: *The Director, Chief Executive* and *Management Today.*

Preface

When one meets business leaders or reads their biographies, one is struck by the dissimilarities between them. There are few common features and no obvious 'types'.

Like great military leaders or leaders in history, successful leaders in industry tend to be intensely individualistic – even non-conformist – in ideas, tastes, lifestyles. They hold strong, sometimes outrageous opinions about their own companies, industry in general, the unions, the government, politics, society.

They have their own ideas about what is acceptable. The managing director of a famous engineering firm makes a practice of relaxing at intervals during the day by stretching out on the boardroom table. One chief executive was wearing a bright pink shirt and suit when he welcomed me into his office.

But as they talk about their careers a pattern emerges. Almost to a man, for instance, they work long hours. Sixty hours or more a week is common. Their drive and diligence helps to explain their success. The president of Goodyear says: 'I don't think I was any smarter than anyone else, but if you're working more than the other fellow you get that much more experience'.

Leaders tend to be extremely competitive, and have an intense desire to succeed. Many seem to regard management as a kind of game that must be won.

They tend to be initiators rather than responders: they act rather than react with regard to markets, employees, policies. And they *want* to lead. They want to be in control, and to organise and influence other people. 'In every organisation, somebody has to be in charge', says one executive, 'and I want to be that person'.

Many leaders transcend their specialisms and eventually become involved in general management. Many have made the shift from administrative management to organisational leadership, the shift being marked by an increasing involvement in the aims and strategy of the entire organisation (or their own parts of it), and in directing the organisation towards new goals. As administrators they controlled the present. As leaders, they feel, they are helping to shape the future of their organisations.

Not surprisingly, most leaders believe that the success of an organisation is determined, above all, by the qualities and performance of its leaders and that, without leadership, the organisation will drift opportunistically, over-exposed to internal conflict and outside pressures.

Robert Scholey, chief executive of the British Steel Corporation, makes the point that although leadership is difficult to define 'we all know well enough the difference its presence or absence makes to an operating crew. In any competitive context, the word leader means the guy who's out in front. It ought to mean the same when we're talking about teamwork in industry.'

Teamwork, as Scholey points out, is rapidly replacing autocratic styles of leadership. But the change, far from eliminating the need for leaders, is having the effect of distributing leadership responsibility among more people than ever before. Today, effective leadership is needed at all levels of management and supervision, as well as among union representatives with their wider responsibilities.

But at the same time that more and more people are finding themselves in leadership positions, the leader's job is getting tougher and tougher. Leaders today have more than the board or the shareholders to please. With democratic norms sweeping across industry, the leader's freedom of action is increasingly circumscribed by employee rights, the powers of the trade unions and outside influences such as consumer groups, public agencies and government controls.

Thus, leaders today need to be far more knowledgeable and much subtler in approach than their predecessors. But the change is not an easy one to make. This fact helps to explain why, according to a recent Confederation of British Industry survey, 86 per cent of employees think that there is a big need to improve the quality of industrial leadership. Arguably, poor leadership is one of the main reasons for the decline in the ability of some industries, such as textiles and shipbuilding, to compete in world markets.

Steps that an organisation can take to improve the quality of its leadership, and steps that the individual leader can take to improve his own performance, are described in the following pages.

My approach to the subject is functional and pragmatic. Managers are far more interested in what leaders do and say, and in improving their own leadership performance, than in academic theories of leadership.

Part 1
THE EXECUTIVE
LEADER

1

'I don't think I was any smarter than anyone else, but if you're working more than the other fellow you get that much more experience.'

Charles Pilliod, President of Goodyear

Profile of the executive leader

Who are the business leaders and how do they reach the top? One survey of the heads of the *Fortune 500* companies (plus the largest non-industrial corporations) reveals that today's top executive is more likely to come from the middle class than his upper-class predecessor – but that he is still *he* and still white [1.1]. More than half are economics or business graduates.

The survey reveals the importance of persistence in the careers of executive leaders. Nearly 30 per cent have worked their way up from the bottom of their present company; nearly two-thirds have switched employer no more than once.

An inquiry by Sturdivant and Adler into the backgrounds of executive leaders revealed that most top executives are middle-aged or elderly [1.2]; 97 per cent were over 45 and nearly 60 per cent were in the 55-65 age-bracket; not one of the 444 executives studied was non-white or female; 96 per cent were college educated, with law degrees and MBAs as the commonest qualifications.

A *Newsweek* report on a hundred top corporate women showed that about a dozen had found a law degree, or a banking or financial services background, a principal tool in their rise [1.3]. This and other evidence suggests that lawyers and financial people are getting to the top in increasing numbers – possibly they learn more about their companies than anyone else and so are better equipped to control them. Conversely, the *Fortune* report shows, the proportion of chief executives with production or engineering backgrounds has fallen – from a third of the total in 1952 to a quarter today.

Leaders in business appear to be remarkably similar in background and characteristics to leaders in many other spheres. For instance, a study of American college presidents shows that these academic leaders are most commonly middle-aged, married, white, Protestant and from relatively well educated, middle-class professional/managerial backgrounds – the conventional elite group [1.4].

The evidence suggests that Clark's comment made in 1968 is still largely valid: 'Although lower and middle management positions are open to the meritocratic, this is certainly not the case amongst top managers and directors. Here, all too often, they are drawn from a tight, homogeneous social and educational group' [1.5].

Qualifications

In Britain, formal academic qualifications seem to be less relevant to success in business than in America and most European countries. A 1971 survey found that only half of Britain's chief executive officers have a degree, compared with 83 per cent in France, 85 per cent in Belgium and 81 per cent in West Germany. In *The Chief Executive* [1.6] Copeman reports that large firms are more likely than smaller companies to have a graduate as chief executive.

In the United States, more than half the chief executives covered in Burck's survey were business or economics graduates, while more than a quarter had studied business in graduate school. British business leaders, clearly, tend to have had a less formal education than their American and European counterparts. Moreover, their qualifications are likely to be less relevant to their jobs – perhaps reflecting partly the tendency of many able youngsters in Britain to shy away from careers in industry.

What do leaders do?

What do executive leaders do? What is the nature of their work? Diary studies by Rosemary Stewart, Carlsen and others reveal the great importance of communication in their working lives. On average, 70-80 per cent of their time at work is spent in various kinds of communication activity.

In *The Nature of Managerial Works* [1.7] Mintzberg points to a number of skill areas which are of prime importance for leaders in business:

1   *Communication skills:* leaders must communicate continually, especially with colleagues and subordinates.
2   *Information skills:* the ability to obtain, edit, present and disseminate information.
3   *Man-management skills:* the ability to handle subordinates and get work out of them.

4   *Disturbance-handling skills:* the ability to solve conflicts, handle crises, put out fires.

5   *Decision-making skills:* the ability to make high-quality decisions from available alternatives and information. The ability to find the best method of reaching a decision, e.g. by consultation, through a committee, an individual decision, etc.

6   *Resource allocation skills:* the ability to allocate time and other resources to competing demands in an efficient way.

7   *Entrepreneurial skills:* the ability to spot opportunities, innovate, take risks.

8   *Reflecting skills:* the ability to think out and plan one's own and the organisation's – or the unit's – future.

McGregor's categories are somewhat broader. In *The Human Side of Enterprise* [1.8] he argues that the major components of the manager's job are communication, planning, problem-solving and initiating action. Presumably, the successful leader is a manager who possesses the personal skills and qualifications needed to deal effectively with these major job components: *thus, the leader must be an effective communicator, planner, decision-maker, innovator and controller. Weakness in any one of these areas could severely reduce his chances of success. The implications for management training and executive recruitment of this kind of approach are enormous.*

Communication networks seem to make an impact on the emergence of leaders. For instance, if a person is in a key communication position in the organisation and much information is channeled through him, his potential for influence is high and he has a strong chance of becoming the informal leader.

What is an effective leader?

When Wofford surveyed 136 managers from 85 companies, he discerned five independent dimensions of leadership behaviour, with leaders constantly swinging from one dimension to another:

Leader's objective	*Leader's behaviour*
1 Group success	Leader attempts to dominate the work by careful planning and organising of work activity; authority often delegated to lower levels.
2 Personal enhancement	Leader attempts to dominate his subordinates, thus emphasising his own power and authority. Forces subordinates to be compliant, and closely controls their work. Decision-making is restricted to upper levels.

3	Personal interaction	Realising that leadership cannot occur without communication, the leader interacts with his subordinates, and tries to influence them via friendly, informal contact. The leader as communicator and socialiser.
4	Dynamic achievement	The leader attempts to be forceful and active, to be where the action is, to get things done. Consciously tries to *achieve*.
5	Security and maintenance	The leader tries to make his team feel happy and secure so that they can concentrate on getting on with the job. Doesn't worry about work or the consequences of error; avoids putting pressure on people.

As this analysis suggests, the effective leader not only influences his followers by means of power and influence, but also produces good results by building a successful and secure team [1.9].

In *A Theory of Leadership Effectiveness*, Fiedler makes substantially this point [1.10]. He defines leadership effectiveness as the success of the leader's group in achieving its goal. Fiedler compares two styles of leadership:

1 Psychologically distant and controlling.
2 Psychologically close and more permissive.

He argues that a close, liking relationship enables the leader to be more decisive and to obtain the co-operation of subordinates without resorting to power.

To be effective, says Schutz, the leader must help individuals in the group to satisfy their needs – for instance, by giving responsibility to those with high power needs, close involvement to those with high 'inclusion' needs, and so on. Arguably, if the interpersonal needs of group members are not satisfied, the leader may fail to spur the group to achieve its task.

To some extent, the leader's effectiveness in the interpersonal area can be judged by the group's practical achievements. In a business context, the practical criteria for judging leadership effectiveness are always the same, irrespective of situation. They include:

1 The leader's ability to achieve *output targets*.
2 The leader's ability to achieve good *financial results*.
3 The state of *morale and discipline* within the leader's area of command.
4 The extent to which the leader helps the organisation or the unit to achieve its *overall objectives*.

Different approaches

The following approaches to the whole question of the leader and his role are those most often used by writers on the subject:

1   *The group approach*   The assumption is that the leader's success is determined by the group. The leader, to be effective, must win his followers' support and acceptance. This is usually achieved by the leader conforming to the group's expectations of him and by adopting and expressing their aspirations, values and goals. Who leads whom?

2   *The situational approach*   The kind of leadership qualities and style that are required depend on the particular situation, e.g. the nature of the task, the preferences of employees, and other variables. To pick the leader, study the situation.

3   *The functional approach* (or 'action-centred leadership') This approach stresses what the leader *does*, not what he *is*. According to Adair's action-centred leadership theory (developed from the armed services 'functional leadership') the leader has three basic jobs:
a   Clarifying the *task* of the group (setting goals, allocating resources, etc.).
b   Holding the *group* together so that it can achieve its task (building team spirit, applying discipline, etc.).

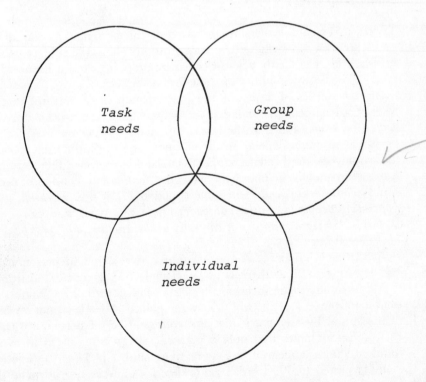

Figure 1   Action-centred leadership

   c   Looking after *individuals'* needs so that they remain in the group and help with the achievement of the task (encouraging, giving recognition and status, etc.).

The functional approach makes no attempt to be analytical but, instead, provides clear and simple guidelines for improving leaders' actual practice. The theory implicitly rejects Argyris's idea of the individual's interests necessarily being in conflict with those of the organisation (see Figure 1).

The functional approach to leadership is an attractive one to anyone involved in management training; it is more practicable to train people to provide specific leadership *functions* than to help them develop leadership traits.

4 The 'traits' approach attempts to explain leadership in terms of the personality and psychological traits of the leader – intelligence, courage, etc. According to this view, the leader's personality is the key to the leader's – and the organisation's – effectiveness.

Leadership traits

Trying to explain leadership in terms of the personality traits of the leader seems a somewhat sterile way of approaching the subject – as the British Army has tacitly acknowledged by dropping the list it once compiled of thirty-two qualities of the effective leader.

After centuries of study of the phenomenon of leadership, there is widespread agreement among investigators that there are no universal leadership traits, and that the leadership characteristics required for any particular situation depend on the nature of the work, the preferences of the employees, the leader's temperament and numerous other variables. Leadership goes to the man who best suits the occasion – and most people could be successful leaders in some situations. *It is thus essential, when appointing people to positions of leadership in an organisation, to consider factors in the work situation as carefully as the qualities and qualifications of the candidates.*

According to Bennis, all the accumulated research in personal psychology suggests that 'there is not one single trait or characteristic that would have any value in predicting leadership potentialities. None – not even intelligence' [1.12]. Gibb makes the point: 'A leader is not a person characterised by any particular and consistent set of personality traits' [1.13]. Lippitt notes that only 5 per cent of the traits listed in over a hundred studies appeared in four or more studies [1.14]. An American study has listed 17,000 words used to describe qualities of leadership that one leader or another may possess.

Qualities that lead to success

Such evidence has not, of course, prevented individual observers from forming their own ideas about the characteristics and qualities possessed by the leaders they have studied or talked to. Thus, McClelland and Burnham conclude that the successful business leaders they met seemed older and wiser, more mature and less egotistic and defensive and more willing to seek advice than the average person – and they had fewer personal possessions [1.15]. After surveying 124 books and articles dealing with leadership traits, Stogdill concluded that the leader generally exceeded group members with respect to, first, intelligence, secondly, dependability in carrying responsibility and, thirdly, communication ability.

J. and D. Rawls [1.16] found that leaders are consistently above average in intelligence and tend to be more dominant, aggressive and self-confident. 'Furthermore, they have demonstrated fairly consistent life patterns of successful endeavours, for example, successful peer and family relationships, above average scholastic achievements . . . involvement in numerous extra-curricular activities.' According to Lewis, the board member requires analytical intelligence; the capacity to evaluate strategy; awareness of the social, political and economic environment; the ability to size up the CEO's chief subordinates; and an understanding of the company's strengths and weaknesses [1.17].

While it is undoubtedly true that there are no *universal* leadership traits, there are a number of recurring qualities that appear to be possessed by many successful leaders *in business*. For instance, when asked 'Which qualities or characteristics are most important for success in business?', those most commonly mentioned by some twenty middle-ranking and senior executives interviewed recently by me were :

1 Intelligence.
2 The ability to win and to hang on to power.
3 Psychological resilience.
4 Decisiveness and self-confidence.
5 Working very long hours.

Intelligence

Many researchers have found that leaders are above average in intelligence compared with the group they are leading. J. and D. Rawls, for instance, reach this conclusion, as does Stogdill, after surveying 124 books and articles dealing with leadership. The board member requires 'analytical intelligence', according to Lewis.

Intelligence seems to be essential for the senior leadership position in business. Copeman has described an executive in a food ingredient factory who was passed over when a new managing director was appointed. The executive had been a good manager for the company, but his level of intelligence was not high enough for a top position: he lacked the ability to grasp new facts and techniques and doggedly resisted every new practice because of his 'inability to understand these practices'. Eventually, he was asked to resign.

High intelligence is less crucial in many leadership positions at lower level. A works manager told me: 'Men who have only average intelligence, or even below average intelligence, sometimes make outstanding supervisors'. He reckons that these men often find it easy to communicate with their work groups on equal terms and approach problems in similar ways.

Work-hunger

Bailey found in all of the twenty-four company presidents that he interviewed a notable capacity for immersing themselves in work [1.18]. All of the executives I interviewed agreed that an appetite for hard work is essential for success in business.

Leader after leader exhibits this characteristic. Lord Ryder, who has headed Reed International and been chairman of the National Enterprise Board, usually got up before dawn and put in a sixteen-hour day. Borel who, until recently, ran Europe's largest restaurant chain, takes pride in working a hundred-hour week. Roche's chairman, Jann, says that to succeed, the business leader needs 'a great capacity for work'. But the work, he insists, 'must be done in the interests of the company rather than in a self-interested way'. Jann reckons that a hard-working leader finds it easier to win the respect of his subordinates.

'Successful chief executives give every evidence of relishing hard work', says one investigator. 'They communicate more, analyse more, travel more. And, with rare exceptions, they work themselves harder than almost anyone else in the organisation.' But he admits, 'It is not always clear whether hard work is the mainspring of their success or simply a reflection of their personal commitment and interest, but either way hard work appears to be a common denominator of success' [1.19].

The hard-working leader is an achiever because he works at the task with such determination and persistence. This generates an atmosphere of urgency and fast movement in his unit and so attracts more work, more responsibility and more success. The hard-driving executive, says Jann, prefers getting the job finished to playing company politics, and empire-building comes second to getting the job done, completing the project and chalking up another gain. Other executives find it hard to stop or to oppose this kind of leader. With so much work being done, with so many projects and proposals being generated, it may be possible to stop one or two – but not all.

According to Nixon, Kissinger, like many other successful leaders, could not stand bureaucratic in-fighting and politicking: he saw it as a time-wasting activity that 'prevented him from getting on with the job'.

Donnelly, chief executive of Donnelly Mirrors, explains the qualities he looks for when appointing people to positions of leadership in the company : 'So many people talk of wanting an *aggressive* leader. Aggression connotes destroying the other. What you really want is a person who can achieve, who wants to get things done. You want work, you want energy, you want a self-starter.'

There is a strong puritanical streak in many successful leaders. Lord Reith felt personally responsible to God for doing a good job as head of the British Broadcasting Corporation. Byrom, chief executive officer at Koppers Company, believes that it is the leader's responsibility 'to use your talents to something approaching your best. Being human, it *can't* be your best. But you don't deserve credit if all you're doing is just using the talents and energy that were given to you. *That's* an obligation.'

Wasserman, chairman of MCA Incorporated, which makes television films, confesses his workaholism with seeming pride. He has never played a set of tennis or a round of golf and has had only one vacation in forty years. He gets up at five every day, and sleeps on a daybed in his study so as not to disturb his wife. His formula for success in business? 'Hard work.'

Estes, president of General Motors, makes the point : 'I think if you come in late every morning, you are going to have all your comployees coming in late before long. If you go home early, they are all going to go home early, so I guess I have the feeling that I have to give everything to my job, and I expect everyone else to do the same.'

Many of the successful executives surveyed by psychologist Maccoby for his book *The Gamesman* paid a high price for their hard-working lifestyles [1.20]. They worked so hard at their careers that they tended to deny all values and urges that would threaten them. Their emotional lives atrophied. One executive reported 'If I let myself feel their problems it would be impossible to deal with people'.

Among the difficulties these leaders experienced were inability to express their feelings to others; uncertainty about what they really wanted from their jobs or from life; anxiety and a tendency to blame themselves; a tendency to avoid people; restlessness and depression. A price that some top executives pay for such a total immersion in work is alcoholism. According to a 1977 report by the National Council on Alcoholism, the most drink-prone members of the population are company directors : they are twenty-two times as likely to suffer health damage from excess drinking as any other occupational group.

Decisiveness and self-confidence

According to the chief executive of a construction company, 'the ability to make up your mind on insufficient evidence' is a vital leadership characteristic. Most managers find it extremely difficult to do this, 'but you have to do it in business, and anybody lacking this ability could scarcely function as a leader'. That is the reason why, according to this executive, decisiveness and confidence in one's own judgement are essential pieces of mental equipment for leaders in industry.

Successful chief executives, says Clifford, 'make fast decisions on new ideas and are also quick to terminate losing or unpromising activities' [1.19].

One chief executive is so convinced of the importance of decisiveness that he actually recommends making 'a decision on every single item that reaches you on the day you get it'.

To lead others decisively, the leader must know where he is going himself : he must be a leader, not merely an administrator. 'I was certain I had a clearer notion of the business than the rest of the board', a highly successful managing director reports. 'I felt my decisions were sounder.' This man knows where he wants to go – and so is in a strong position to lead the rest of the organisation. He possesses the self-confidence that is needed for taking difficult and risky decisions; and the decisiveness that is needed for leading subordinates who, generally speaking, want to work for a boss who knows where he is going and in whom they can believe.

Maccoby says that the true leader is compassionate, but still does not shrink from taking tough but necessary decisions – such as laying people off or closing a plant. This ability to take tough decisions distinguishes the leader from the talented, sensitive person who lacks the inner toughness or conviction that is needed to stand up to the pangs, and the conflict and in-fighting, which many unpleasant decisions trigger off.

Decisiveness, which is based on self-confidence plus a clear sense of direction, is quite different from the mechanical skills of the 'numbers' man. It is a temperamental trait that equips a leader to deal with situations and problems where numbers are of little help. This trait is, arguably, essential in top-level leaders : the chief executive *must* be decisive and trust in his own judgement because there is nobody above him to check or advise him on a day-to-day basis.

Margaret Thatcher has talked about the loneliness of leadership : 'I have a new definition of a leader. It's someone who's got no shoulder to cry on. . . . You have to make the decisions alone.' But she added : 'Curiously enough, I still like making the decisions'.

Moreover, successful leaders have enough self-confidence to be themselves. Brouwer [1.21] points to some of the strong men of history who 'seem always to have been themselves as persons : Michelangelo, fighting against odds for a chance to sculpt . . . Beethoven, continuing to compose after he became deaf . . . Milton, who didn't allow blindness to interfere with his writings'. Brouwer argues that what distinguishes the strong man from the weak man – the leader from the follower – is 'self-concept' :

> The difference between a strong man and a weak man may not be a difference in ability, for many clerks have keen intelligence; or in

drive, for many ambitious men get nowhere; or in opportunity, for somehow, strong men *make* opportunity. No, the difference lies in self-concept. How much do I value my life? What do I want to do with it? What must I do to be myself? Strong men have emerged with clear-cut answers to such questions; weak men equivocate and temporise and never dare.

Bass argues that those trying to gain leadership position are individuals with much confidence and high self esteem. [B. Bass, *Leadership, Psychology and Organisational Behaviour*, Harper (1960).]

Psychological resilience

Psychological toughness equips a leader to cope with such inescapable aspects of executive life as stress, risk and conflict and is therefore – at least, according to P & A Management Consultants – an essential requirement for executive leadership. It means that the leader feels strong enough to fight for what he believes in – to press for necessary decisions and policies even when this triggers off much conflict and in-fighting, and even when it damages his own prestige or career.

Bailey found this resilient quality in the twenty-four company heads that he interviewed: they would be willing, for instance, to resign rather than back down on really important issues. One manager told me: 'I'll always compromise on the unimportant issues – never on the vital ones' [1.18]. Perhaps if an executive is not tough enough to risk losing his job when necessary – with the consequent loss of status and income – he is not tough enough to be a leader anyway.

For the leader at any level, the willingness to lose his job frees him from dependency on his boss. As Bailey points out, it enables him to take tough decisions free from too much anxiety about the effect on his own career. 'That bridge he has crossed beforehand.'

Conflict occurs in all organisations and can be a means of establishing stability once the combatants have tested each other's strengths. Some organisation development specialists such as Beckhard, Lawrence and Lorsch, believe that organisations should actually encourage the open expression of conflict between departments and groups, and that this is a way of reconciling differences, achieving higher-quality solutions to problems and of accelerating the emergence of natural leaders. The leader, they believe, must be tough enough to marshall his forces, take a stand – and fight. He must be able to stand up to other people's aggression without becoming too anxious about it. This kind of resilience could be regarded as an essential quality in coming to terms with the tough competitive environment of modern business. Leaders must also be sufficiently resilient to tolerate the feelings of loneliness or even isolation that many leaders experience.

As McGregor points out in *Leadership and Motivation*: 'Since no important decision ever pleases everyone in the organisation (the leader) must also absorb the displeasure, and sometimes severe hostility, of those who would have taken a different course'. The role of the leader often produces a separation between leader and led, and precludes the leader from establishing close personal relationships with his subordinates. Clearly, the leader must be psychologically tough enough to cope with the feelings of guilt and anxiety created by this situation.

Sexy leaders?

Research suggests that successful business leaders not only have more opportunity but also a good deal more sexual activity than their less successful colleagues. According to the findings of sociologist Centers, published in 1972, women are predisposed towards men belonging to top management; the higher up the scale the better the opportunities for sexual activity. Interestingly, though, some research among top business-men in 1975 showed that despite this greater opportunity, they were no more unfaithful than the average.

'Women gravitate towards men of leadership, achievement, occupational and economic ability', says sexologist Gosselin [1.22]. By contrast, men are drawn to women who are physically attractive, are erotic and affectionate, and have good social skills.

Power needs

Most successful executive leaders seem to have a notable power urge, a need to take control. Frey, Bell and Howell's chief executive, candidly admits: 'I just have to be in charge of a whole business – it's in here, a gut-feeling . . . you could say it's a need for power. In an esoteric sense it's a need for completeness. I'm not happy unless I'm dealing with all the pieces.'

Hanley, Monsanto chief executive, says he has always had an intense inner drive to take charge. That is why, when he was passed over for the top spot at Proctor and Gamble, where he formerly worked, he quickly left to become Monsanto's chief.

Researchers McClelland and Burnham have discovered that effective leaders in large companies tend to have stronger power needs than their less effective colleagues: presumably to be effective the executive needs to be strong and influential within his organisation. In a product development division, 73 per cent of the better managers had a stronger need for power than a need to be liked. This compared with only 22 per cent of poorer managers [1.15].

The executive leader seeks power – or at least needs power – so that he can impose order on his unit or organisation, get better efficiency, introduce necessary changes. When one executive took over as managing director of a small engineering company, he soon discovered that results were poor because of ineffective leadership at all levels of management. So he used his power to dismiss one manager, demote two others, and move several more to different jobs. He revitalised the company at a single stroke – but he needed power to do it.

Strong feelings of competitiveness are closely linked to the power-drive and are a striking characteristic of many successful business leaders. For instance, Estes, GM president, admits to being very competitive in his approach and says: 'The competitiveness of our industry maybe develops this intense feeling. I think if you talk to our competitors, you might find the same kind of feeling there.' He adds: 'In fact, we have internal competition. When I was at Oldsmobile I was dedicated to having a better car than Buick, Pontiac, Chevrolet or Cadillac. It was going to be the best car in General Motors.'

The urge to make a difference

Successful executive leaders are people who want to lead, who have a drive to get things done – and for this they need power. Acceptance of responsibility, says Fiedler, the 'impelling urge to make a difference', is the crux of leadership. When asked why he wanted to hold a difficult and dangerous job – the United States Presidency – Kennedy said that difficult and dangerous decisions had to be made that would affect the lives of his family, and he preferred to be in a position to make those decisions. As Kennedy's words imply, there must be a genuine commitment to action underpinning the power-urge. Major policies cannot be effectively advanced without conviction in the executive who proposes them. Much lip-service is paid to team effort and collective leadership, but often the reality behind the rhetoric is power struggles and ruthless competition. Organisations, like ancient kingdom, are racked by continuing conflict and struggles for influence. It is easy to understand why. Controlling and influencing other people is an essential part of the leader's job. Worker participation may be in vogue but managers still have to manage, still have to think in terms of power and authority. Without these there can be no discipline and no survival. 'An executive without power', says one consultant 'is all too often a figurehead – or worse, headless.' The general manager of an electronics supplies firm makes the point succinctly: 'Managers who don't think constantly in terms of power and influence don't survive'.

Leaders need power

Arguably, the most effective leaders are those who are capable of dealing with the group's problems: this depends on the leader's ability to persuade and influence his followers which, in turn, depends largely on how much power the leader possesses. McClelland and Burnham [1.15] point out : 'The manager's job seems to call more for someone who can influence people than for someone who can do things better on his own. In motivational terms, then, we might expect the successful manager to have a greater need for power than a need to achieve.' Thus a major characteristic of the leader in industry is that he believes strongly in the need for centralised power and authority – even if this means sacrificing some individual rights, including his own.

Leadership and the power-urge are closely linked : leadership involves 'the control of others for the purpose of achieving a common task'. Thus leaders strive to reach positions in the organisation where they can exert authority over others. Individuals who don't are not likely to rise very high in management or to make very effective leaders. The power game is a part of executive leadership, so perhaps leaders should be selected partly on the basis of their fitness and need for power.

The pursuit of power involves alliances at all levels. These are often formed during furtive meetings behind closed doors where common goals and tactics are agreed and common enemies identified, and where horse-trading is carried out. I was present at one session where a promise of a particular organisational reform was offered in exchange for support over some issue.

This kind of wheeling and influence-peddling swirls round the executive corridors of every large organisation. How many corporate decisions are spun out of it? An executive may involve himself in this kind of power-seeking behaviour because he is not influential enough to push through a decision on his own. He thus has recourse to the 'plural executive' – a clique of managers conspiring to achieve common goals. In this way, many a managerial clique gets a stranglehold on decision-making.

Desire to excel

Leaders must have power to do a good job – to control subordinates, to ensure the proper allocation of resources, to ensure that the right appointments and promotions are made. But when talking to successful business leaders, it is impossible to avoid the conclusion that the thrust for power owes more to the personality of the leader than to any management theory. Motivations and styles vary, but one discerns the same strong urge for power and status, and to put one's ideas into practice.

Borel, the brilliant French catering entrepreneur, has an undisguised lust to dominate. He enjoys trials of strength with competitors, and rejoices when they lose. Borel points out that managers who *don't* think constantly in terms of power don't survive. 'One must always come first.' This philosophy helped to make his restaurant group the largest in Europe. With his company serving nearly half a million meals a day he got where he wanted to be – the top – and the pursuit of power got him there.

Pilliod, Goodyear's president, is another leader who always wanted to be a winner. Pilliod attributes his success to 'a desire to excel – a drive to do better than the other guy', though he admits that hard work helped too. 'I worked more than the others. I put in more time. I don't think I was any smarter than anyone else, but if you're working more than the other fellow you get that much more experience.'

The pursuit and wielding of power is so important in organisations that, according to some, one of the aims of management training should be to tutor aspiring leaders in the arts of winning and holding power. Cohen [1.23] reckons that the Harvard Business School has already got the message : 'You learn in school not to give a shit if the people you climb over are weak or sick or small or blind. You learn that everyone is your enemy and you learn to hate and fear people, to live in crowded isolation for the rest of your days. But above all you learn never to show your weaknesses and to put up a front at all times.'

Displaying authority

Power-seeking is often attacked as an irrational kind of anti-social aggression. But as Lorenz has shown, power and authority depend on force, yet lead to law and order by imposing a pecking order. Power struggles in organisations may be a sign of health – even a biological principle. In any case, employees expect or even demand leaders who are powerful. They feel stronger and more secure when they feel that their boss can exert influence over *his* boss. That is why McMurry advises the ambitious executive to *display* signs of his power and authority, since modesty and a democratic style may simply be mistaken for lack of power and authority. Be friendly with subordinates, Mc-Murry counsels, but never intimate. Open your door, but never too wide.

McGregor, referring to his experiences as president of Antioch College, says : 'It took a couple of years, but I finally began to realise that a leader cannot avoid the exercise of authority any more than he can avoid responsibility for what happens to his organisation'.

A Swiss executive who was promoted to a top leadership position in his company was soon made aware of the importance of display. He was told plainly to stop coming to work in his two-year-old Peugeot and to get something better. Individuals who occupy similar positions in similar organisations vary widely in the way they utilise the power of office.

Ploys that are used by some power-conscious executives to consolidate their power include divide-and-rule tactics when confronted by coalitions of subordinates or colleagues. Opponents can usually be bought off by making concessions to them – saying yes to some of their demands – or by coopting them into the central leadership group or key management committees.

In his executive-survival manual, *Power: How to get it and how to use it,* Korda says that anyone can win at the power game if he is determined enough. In the power office, for instance, there might be several phones on the desk to signal the executive's status and far-flung empire. Paintings, cartoons, cut-outs on the wall, signal the executive's territorial rights. The desk, advises Korda, should be placed as far away from the entrance as possible with objects such as chairs and tables strewn along the way to impede a visitor's progress, with the visitor's chair placed directly in front of the desk. The more aggressive power players, says Korda, invade other people's offices and challenge *their* power by such moves as putting their feet on the desk or flicking cigarette ash on the carpet.

Maccoby's new-style leader, the Gamesman, is very common in the senior ranks of most management teams. Maccoby interviewed 250 managers at all levels and found that Gamesmen formed the largest category. The Gamesman regards his career as a game and to win the game he needs power. 'The contest hypes him up' and 'he communicates his enthusiasm, energising his peers and subordinates, like the quarter-back on a football team'. The Gamesman is compulsively driven by a need to succeed. He wants power not as an end in itself but so that he can achieve the exhiliration of victory and be known as a winner.

Neurotic power drives

There is a need to distinguish between the constructive pursuit of power – power as a rational means of exercising organisational control – and power-seeking as an irrational, neurotic drive. Some individuals pursue power and influence as ends in themselves. Richard, formerly personnel director at Polaroid, points out that 'some men get real satisfaction from manipulating and controlling people. For some men there is challenge and excitement in the domination game'.

Power motivation is frequently defined as gaining satisfaction from manipulating others as a way of avoiding feelings of weakness and loss of control [1.24]. A neurotic power drive may stem from lack of love (Fromm), or from feelings of inferiority (Adler) or from continual anxiety and feelings of anger and hatred (Horney).

The kind of individual who gets undue pleasure from controlling, manipulating or punishing others should be screened out at the appointment stage. Brown has said: 'There are good reasons why self-centred and power-loving individuals should not be placed in positions of responsibility; for the power-loving man is a sick man who seeks to compensate for his own inadequacy by gaining control over others' [1.25].

The leader who uses power for rational, constructive ends makes his subordinates feel stronger, more confident, better motivated to strive to achieve the organisation's goals. The executive who wields power for

self-centred, or neurotic reasons makes his followers feel weak, defence-
less, constantly at risk.

To guard against possible abuses of power or the possibility of too
much power becoming concentrated in only a few hands, many organisations create formal structures that have the effect of sharing and distributing power. Examples are committees, participation in decision-making,
workers on the board, consultative machinery, and a separation of power
between the executive (management) and the legislature (the board).
Such checks and safeguards make the leader's life very difficult, but they
are better than the sort of unchecked power that can close a plant or
throw people out of work just because some top executive says so.

Distrust of power

In recent years, numerous cases of the abuse of power by political and
business leaders have fuelled the deep suspicion of power seeking that
exists in the public mind. The Opinion Research Centre has found that
only a third of Britons have much confidence in big business. In the US,
the Opinion Research Corporation found that business leaders came low
in public esteem: the ratings of various occupations in order of esteem
were scientists, doctors, college lecturers, lawyers, government officials,
small businessmen, PR executives, average workers, local officials, company executives, advertising executives, union leaders. A recurring criticism is that business executives have too much power. In psychological
tests, people are pleased to be told that they have high achievement
needs, but generally dislike being told that they have strong power needs.

Clark, former president of the American Psychological Association,
sees the power urge as a primitive, aggressive drive that must be checked:
he urges that important political leaders should be required to take drugs
while in office so that they won't be tempted to use their power for selfish
or aggressive ends. The drugs would inhibit the leader's primitive, aggressive urges. (No less an authority than Kissinger has extolled power as the
ultimate aphrodisiac.)

Rohatyn, a partner in Lazard Freres merchant bank and chairman
of Big MAC, the body that saved New York from default in 1975, says
that he has succeeded in New York because he has made it clear that
he covets no position of power there. True power, he claims, lies in having
ideas that are sought after by others and in the ability to convince people.

Power as influence

A journalist who has interviewed such outstanding football managers as
Bill Shankly, Sir Alf Ramsey, Bertie Mee and Sir Matt Busby, has said:
'I found no common factor except the ability to make people believe
what they wanted them to believe. When Shankly roared that Liverpool

had been robbed of two points it didn't sound outrageous. The man had authority and true power.'

As this case suggests, leadership today is an influence activity. Business executives no longer find it easy to get results by means of naked command. Bulmers chairman, Prior, defines leadership as 'the art of getting someone else to do something you want done because he wants to do it'.

The leader's effectiveness, say researchers French and Reven [1.26], depends on the kinds of power available to him and the strength of each. They contend that leaders, to be effective, require five main kinds of power:

1 *Reward power,* enabling them to reward followers who serve their purposes.

2 *Coercive power,* enabling them to punish followers who fail to serve their purposes.

3 *Legitimate power,* which gives the leader the full backing of his organisation.

4 *Referent power,* which is based on the follower's identification with and admiration for the leader.

5 *Expert power,* which is based on the leader's expertness in some field or on some specialised skill or knowledge.

Limits on power

How powerful are leaders? In *The Managerial Revolution,* Burnham predicted that managers were destined to become the primary holders of power in society generally. But today the power of executive leaders is being increasingly circumscribed – and very few of the executives I have talked to see themselves as having much power. They see their power of decision and action checked by legislation such as the Health and Safety at Work Act and the Equal Pay Act; by government regulations; by consumer pressures; and, above all, by growing union power. One general manager told me: 'I'm safe as long as my results are good. As soon as they stop being good it's goodbye and good luck.' Most of the managers I interviewed were very aware that they must *keep* producing results, that they can never stop. No matter how powerful he may be at the present moment, the leader must continue to earn his position, otherwise he may lose it.

One manager says: 'At one time employees were behind the company. Now they've transferred their consent to the unions.' Barclays Bank chairman Thompson believes that the 'best way to head-off trade union militants is to show a much more positive approach to dealing with the unions, and to give much more encouragement to union work. Sharing decisions with the unions encourages the silent majority to take part in union activities.'

Leaders used to be able to make decisions but today, in order to function effectively, they need to involve the unions in those decisions.

Leaders are also vulnerable to numerous external pressures, such as those exerted by the financial institutions: Howard Hughes was dismissed from his control of Trans-World Airlines by banking interests. There are also legal pressures to contend with. Following its illegal payments to Nixon's 1972 election campaign, Northrop had to agree to the settlement of a suit which provided for the revision of the executive committee of the company so that five of its six members were outside directors. The effect of this action was to make the internal management more *accountable* for its actions.

Trends such as these contribute to the sense of powerlessness that many executive leaders feel. At one time, says Professor Carlson in *Executive Behaviour,* the executive leader was like the conductor of an orchestra – in overall control. Today, he is 'a puppet in a puppet-show with hundreds of people pulling the strings and forcing him to act in one way or another'.

Bennis [1.12], a college president, has said:

As a supposed leader I watch with envy the superior autonomy of the man mowing the university lawn. He is in complete control of the machine he rides, the total arbiter of which swath to cut, where and when. I cannot match him.'

2

'Effective leaders are those who are capable of behaving in many different leadership styles, depending on the requirements of reality.'

Chris Argyris

Varieties of leadership

With the enormous diversity of organisations, there can be no such thing as the archetypal leader, the ideal executive who is right for all situations. Surprisingly few executives in fact, measure up to the common or Hollywood conception of leadership. This portrays a thrusting dynamism that observation rarely justifies. In business, the all-purpose leader has escaped detection.

Indeed, in many business situations there is no clear separation of leader and led. Consider what happens in a discussion. One man explains an idea and the others listen. The man with the idea becomes the momentary leader. When someone else speaks and develops the point, leadership passes to him. A third person outlines an alternative method . . . thus leadership is as momentary and shifting as the flow of discussion itself.

Leadership depends on the ability to control and motivate others and to coordinate their efforts – and this can be achieved through a variety of leadership styles. Leadership goes, in fact, to the man who best suits the occasion. At normal times the leader may be the steady, reliable man. At times of crisis the awkward, aggressive individual may emerge as leader. In Bion's studies of groups of neurotics during the war, often the man with the most problems was the leader. Insane or neurotic politicians are catapulted into leadership positions in convulsive periods of history.

Thus, leadership is not a set of permanent qualities enabling one man to march others smartly through the business jungle. For the good leader in one situation may be reduced to stumbling ineffectuality in another. Klein sees leadership as the ability to elicit the required response – and this may require the gentle touch, or even self-effacement.

For instance, Cefio, president of Italy's largest industrial corporation, is so shy and retiring that he is known as 'the ghost'; so unassuming that he signs 'the president' on company documents, not his own name. He leaves the speech-making and the news conferences to subordinates be-cause, he says sourly, 'It's the middle-ranking people who want to be the prima donnas'. His record shows clearly that you don't have to be a hip-shooter to hit the target ten times out of ten. Leaders occupying similar power positions often exhibit very different styles of leadership. President Eisenhower, for instance, is reputed to have set up an Army-type 'staff system' in the White House which screened and decided many issues before they reached the desk of the President. Each cabinet member was given complete authority in his own area which enabled him to act with military efficiency and precision – and which removed much of the load from the President. A similar style is utilised by senior executives in many large organisations.

President Roosevelt, however, adopted a very different style which enabled *him* to take the initiative and make the decisions. A favourite technique was to keep giants of authority incomplete, jurisdictions un-certain, charters overlapping. 'The result of this competitive theory of administration was often confusion and exasperation on the operating level; but no other method could so reliably ensure that in a large bureaucracy filled with ambitious men eager for power, the decisions and the power to make them would remain with the President.' [2.1].

According to Fiedler's Leadership Contingency Model, which is essen-tially a *situational* approach to the leadership question, three major vari-ables determine whether or not a given situation is favourable or un-favourable to a leader:

1   The amount of *structure* in the task facing the group.
2   The amount of *power* that his position gives him.
3   His *personal relations* with the group members.

The manager is in a very favourable position to influence the group and exert powerful leadership when he is managing a well-defined job with much structure, has much power, and gets on well with group members [1.10].

Organisational requirements

The style of leadership required depends on the nature of the organisa-tion. Taking a company from zero to £$\frac{1}{2}$ million turnover requires a

different kind of leadership from that required to take the company from
£$\frac{1}{2}$ million to £10 million, as Figure 2 illustrates. The first generation
may require an expansionist entrepreneur; the second generation is more
likely to require an efficient administrator who can apply the controls
and create internal order.

	Small company	Large company
Primary task of company	Survival and growth	Control and allocation of resources
Levels of management	One or two levels	Three or more levels
Organisational structure	Informal, direct	Different functions and levels held together by formal systems
Leader's primary task	Direct supervision of employees, production, sales and all other activities	Control of work force and different functions via intermediaries and 'systems';financial control
Authority	Often clear-cut, undisputed	Often ambiguous and uncertain

Figure 2 Leadership styles in small and large companies

An interesting point about leaders in companies of different sizes was
made by Albert Porter [2.2] who found that in small organisations a
'masculine' pattern of interests helped to explain the success of many
executives, but that in larger organisations, masculine interests could
damage executive careers. The bigger the company the suaver the
leaders.

As the company grows in size, the leader acquires wider responsibilities
and requires new talents – for administration, budgeting, liaising, and the
like. Perhaps this simple fact lies behind many of the observed cases of
the Peter Principle, which is about the executive who rises then flops
because he or she fails to cope with the changed demands of the new
job.

Just as common are those cases where a manager moves from a small
to a large company and fails to cope with the new responsibilities, which
may be of a different kind from those encountered in the smaller company. In the past, the manager may have been responsible for everything

that happened in the small company, with personal control over every aspect, so that there were no problems in establishing one's authority or understanding one's role. It is relatively easy to exert control over a small empire, 'but in groupings of a more federal nature where other managers hold sway control demands the willing cooperation of colleagues' [2.3]. A completely new, subtler kind of leadership is required – and the manager may not have it.

The small-company leader

Kneissl runs a small ski-making factory in Austria. He personally supervises every aspect of the company's activities, initiates all its plans and policies. He runs the place with paternal and undisputed authority – and the shop-floor slogan he prefers is 'Wages are the best guarantee of production'. Kneissl is decidedly gloomy at the thought that modern management techniques might some day invade his industry – understandably so, for his decisive, individualistic style of leadership really works. The factory has doubled its output in the past five years.

But this kind of small, rapidly expanding company requires a different kind of leadership from the giant, steady-state corporation. The small-company dynamo needs to be energetic and direct in his approach because he is responsible for all plans and activities and involves himself closely in every functional area. And he needs to be good at making decisions alone. The managing director of one small company reports: 'I require growth plans by all managers, approve all plans, review progress, change directions – and enthusiastically lead'. The small-company leader is likely to be more opportunity- and expansion-minded than his big-company counterpart.

The bigger a company becomes the more tolerant of formal structures and systems the workforce become. Indeed, the leader is almost expected to assume certain formal types of power – the chairmanship of committees, reviewer of reports, and so on.

The big-company controller

The big-company controller has little *personal* involvement in operations, or in individual functional areas. At senior levels, the leader's principal roles are strategic planning and financial control. These require a general rather than a specialist approach – even a certain remoteness from operations. This is so especially in a company with many divisions, or in a multi-national company. The chief executive of a large conglomerate points out: 'Our company is a multi-national corporation. The leadership's role is therefore no longer one of managing resources within a single business, but managing the *corporate* resources and deploying them among the existing businesses – i.e. resource allocation'.

The chief executive of one large company says: 'Most of my time is devoted to business planning and financial policy', and he points to four specific leadership activities:

1 Setting specific goals and objectives.
2 Establishing responsibility for plans and projects.
3 Monitoring the implementation of plans and projects.
4 Coordinating the activities of different departments and functions.

Since most of this man's time is spent developing policies with other executives, the skills required are those of the communicator, the committeeman and the controller. There is much evidence, indeed, to show that the higher a manager climbs the more committees and informal discussions he attends. It is not uncommon for senior managers to serve on ten or more committees, and to spend nearly a half of their time at work discussing plans and policies with other executives.

Committee skills

A director in a large engineering company reports: 'Almost every week the executive advisory group, consisting of principal officers, meet to discuss problems of corporate growth, both internal and external, such as new facilities, new processes, possible acquisitions, and so on'. At Daimler-Benz, the top management team get together at least once a week to talk about policy. Invariably, disagreement surfaces in these meetings – 'if it didn't, the yeast would be missing', says one director, then adds: 'The important thing is the manner in which such disagreements are handled, and here they are handled with considerable subtlety and tact by the chairman'.

This point is supported by personnel director Schleyer, who claims that the discussions always lead to unanimous decisions because of chairman Zahn's leadership style. Zahn, it seems, goes all out for harmony, using every device open to the practised committeeman to reconcile the different viewpoints and convince individuals of the merits of each other's proposals. The leader as diplomat and conciliator.

In the large company, the main barriers to efficiency are the problems of organisation and communication, especially when there are more than three or four hundred employees. Below this level, the leader can maintain control by *direct* action – he looks out of the window and sees for himself that a delivery is leaving on time; he walks through the workshop and sees for himself that there are no machines or men standing idle. But above this number he has to rely on systems, intermediaries and formal reports for a picture of total operations; and problems of organisation and communication multiply. *Thus, the leadership skills required in a big company are those involving organisation, coordination, control and the setting up of systems.*

Like military leaders, the leader of the large industrial unit often finds that it is easier to stamp his authority and control on his people if he maintains a psychological distance from them. This makes it easier to discipline them, give unpopular instructions, reassign, or lay people off. In a large company, the leader must coordinate the contributions of numerous specialists; he must communicate and cooperate with different department heads; and he must think about money and budgeting in a new way.

In a very small company, there is less need for coordination and co-operation. For the boss himself is in touch with every aspect and co-ordinates everything in his own mind. Every day he is seeing people and talking to people, and becomes so involved in every aspect of the company's activities that there is little need for coordination or consultation.

Successful leadership in a big company requires :

1 Delegating skills In a large or medium-sized company, there is a tremendous number of things to do. The job can easily become un-manageable if the boss tries to oversee all aspects, or carry them all out personally in the manner of the small-company leader. An employee in a large engineering factory said wryly about a new department head : 'He can't be successful without our help'. Thus the leader may have to delegate work in most areas to subordinates while involving himself more deeply in key areas or in areas in which he is personally expert.

2 Coordinating skills The leader must work closely with numerous specialists and functional heads and coordinate their contributions so that projects are fulfilled and objectives achieved. The general manager of a food processing factory told me : 'If I couldn't get our production people to work closely with sales, I wouldn't last two minutes in this job'.

3 Agreeing on spheres of influence and areas of cooperation with other managers Often in a large company an individual executive is not heavy enough to push a decision through on his own and so must rely on the plural executive – a group of managers cooperating to achieve common goals. Thus, in a large company the leader's greatest asset is friends in other parts of the company. The pursuit of big-company power involves alliances at all levels, formed for the purpose of identify-ing common goals and tactics and carrying out agreed programmes.

Some of the different aims and approaches required in small and large companies have already been listed in Figure 2.

As the manager climbs

As the manager climbs up the hierarchy, the leadership skills required progressively change. His expertise must change from a strong functional orientation (at first-line level) to broader areas of general business ex-pertise and grasp of policy and strategy.

The first-level manager concentrates on carrying out today's activities

smoothly and efficiently. The skills required are practical ones, such as
the ability to control work-flow and the management of people.

The middle manager must have a longer time-horizon than today's activities. He plans activities in monthly, quarterly, or even annual periods. But he also requires a thorough functional expertise and an understanding of the work process so that he can take sound operational decisions.

The senior manager needs to understand the total business system or process required. He must understand the interactions of all the functions within the company and their impact on the total business. This understanding allows him to coordinate the activities of various specialists and departments.

The 'new' leaders

Traditional ideas of leadership as seen, for instance, in the civil service and the Army, spring from the belief that a senior individual can co-ordinate in his own mind the work of all his subordinates. It is McGregor's Theory X, management by control, the pyramid and chain. The problems facing the leader are broken down into specialisms. Subordinates are controlled by instructions and decisions issued by the leader. Management is visualised as the hierarchy of the organisation chart.

The system produces excellent paper organisation, but often neither leaders nor followers are used to the best advantage since personal initiative has little scope, and staff relationships and lines of communication are rigidly structured. However, traditional leadership styles are reasonably suitable for organisations operating in a context of stable market and technological conditions; and for managing standardised, routine operations of the assembly line type. The vast sums spent by large companies on research, the trend to mergers, and the increasing number of specialists have underlined the unique role of the business leader as a coordinator.

However, when a company is operating, in a dynamic, changing environment, more and more problems are thrown up that a monolithic, over-structured leadership cannot cope with. In these conditions, a 'new' type of leader is needed – one who can stimulate subordinates and colleagues to work in teams and who can integrate the work of numerous specialists, for modern industrial problems are very complex and no one individual has all the technical expertise that is required. Thus cooperation, teamwork and participation in decisions are more important than they sometimes are in a stabler environment.

But in the dynamic environment of a firm like IBM, say, or Ferranti, conditions make it essential to distribute leadership far more widely than when technologies were simple. Different people become leaders at different times. Everybody has several different leaders – or no leader.

To some extent, employees choose their own tasks and methods – this taps talent and keeps morale high. Also, participation relieves the leader's workload because employees learn to think in terms of what needs to be done and how to do it.

Traditional leadership methods with their neat chains of command, their rules and their rigid procedures, are ill-adapted to the dynamic environment in which many firms now operate.

Choice of style

The correct style of leadership in any particular situation depends on the nature of the work, the preferences of the employees and the manager's own temperament.

1 The nature of the work As Joan Woodward, Morse and Lorsch and others have shown, large-batch and mass production require tight supervision and control : the job *has* to be done in a certain way and the leader's primary task is to apply the necessary controls. On the other hand, high-level, abstract work, as in the R & D department, requires conditions of greater autonomy. Highly structured organisations, such as the armed services, require an autocratic style of management for efficient operation.

2 The manager's temperament Generally, leaders are more effective and come over more strongly if they have scope to operate in the way that comes naturally to them. Thus, accurate selection and placement of managerial personnel is essential so that, first, the leader's job is either precisely defined or general, according to his preference and, secondly, managers are placed in departments or units in which their 'natural' style of leadership will have most scope. This may mean placing the tough, no-nonsense executive in production; the cheerful extrovert in sales; the sensitive, one-to-one communicator in personnel, and so on. As Harriman points out : 'Too many times higher-level managers have worked hard to change a tough guy into a human relations star or a reserved person into a tiger only to wonder later what went wrong' [2.4].

3 The preferences of employees Many employees prefer a democratic style of leadership and the opportunity for participating in decisions. Others prefer the security of clear structure and firm direction so that they know exactly where they stand. Some leaders are flexible enough to be able to make an assessment of the employees' preferences, then cater for them. A survey at the Maytag Corporation showed that most employees there preferred hard-line foremen who made workers follow instructions to the letter – an approach that could whip up labour unrest in other companies. People who have got used to working in an autocratic organisation often find it very difficult to adjust to a different kind of regime. Polaroid employed five ex-convicts, but all except one man failed in their jobs. After the controlled environment of the prison where there was little pressure, few demands and just one boss, they failed to adjust to the new – and unwanted – freedom of the Polaroid plant.

A research team from the Ashridge Management College has found that the consultative style of leadership is the most popular among employees : but only a quarter of the respondents thought that their own boss's style was consultative. The Ashridge study also found that autocratic managers were the ones most likely to be described as 'running things efficiently'.

Obedience to authority

Vroom found that those with high needs for independence are more likely to respond to a democratic and participative style of leadership, while those with high dependence needs want structure and clear guidance. Some people *want* to be told what to do [2.5]. Thus, when there is a mismatch there is bound to be tension or conflict and a drop in morale. Most groups have some members who fight against all attempts by the 'parent' to control them. Other people behave like docile obedient children, and refuse to take the initiative or accept responsibility even though a 'democratic' leader offers it to them. They love to fall back into the safe role of follower so that, like children, they can enjoy the security of a dependent relationship. This pushes all the leadership responsibility – for decision-making, ideas, enthusiasm – onto the boss. An effective antidote is to give the dependent individuals particular responsibilities, specific problems to solve, areas in which *they* have to provide the ideas and make the decisions. This forces them to play a positive, active role and thus develops their management potential.

Milgram's studies in the 60s showed the astonishing power that authority had over many individuals. Volunteers, who believed they were partaking in a study of memory and learning, were stood in front of a row of thirty switches labelled from 30 to 450 volts and told by the stern, authoritative 'experimenter' in his white coat to give increasingly severe 'shocks' to a learner-victim, who was strapped in a chair, if he answered questions wrongly. The victim gave incorrect answers to three out of every four questions.

When the shock (as the volunteer believed) reached the 300-volt level, the learner-victim, as prearranged, kicked on the wall of his room next door. When the volunteer asked the experimenter for guidance he was told authoritatively to carry on right up to the maximum voltage and to ignore the pounding. Two-thirds of the volunteers went on to administer 450 volts to the victim although in many cases they were sweating, laughing nervously, stuttering, and showing other signs of severe emotional disturbance. The degree of obedience to the authority figure seemed incredible to Milgram and his colleagues.

In many industries, autocratic management methods appear to be more and more of an anachronism, completely out of synch with the democratic, liberated age that has arrived at the other side of the factory gate. While autocratic leadership styles may flatter the egos of the few top men, just how stultifying they can be for everyone else many a loss-laden annual report has shown. Often they produce high levels of frustration combined with low levels of accomplishment – not least because autocratic leadership is likely to reflect a negative, pessimistic view of man, and people tend to live up to other people's expectations of them.

It is easy to recognise the symptoms of autocratic leadership methods:

1 There is no criticism of top management; decisions are never challenged.
2 Yes-men abound.
3 Individuals are extremely status-conscious.
4 Individual executives are reluctant to take decisions.
5 Everybody sticks to the rules. Requests and suggestions are forwarded through the proper channels and procedures.
6 Feelings of powerlessness in face of the central bureaucracy.
7 Apathy and bewilderment among managerial staff.
8 Too many committees, too much buck-passing and referring problems and decisions up the line.
9 Managers show little concern for efficiency or profits.

A tough, hard-driving leader is needed, says Levinson, when 'a situation is such that it calls for heroic rescue or rebuilding efforts by a single person. . . . My own observations suggest that a heroic organising or rebuilding task takes from three to five years.' After the initial building period, 'a whole new group of managers must be introduced whose talents lie less in their own vigorous attack and more in coordinating and supporting the problem-solving abilities of groups' [2.6].

Why do so many tough, aggressive business leaders behave meekly and submissively at home? Perhaps they are simply trying to restore the balance. At work, the boss is forced by his role to command, to domineer, to be unnaturally aggressive and competitive, his basic business aim being to drive rivals out of a job or even out of business. On returning home, the manager tends deliberately to correct the balance by playing a more gentle, submissive role with his wife.

Sizing up the situation

Leaders need to be sensitive to employees' preferences and needs; to adjust their style to meet employee preferences. Effective leadership begins when the manager sizes up the situation, decides what kind of leadership is required, then slips into the appropriate gear. Pushing ahead with participative devices when the workforce is looking for firm direction combined with low levels of performance.

Status-stripping is an example of this kind of miscalculation. The status-stripper is a leader without direction, a boss who, in effect, denies his authority and lets subordinates run things in their own way, set their own objectives, make their own decisions – even when the objective situation cries out for firm direction and control. A college department head let staff decide to drop a highly successful course because lecturers were 'not interested' in the subjects covered. A director of research let staff decide to work on a project which interested them but where the prospects of commercial application – and therefore financial return – were minimal. This kind of leader argues that leadership does not mean getting your own way but learning from others, giving subordinates their head, always accepting their ideas and decisions.

Such an approach works well in certain organisations, such as advertising agencies or some academic institutions, where much high-level creative work is being done : creative people often work well in a free, wide-open environment and the leader's job is therefore to create this kind of environment for them. Creative performance generally can't be commanded. 'An unstructured task seems to call for permissive, non-directive leadership' [2.7]. But in other situations, the permissive style of leadership can lead to disorganisation and loss of control, with individuals pursuing personal instead of corporate goals.

Status-stripping

If the leader tries to deny his own power and authority by stripping himself of status and authority, employees may join in, so that the leader becomes an object of open or secret ridicule, and decision-making becomes one long argument.

As Zaleznik [2.7] points out :

> 'All these attempts at status-stripping fail sooner or later. The executive may discover that his subordinates join in gleefully by stripping his status and authority to the point where he becomes immobilised, is prevented from making decisions . . . problem-solving and work become terrorised.'

In one department, the boss was a democratic nice-guy whose basic error was never to assert his authority and slap down the fifth-column. Some of his subordinates, sensing his uncertainty and self-doubt, seemed to take delight in questioning his instructions and openly ridiculing his decisions. Later, one clique arranged to take it in turns to complain to the head of the organisation about the manager's incompetence. Eventually he was transferred and one of his critics became department head.

Like individuals, organisations pass through different stages of maturity, and at each stage a particular kind of leadership is required.

In the early stages of a company's growth, organisational requirements are less sharply defined and understood than they are at later stages. Hence the requirement for 'strong' leaders who can provide structure, direction, positive authority and clear guidelines for action.

But as the organisation grows, stable patterns and policies develop, the number of specialists increases and leadership passes into many hands. Thus administrative and coordinating skills are required. During the early stages of growth, the leader is often an individual taking solo decisions and independent action; but at a later stage, the committeeman and the 'company man' are likely to emerge as leaders because the top executive group as a whole must *collectively* solve problems, take decisions, set policy and control spending.

Mature groups often do well under *laissez-faire* leaders who exert a minimum of supervision and control: the members of the group understand better than the boss what needs doing and what methods should be used. Moreover, mature groups have worked through their most serious emotional problems, and usually work well together without the need for close supervision and control. The main requirement is that they should be left to get on with the job – with the leader taking periodic audits on progress. Immature groups, on the other hand, i.e. groups that are still experiencing serious interpersonal difficulties, need control and structure to allow them to operate without being torn apart by tension and conflict or paralysed by inhibition and withdrawal.

A group's development, like an individual's development, may be arrested by overstrong leadership and control. It has been suggested that all groups pass through four 'natural' stages of development:

1 *Forming:* much anxiety because of uncertainty about roles, objectives, relationships, etc. Thus much dependence on a 'strong' leader.
2 *Storming:* members experiment with relationships and roles; conflict between sub-groups; polarisation of opinion; rebellion against the leader.
3 *Norming:* members settle into roles; conflicts are resolved; norms emerge; group cohesiveness grows; a more democratic type of leadership is often required at this stage.
4 *Performing:* inter-personal difficulties are resolved; the group is able to concentrate on doing the job and achieving results.

The theory implies that before a group can perform effectively it must first pass through the preliminary tense and conflict-filled stages. In some cases it might make sense to appoint a permissive kind of individual to head a new department or division, somebody who will permit conflict and allow – even encourage – the open expression of feelings. This kind of leadership might well have the effect of expediting the process of group

development and, in the long run, improve the new unit's performance –
though the price to be paid is short-term conflict and disruption.

Predicting the leader's performance

A considerable body of research evidence suggests that the leadership
qualities needed in any particular situation are not concentrated in one
individual but spread among several. Thus, in filling a top-level vacancy,
the strength and weaknesses of the person being appointed should be
considered along with those of the people he will be working with.

In considering candidates for promoted positions at Tandberg in Norway, evaluations by the man's colleagues and by his subordinates are
carefully considered. The company reckons that a man's colleagues and
subordinates see many aspects of his behaviour of which his boss is not
even aware – his leadership and communication styles, for instance and
his team-building ability – and that they are therefore in a very good
position to advise on his suitability for leadership responsibility.

Valuable clues on predicting the future performance of appointees
come from Ohio State University research. A group of investigators tried
to predict how naval officers would perform in new jobs on the basis
of, first, previous job performance and, secondly, the performance of their
predecessors in the job. They found that the way a man would perform
in a new job could be forecast almost as well by looking at the behaviour
of the previous job holder as by examining the new leader's past performance. One of the researchers concluded that 'less than half' of the
leader's performance 'could be ascribed to the man and a little over half
to the demands of the particular job'.

Leaders at different levels

The unique characteristics of an organisation may be crucial in determining which of two equally competent executives will become a 'leader'.
Often, these organisational characteristics – the preferences of subordinates, perhaps, or the nature of the production process – vary according
to the leader's level, department or location. Thus traits and characteristics that spell success at one level may lead to frustration and failure
at a higher level or on a different site.

The ability to control and organise is often highly valued at middle
levels of management, but when the middle manager is appointed to a
senior executive position he may find that he is judged for risk-taking or
opportunity-seeking, and that nothing in his previous experience has
prepared him for these activities. He has arrived at his level of incompetence.

Top leaders must be able to control the organisation as a whole. That
is one of the reasons why nuts and bolts business experience is becoming

less important at top management levels. A 1976 *Fortune* report shows that the proportion of chief executive officers with primary experience in production, engineering, design, or R&D has fallen from a third of the total in 1952 to a quarter today [1.1]. Instead, accountants and lawyers are getting to the top in increasing numbers, heading about two-fifths of the largest companies in the US. Presumably they have become so involved in virtually every facet of modern capitalism, says the report, that they learn more about their companies than anyone else and so are better equipped to control them. One CEO, an accountant, reports : 'I'm "in" on every function so I know the right questions to ask and when to ask them. I can keep track of everything.'

Identifying leaders

These are some of the reasons why, when appointing people to leadership positions at any level in the organisation, it is essential to take into account not only the individual's qualities and qualifications but also the situation in which he will be acting – now and in the future. The approach used by many companies – particularly in the US – is to evaluate the job, identify the need for a particular kind of leadership, then use psychological tests to help select the candidate with the most suitable profile. Guetzkow and Stogdill [2.8] conclude that it is not difficult to find people who have leadership qualities, but that it is more difficult to place these people in situations where they will be able to function effectively as leaders. *Perhaps the key to effective placement is to take great pains (by bringing in outside consultants or process development experts, perhaps) to place newly appointed managers in units which will be likely to respond favourably to the new man's 'natural' leadership style.*

Fortunately, the size of the problem is reduced because of a natural selection process which seems to occur, with leaders gravitating towards the kind of jobs, units, companies and roles that most suit them. A tough leader might be attracted to a job involving a lot of hard bargaining with the unions. A human relations specialist might apply for a job requiring diplomacy, tact and the ability to get on with the rest of the team.

Individualistic leaders the best?

Leadership is a highly individual process. A style that works well for one man may not work for another man in the same situation – or even for the same man in a different situation. Thus every manager must discover for himself his 'natural' leadership style – what does and does not work in his own work situation.

Ghiselli concluded, after studying managerial behaviour, that those the best leaders.

Bulmers encourage distinctive styles of leadership at all levels of management, and strongly encourage managers to do their own thing and develop their interests. These interests currently include free-fall parachuting, cross-Atlantic sailing, and kyacking. In a recent annual report, Bulmer's chairman, Prior, said : 'I have never been a great one for tradition. I have long felt it was at the root of many of our industrial ills. Indeed, in some ways I have felt that non-conformity was almost a positive virtue; one which promoted virtue in industry and, very often, greater productivity.' The approach seems to work at Bulmers where production has been rising steadily for several years, with no time lost through disputes.

Walden, who runs Capricorn Records in Georgia, has a highly unorthodox – and successful – leadership style. He comes to the office when he feels like it wearing jeans, T-shirt and sneakers, with hair down to his shoulders. He wanders round the building joking, chatting up the chicks. He opens a business meeting with a round of scotch highballs. The point is that his style suits the pop world in which he operates. As he says, 'If you can make money *and* have fun and power, that's what it's all about'.

Formidable individuals

Ogilvy, head of the successful New York advertising agency, Ogilvy and Mather, has said :

> I have observed that no creative organisation, whether it is a research laboratory, a magazine, a Paris kitchen or an advertising agency, will produce a great body of work unless it is led by a formidable individual. The Cavendish laboratory at Cambridge was great because of Lord Rutherford. The *New Yorker* was great because of Ross, The Majestic was great because of Pitard. Few of the great creators have bland personalities. They are cantankerous egotists, *the kind of men who are unwelcome in the modern organisation.*

Ogilvy supplies a good reason for tolerating, even encouraging, the appointment of mavericks to positions of senior responsibility in the organisation. But in most organisations there are strong pressures to conform to the ruling philosophy and value system. To rise to a senior position in a large organisation may demand decades of toiling alongside other sober, professional managers or administrators; rising by means of careful manoeuvres and tactics through a tough management evaluation system that weeds out the individualists and the non-conformists. By the time these leaders have risen to the top, they are part of a homogeneous group where non-conformist views and behaviour are definitely not acceptable. General Motors chairman, Murphy, makes the point succinctly: 'If you become an earache you just get turned off'. A few years ago, when some GM managers tried to persuade the company to scale down the size of some of its models in response to the small-car trend, they just got turned off.

New kinds of leadership

The rapid transformation of work during the past few decades has, arguably, created a need for a fresh cast of characters at the corporate summit. In 1900, 80 per cent or more of the workforce in industry was blue-collar. Today, the proportion has shrunk to less than half. Nearly a third of total employees in most industries today are professional, managerial and technical people. Studies by Baker and Davies suggest that about 30 per cent of manufacturing employees are concerned primarily with producing and processing information. There is a different kind of workforce: is a new kind of leader needed to manage them?

Consider how the technology influences the kind of leadership required. For instance, unit or small-batch production usually requires a supervisor with plenty of technical or craft skill so that he can help employees with the frequent non-routine problems that crop up. The supervisor must also be capable of exercising general rather than close supervision.

On the other hand, a mass-production factory where the average skill levels of employees is low, needs 'traditional' supervisors who will exercise close supervision. The supervisors are not necessarily highly skilled, but they do need to be able to plan and organise work – i.e. to be 'production-centred' rather than 'employee-centred' in their leadership style.

Task determines management style?

Morse and Lorsch studied two R&D units and two units manufacturing standard containers on automated production lines [2.9]. The successful manufacturing unit had a pattern of formal rules, procedures and control systems. 'We've got rules for everything', said one manager, 'from how much powder to use in cleaning the toilet bowls to how to cart a dead body out of the plant!'.

The management style was directive. Another manager made the point: 'We make sure each man knows his job, knows when he can take a break, knows how to handle a change in shifts, and so on. It's all spelled out clearly.'

The investigators conclude that structured practices and 'traditional' leadership were suitable for the plant because behaviour had to be rigidly controlled around the automated production line. There was only one way to accomplish the plant's routine, programmable task – and it was the leaders' responsibility to define and control it by means of clear instructions, checks, formal reports, operating review sessions, and so on.

There was, however, noticeably less structure and control in the less successful manufacturing unit, the implication being that this unit had failed to find the leadership style most appropriate to the production process.

In the successful R&D unit, there was very little structure, and little control over the behaviour of research workers. The effect was to encourage the individualistic and creative behaviour that the uncertain, rapidly changing research task needed. There was notably more restraint and structure in the less successful research unit: a researcher there complained, 'There are rules and things here that get in your way regarding doing your job as a researcher'.

The conclusion is that one of the main responsibilities of the top-level leadership in any organisation is to tailor the management style to fit the task and the people. Argyris goes a stage further: 'Effective leaders are those who are capable of behaving in many different leadership styles depending on the requirements of reality . . . I call this "reality-centred" leadership' [2.10]. Certainly, the rigid person who cannot, to some extent, adapt his style to the situation will find it difficult to succeed in a changing environment.

Subtler methods needed

'A company needs leadership, not communication', mutters one dictator who refuses to accept the fact that times – and employees – have changed. A strong believer in the whip and the carrot, he sent his employees this memo:

> As from today you must let me know your movements when leaving the office, your estimated time away, the purpose of your visit, your contact, and the telephone number where you can be reached. Failure to comply will result in disciplinary action being taken.

Two days later came another mortar-bomb restricting the use of company cars and threatening to take them away unless the instructions were carried out to the letter. But when strike action was threatened, he blamed 'troublemakers', not himself.

In offices, and in factories concerned with the high-technology end of the spectrum, jobs and workers are generally so sophisticated that general rather than close supervision and a more democratic style of leadership is required. In many organisations staffed largely by advanced technical and professional personnel, the leader can no longer function effectively by means of traditional supervision and control. Join me in a plant where a machinist is setting up a new stop valve – the valve must be able to close instantly in case of a power failure, otherwise an entire turbine-generator system will be ruined. Overhead is a computer readout which gives the man the information he needs to do his job. The supervisor wanders up, has a chat about football, walks away. It's hard to imagine occasions where he, or any other manager, would want to tell this machinist how to do his job. And in modern industry there are millions like him. Their sophistication, responsibility and know-how limit the kind of leadership-styles which a boss can successfully use.

Mirabel, an executive with General Electric, remembers that when he first joined GE 23 years ago, women working on components for generators painstakingly wrapped three layers of resin-soaked tape round each metal conductor bar. Now this task is done by operators controlling machines worth nearly a third of a million dollars each. The job has moved four or five rungs up the sophistication ladder – and the manager's style has had to change too. A man with a Coca-Cola style of leadership wouldn't last long at GE today. Sophisticated employees judge the boss not by the size of his fist but by the size of his brain, and on the basis of his technical, administrative and structuring ability, and his ability to talk freely and on level terms about job problems.

Range of styles

Tannenbaum and Schmidt (1958) postulate a kind of leadership continuum with at least four leadership styles located on it :
1   *Autocratic*   the leader forces compliance.
2   *Persuasive*   the leader sells his ideas and whips up support and enthusiasm among his followers.
3   *Consultative*   the leader confers with subordinates – then takes the decision.
4   *Democratic*   the leader involves subordinates in policies and decisions.

The range of possible leadership styles is shown in Figure 3. This shows the different degrees of authority assumed by the leader and the different degrees of 'participation' allowed to subordinates. The particular point on the scale that the leader should opt for depends largely on the characteristic working situation. Answer the following questions to help determine which kind of style your own situation demands :
1   Is the workforce skilled or unskilled, technical or non-technical, sophisticated or unsophisticated?
2   Would it increase your own time-efficiency to involve others in decision-making? Could those others afford the time? Leaders often strive for extra participation without appreciating the extra time-investment that is required.
3   Have you enough information, experience and know-how to make the decision alone? Decisions made on inadequate information may need to be corrected or cancelled at a later stage.

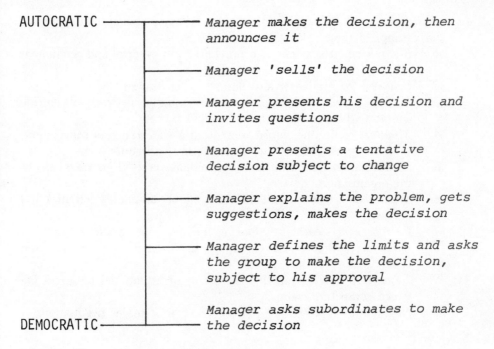

```
AUTOCRATIC ─────┬───── Manager makes the decision, then
                │       announces it
                │
                ├───── Manager 'sells' the decision
                │
                ├───── Manager presents his decision and
                │       invites questions
                │
                ├───── Manager presents a tentative
                │       decision subject to change
                │
                ├───── Manager explains the problem, gets
                │       suggestions, makes the decision
                │
                ├───── Manager defines the limits and asks
                │       the group to make the decision,
                │       subject to his approval
                │
DEMOCRATIC ─────┴───── Manager asks subordinates to make
                        the decision
```

Figure 3   Styles of leadership

4   Should other people be involved in decisions to win their commit-
    ment to the decision and thus increase the chances of smooth
    implementation? Could you win their commitment even if you took
    the decision alone?
5   If you involved subordinates in a particular decision, would there
    be conflict and disagreement?
6   Would the involvement of others increase the quality of the deci-
    sion?

Clearly, some situations require one style of leadership, different situations require another. Yet research suggests that managers tend to use
one preferred style, irrespective of the situation – understandably so, for,
arguably, subordinates need a consistent relationship with their boss so
that they know where they stand. Subordinates often become anxious
when they are not sure what the boss's style is, or when that style changes
constantly.

Ten roles

Several diary studies – by Stewart, Carlson and others – have revealed
the wide range of leadership skills that executives need to deploy. In *The
Nature of Managerial Work*, Mintzberg describes ten roles which the

42 manager should be capable of playing – though obviously the relative importance of these roles varies from job to job:

1 *Figurehead* – the symbolic head. This requires social and ceremonial skills.
2 *Leader* – the motivator and director of employees.
3 *Liaison expert* – building and maintaining a network of outside contacts who provide information and favours.
4 *Monitor* – collecting information from a wide range of sources and thus acting as a kind of nerve-centre in the organisation.
5 *Dissemination* – transmitting information received to members of the organisation.
6 *Spokesman* – telling outsiders about the organisation's activities and results.
7 *Entrepreneur* – constantly looking for new opportunities.
8 *Disturbance-handler,* overcoming unexpected disturbance and crises.
9 *Resource-allocator* – distributing scarce organisational resources between competing claims.
10 *Negotiator* – representing the organisation at major negotiations.

3

'The organisation is a system with a logic of its own, the weight and tradition of inertia. The deck is stacked in favour of the tried and proven way of doing things and against the taking of risks and striking out in new directions.'

John D. Rockefeller

Leaders and administrators

What makes the really successful organisation stand out from all the rest? Dynamic and effective leadership.

What makes Volvo, for instance, or Marks and Spencer, or Josiah Wedgwood & Son, prosper and expand while their less successful rivals are fighting the unions, closing factories, laying off thousands of employees? Strong and effective leadership.

In the highly competitive world of business, decisive leadership can mean the difference between survival and failure. Yet decisive leaders seem to be in extremely short supply.

In preparing this book I talked to scores of executives in a wide range of industries. Almost all agreed that there is no shortage of managers who are capable of doing the routine work – the administrative chores; but that there is a real shortage of managers who are capable of exercising such decisive leadership, via innovation, motivation, opportunity-grasping, that they actually make a significant difference to results.

Perhaps one reason for the shortage is that strong leaders are rarely comfortable people to have around. They are often abrasive, disruptive, idiosyncratic people who fail to fit comfortably not only into their own organisation but into any organisation. How many potentially outstanding leaders never make the grade because they are held back by the establishment, or branded as non-conformists, or trouble-makers, at an early stage in their careers?

Every day the manager is confronted with new problems and conditions. Yesterday's solutions do not fit today's problems – even less, tomorrow's. Thus the ability to enjoy and participate in change is an important aid to leadership in an environment which is growing in uncertainty and complexity. Sloan, General Motors' chairman in the 1920s, has said: 'We had no stake in the old ways of the automobile business. For us, change meant opportunity.' Contrast this approach with that of today's top management. When asked during the oil crisis if GM ought to reconsider its policy of making only big cars, Terrell, a member of the executive committee, retorted: 'I don't see any difference in the size of people walking round here'.

The experience of Polaroid and Edwin Land demonstrates how business leaders operate. Nobody demanded a camera that also printed the pictures, but that didn't stop Land giving it to them. Years later, Land made another big decision: to spend big money developing the SX-70 instant colour camera. An impatient, pushing man, Land insisted on speedy development. This meant that Polaroid was first to market. But it also led to many technical problems that dented the company's profit graph. But Land remains unrepentant. He *knows* he was right: 'I represent a framework of ideas. The men who have come with us know this framework and have chosen to live with it'.

Outstanding business leaders are initiators rather than responders. They act rather than react with regard to the market, employees, policy. Read the biography of any great business leader from Edison to Henry Ford and you find the same irresistible drive and determination to put ideas into action, to do your own thing, to convince other people.

The leader *wants* to lead the way, to explore opportunities, to discover new markets, methods and techniques. Ansoff argues that the leader is a divergent thinker, a risk-taker, with a positive attitude to change [3.1].

Lone-wolf leaders

The leader often turns out to be an individual who is somewhat separate from his environment and from other people. He may work in organisations but he never belongs to them. Force this kind of individual to immerse himself in administrative detail or to fit into a team and all the energy and initiative drain out of him.

Ford and Rockefeller were essentially lone-wolf leaders with a keen money-scent. They piled up their fortunes not by fitting comfortably into some organisation but by pioneering completely new industries. Rockefeller has said: 'An organisation is a system with a logic of its own, the weight and tradition of inertia. The deck is stacked in favour of the tried and proven way of doing things and against the taking of risks and striking out in new directions.' The leader, he implies, must from time to time resist or defy the organisation if he wishes to lead in ideas or action. Especially at times of rapid economic and technical ferment, organisations need innovation as well as control. Companies need mavericks as well as good team-men, chancers who can pluck opportunity out of crisis.

Johnson, former president of MIT, says that more organisations need more leaders – risk-taking individuals who are receptive to change, and with the capacity for translating their ideas into action. Leadership, says Johnson, 'requires boldness, aggression, and a willingness to take risks' – qualities which may trigger off resentment and suspicion in the organisation.

The leader, says Johnson, sets challenging goals, strikes out in new directions and communicates a sense of excitement about them to his colleagues and subordinates. He makes people think that this is the way to go, and that the new direction is not only exciting but essential. He fights until his ideas win acceptance. He must have the drive, determination and egotism to convince people, in spite of widespread scepticism and opposition, that something new and exciting has arrived. Gillette *knew* he was on to a winner with his idea of a cheap disposable blade. When the steel men told him his idea was dud he refused to believe them. He kept trying – and eventually won the support of a lamp manufacturer.

'Balanced' management

In a way, leadership is an anachronism in the modern world, for it appeals to 'the sheer humanness of man as an utterly radical alternative to the oppressiveness of advanced technological society'. Modern society, on the other hand, strongly believes in rational, structured methods of problem-solving – in organisation and methods and management 'techniques' which can be used impersonally and precisely. Perhaps the business world is *over*-rational, *over*-administered and, as Wilson has argued, leaders are needed to re-enchant it and as 'a reassertion of faith in human virtues' [3.2].

Certainly many organisations seem to over-value the technical specialist and the administrator and to undervalue the leader. Indeed, an over-valuation of administrative skills is opposed to leadership. As Barnard explains [3.3] such an over-valuation 'opposes leadership whose function is to promote appropriate adjustment of ends and means to new environmental conditions, because it opposes change either of status in general or of habitual procedures and habitual routine. This over-valuation also discourages the development of leaders by retarding the progress of the abler men and by putting an excessive premium on routine qualities.'

Arguably, the modern industrial organisation needs a combination of the protective management of, say, General Motors or Courtaulds, and the bold, expansionist leadership of Lourho, Cavenhams or Sears, Roebuck. In some companies, this would mean adjusting appointment and promotion policies to ensure a *balanced* management team consisting both of administrators and aggressive, innovative leaders – of 'proactive' as well as 'homeostatic' managers [3.4].

The proactive leader is aggressive, outside-oriented and much concerned with seeking outside opportunities in the environment. The homeostatic manager (or administrator) is more concerned with the efficient functioning of the internal system, with maintaining stability and balance among people and forces. Both kinds of manager are needed. Thus the Catholic Church alternates between homeostatic ('religious') and proactive ('political') Popes, and a similar pattern is discernible in the American Presidency.

Unbalanced management – for instance, too many administrators and excessive conformity within the management team – can lead to stagnation and decline, as the failure of many large, bureaucratic companies, such as Penn Central, has demonstrated.

The leader himself needs to strike a balance – not necessarily in his personality, for almost every leader is 'lop-sided' in some way or another, but in the way he allocates his own time to competing demands. Many of the leaders I have interviewed seem to have achieved such a balance – typically, by reserving particular parts of their daily and weekly time-tables for different functions. For instance, many executives move from fairly routine, administrative jobs early in the day to more diffuse, long-term problems, such as planning activity, later in the day. Other leaders concentrate on their administrative role early in the week, switching to a 'leadership' role (planning, innovation, meetings with subordinates, etc.) later in the week. Cohen and March found that this balanced, cyclical allocation of time was followed by most of the college presidents they talked to [3.5].

Leaders and administrators play complementary roles in the organisation. Each needs the support of the other. Once the leaders have set the objectives and planned the strategy and tactics, so that decisions can be made on the basis of clear-cut criteria, the administrator can take over. A clear, consistent and widely understood corporate plan is, in fact, one of the best guarantees of effective administration. But it is easier to set objectives and plan strategy in the first place when the organisation is already efficiently controlled by the administrators. 'Old activities can be abandoned without excessive strain if, for example, the costs of relatively inefficient but morale-saving transfer and termination can be absorbed' [3.6].

Leading by example

A highly personalised management style is a mark of the successful leader. Ghiselli concluded, after a study of managerial behaviour, that the managers who were judged the best leaders were those with the greatest individuality of style. The administrator or bureaucrat controls affairs impersonally, from a distance, via systems, procedures and intermediaries. But the *leader* is generally too pushing and impatient to wait for the normal procedures to take effect; finds it more natural to lead by persuasion and personal example. Nearly all of the leaders I interviewed admitted that they are more comfortable when dealing with matters directly and personally, rather than indirectly through 'systems'.

Typically, the leader projects himself into any situation where problem-solving by persuasion or example is needed. 'He is not everywhere in the company, but he *is* where the action is' says Hanan [3.7]. He has the knack of appearing at the decisive moment – when a problem is looming or a decision is pending; he may avoid committee meetings as a rule, but he always attends the crucial ones. In the past, great military leaders were often seen in the front line at one moment and at the best overall vantage point the next. They regularly stood back and took an objective look at operations, but they also knew when it was necessary to get involved with people and action, when to get their hands dirty.

The administrator (or conventional manager) has the routine operation and systems under control. But he never questions whether the routines should be done at all, whether the rules need changing. He concentrates on the routine aspects of his job because these are the easiest and safest to deal with. An executive in an electronics firm candidly admits that whenever he is faced with a controversial or high-risk decision he refers it up the line because 'if you stick your neck out in this place you get your head chopped off'.

Most managers are administrators

Leavitt, Stewart and other investigators have identified the tendency of most managers to respond to the routine, programmed tasks facing them (administration) before tackling the unprogrammed ones (innovation, planning, opportunity-seeking). Thus, most managers are, in effect, administrators. The unprogrammed activities – the opportunity-grabbing, and so on – are the creative aspects of the manager's job. Leaders are intensely involved in these activities while 'administrators' tend to avoid them.

One reason for their avoidance is the kind of Gresham's law that seems to operate in many companies, with routine work driving out the non-routine. Often managers are so overloaded with routine work, so immersed in day-to-day operations, that they never find time to stand back and ask themselves fundamental questions about the organisation's purposes and objectives, where it should be heading, what radical changes are needed. This explains why so few organisations have ever studied their own administrations – and why the management of time is an essential prerequisite for effective leadership.

As several investigators have discovered, the manager's work is not systematic or planned but, instead, is characterised by brevity, variety, discontinuity. Most managers are, in fact, strongly action-oriented, with a positive dislike of reflective activities or of rational, systematic methods of decision-making. Yet the leader at every level *must* reflect, *must* have vision and a sense of perspective so that he knows where the organisation is heading (otherwise how can he lead it there?). He needs time for reflecting on the future forces that may impinge on the organisation, time for assessing the organisation's goals and performance, time for planning new directions and clarifying problems.

Opportunity-seeking

One of the leader's main functions is to act as the dynamic change-bringer and opportunity-seeker in the company; to select new areas to penetrate, new ways of doing things, new things to do. This is the leader's role. (The administrator's role is to examine the leader's ideas and plans for viability prior to implementation.)

Administrators have to be hot on detail; leaders often are not. One researcher discovered that leaders try to avoid getting over-involved in details so that they can concentrate on wider, strategic matters [3.8]. They often make poor administrators because they are careless about details and disrespectful of procedures, structures, protocol. The leader is often far more interested in building than maintaining, careless about controlling what he has created. His projects and plans, once implemented, often run into financial and organisational trouble. It is at this stage that the administrators should take over.

Administrators feel at home in a big-company climate, and seem to enjoy seeking agreement from each other, making compromises and deals, playing politics, attending committee meetings and so on. The leader, on the other hand, often feels impatient with and contemptuous of these 'procedures', and uncomfortable in a large bureaucratic organisation that just seems to grind along under its own momentum. That may be one of the reasons why an increasing number of Business School graduates are expressing a preference for more open, informal companies instead of the staid corporate giants. The managing director of a firm of builders' merchants says: 'I much prefer working in a small company because one must do in person many of the things the big firm would do via a system'. Leaders like to feel that they are personally in control and can take the decisions.

Fitting in

The administrator or steady-state manager, on the other hand, gets to the top by fitting in, by not rocking the boat, by being a good committee man. As Mills has pointed out, 'The stress is on agility rather than

ability, on "getting along" in a context of associates, superiors and rules
. . . on who you know . . . on techniques of self-display and the
generalised knack of handling people' [3.9].

Whyte has, somewhat satirically, described Organisation Man's way of
getting ahead :

> For a young man on the make there is no better vehicle than the
> conference way . . . via the conference he can expose himself to all
> sorts of superiors across the line of command. Given minimum com-
> mitteemanship skills, by an adroit question here and a modest
> suggestion there, he can call attention to himself and still play the
> game [3.10].

The rewards for playing the game, for fitting in and accepting the
bureaucracy and its values, are good. They include high salaries, status,
perks, a secure job. But the price to be paid is excessive conformity.
IBM's founder, Watson, once complained that 'all IBM men look the
same to me'. A consultant psychiatrist at IBM has, in fact, pointed to
intense conformist pressures on executives and 'an underlying and un-
healthy mental attitude throughout the corporation'.

What the administrator or establishment manager most needs for
success is 'maze brightness' – sensitivity to the organisation's value system
and a willingness to accept it, an awareness of political and power
systems, knowing which individuals and which departments have got the
most weight and how they should be approached. Thus the administrator operates essentially *within* the system and succeeds by adjusting to it.
The leader, by contrast, is always somewhat *outside* of the system, and is
more willing to challenge power cliques and the organisation's values.

Avoiding change

Bureaucracy, according to Fromm, is 'a method of managing in which
people are dealt with as if they were things'. Bureaucracy is easy to
criticise but it is necessary : all large organisations and all states are
managed in a bureaucratic way. The achievements of the Tudors, the
Romans, the Church, would have been impossible without bureaucratic
organisation.

But since bureaucrats and administrators are responsible for maintaining stability and order in the organisation, they tend to be cautious and
preoccupied with fire-fighting and daily operating problems. They instinctively distrust change and often oppose decisions and projects which
threaten to disrupt the customary workings of the organisation.

Organisations which are dominated by the administrators are cautious,
conservative and slow-moving. Administrators, as a type, will gladly
support all new proposals as long as they combine low investment risk
with guaranteed commercial success, i.e. none of them. They know the

cash value of everything and the true value of nothing and so instinctively clip the wings of high-flyers.

Administrators are change-avoiders because they realise that innovation is a high-risk activity : the greater the departure from present practice the less chance of the innovation working.

Disruption is an inescapable aspect of the change process. New products and systems are conceived in anxiety and delivered in pain. Introducing a new technique or restructuring a division can be a painful business which triggers off serious social and psychological consequences. Thus, creative, innovative leaders make for a less stable and secure, more disturbing environment.

Radical decisions are risky decisions because they may turn out to be wrong or unpopular, and the administrator cannot afford to be either. Radical decisions may lead to people and groups losing power, influence and status; they shake up the social and political system of the organisation. Thus, the administrator develops ploys to counter such decisions, such as delaying tactics, or rigid application of procedural rules so as to delay and discourage the decision-makers.

As a result, the decision-making machinery works very slowly in some firms, with new ideas proceeding slowly up managerial levels until they emerge at the top, fully packaged, as a business plan or request for capital. Sometimes there is an elaborate screening procedure :

> In some companies the 'new idea forms' which must be filled out by innovators require a fullness and precision of detail impossible early in the life of a new product idea. Such screening mechanisms require that each idea be developed verbally before support is given for its development; they have the effect either of discouraging submission of new ideas or of forcing development work underground [3.11].

The most usual kind of screening apparatus set up by administration is a system of interlocking committees through which all major proposals must pass. During the process they stand an excellent chance of being outdated by events or changed beyond recognition.

Faceless companies

Administrators aren't leading, says Bennis, they're consulting, delaying, temporising – administrating. 'They've got sweaty palms and they're scared. One reason is that many of them don't have the faintest concept of what leadership is all about' [3.12]. The administrator identifies closely with the organisation and rarely questions its goals. He thus often takes a somewhat narrow view of his work that may confine him to the ranks of middle management.

Instead of providing leadership – setting clear objectives and motivating employees to achieve them – the administration takes refuge in cosmetic devices – consultative committees, 'participation' exercises, and so on. Consultation is important, but not when what is most needed is a strong initiative from the boss. When clear guidelines and decisive actions by the boss are needed, all that democratic devices may mean to the shop floor is that the boss cannot make up his mind.

Vernon, managing director of engineering company Ash and Lacy, says: 'Britain has the best potential workforce in the world – ruined by bad leadership. British industry is failing simply because there has been a failure of leadership in every sphere, political, trade unions and industrial. As a result the workforce at every level is confused and disillusioned.'

Vernon adds: 'Big-company management has abdicated its responsibility in recent years, has failed to lead, has failed to speak out and has lost contact with its employees'.

An executive in a large electronics company attributes the recent dent in his company's profit graph to uninspired leadership: 'There are no leaders in the company – it's faceless. Everybody is hiding behind somebody else. The company is run by committees, not individuals. Even the general manager has to refer everything to a committee'.

Leadership, says General Sir John Hackett, depends on two basic qualities:
1   Professional competence – the ability to solve problems in your own area.
2   Managerial ability – being able to get other people to act; encouraging employees to climb over obstacles in achieving their objectives.

To these two qualities, perhaps a third should be added: entrepreneurial flair, that inbuilt antenna possessed by business leaders such as Laker, of Laker Airways, and Rowlands, of Lonrho, and by political leaders, such as Jimmy Carter and Margaret Thatcher, that tells them where the opening is, where the opposition has blundered, which issues carry a heavy political payload.

Is leadership an art?

The leader needs both *professional competence* – the ability to solve problems in his own functional area – and also *managerial ability* – the ability to motivate other people to perform the task, and to climb over obstacles in achieving corporate goals. He must have the enthusiasm and communication ability to inspire his team so that they feel stronger, more competent, better able to accomplish their goals. While the administrator is talking about procedures, rules and form, the leader is talking about growth, challenge, new opportunities. He creates excitement in work by the way he talks about it. 'A leader, like an artist, can communicate his vision and create a response in those around him' [3.13].

Bulmers chairman, Prior, makes the point that successful executive leaders 'state clear objectives and encourage a sense of security by defining territories for individual action. They delegate real authority, do not interfere, and they praise more often than they criticise.'

The executive leader must be *action-oriented,* mobilising his team for action by boosting their confidence and enthusiasm. When one researcher tested an audience's reaction to the film of a speech by President Kennedy, he found that they felt strengthened and uplifted by the experience.

The group's representative

One of the leader's responsibilities is to express 'vivid goals which in some sense they want. . . . His role is to make clear which are the goals the group should achieve and then to create confidence in its members that they can achieve them' [3.14]. Thus, in a sense, the leader is somebody who crystallises his followers' aspirations, goals and interests. When the leader is dealing with some other group or organisation he must be able to communicate his own group's interests and viewpoint with forcefulness and clarity.

Followers depend on their leader
1   To identify their goals.
2   To make those goals sound worthy and exciting.
3   To plan ways of achieving the goals.
4   To lead the group towards them.

Gibb defines leadership as one of the mechanisms devised by groups for the efficient pursuit of their goals. 'It is to groups rather than to individuals that the concept of leadership is applicable' [3.15].

This may be an oversimplification, but the fact remains that a leader without followers stops being a leader; and a leader without enthusiastic, strong followers must be considered, in many ways, a weak leader whatever his personal qualities. Aristotle said that kings have the least freedom of all because they must conform to the common expectancy. Military leaders are trained to put their men's needs and welfare before their own. The leader must live up to other people's expectations and not offend their values. When Docherty, the successful former manager of Manchester United, left his wife to go and live with the wife of his club's physiotherapist, he offended both the club and its supporters (many of them are Roman Catholics). His leadership was rejected and he was dismissed. Rice has pointed out that a leader's authority comes from his followers. He must be able 'to carry his followers with him, inspire them, make decisions on their behalf, with or without their collaboration, and communicate the decision to others' [3.16]. The leader's conformity to the norms and values of the group attracts people and gives the leader his authority and influence. *A leader who exceeds his followers by too much loses his following and therefore his leadership.*

The leader is somebody whom his followers choose to follow because he fulfils their purposes and expresses their goals. Contrast the administrator who simply does what he's told by senior management.

Taking personal risks

What makes a successful leader? A recurring characteristic is that, like great military commanders, leaders know where they are going, then go there *despite any personal risk*.

When Byrom, now chief executive at Koppers Company, was a plant manager he made a decision to spend half a million dollars on new equipment for distilling coal tar. He was authorised to spend no more than $10,000 on his own, but he *knew* the plant had to have the equipment. He also knew the request would be rejected if referred to headquarters. So he installed it secretly. It could have cost him his job, though in the event it turned out to be a big success.

The entrepreneurial kind of leader is comfortable in the presence of a high risk/reward ratio and, conversely, is very uncomfortable without it. Both the risk and the reward must be high, says Hanan. 'Entrepreneurs climb the wall whenever there is too much reward for too little risk' [3.7].

Many successful leaders hate doing routine, mundane work and are temperamentally disposed to seek excitement and risks in their jobs – especially when there is a chance of high rewards. In this respect they resemble many sportsmen. Bonington, for instance, describes the various unwritten rules that climbers impose on themselves : 'A large number of rock-climbers in Britain and the Alps, which were first climbed using pitons for aid, have since ascended completely free, using only what the natural rock offers. . . . These self-imposed rules change in time, usually becoming more rigorous as the sport develops and frontiers of the unknown become more limited' [3.17]. For many mountaineers as for many business leaders, difficulty and risk is the name of the game and a high risk-reward ratio is an irresistible attraction.

For Bonington, one of the most attractive features of the 1975 British Everest expedition was that 'no matter what steps we took in our attempt to solve it – size of team, improved equipment, better food – our chances of success still seemed very thin'.

Opportunism

Opportunism is another strong characteristic of many leaders such as Kinney, General Mills president, who started his business career by borrowing $300 to gamble on a new idea. He bought crabs from fishermen – the sort that climb into lobsterpots and get tossed away – for a penny a piece, packaged the meat and sold it to the big companies. In ten years his company was grossing $2 million. Later, he turned fish into convenience food by packaging it in sticks and pre-cooked dinners. As he says: 'I wouldn't be here today if I weren't a risk-taker' [3.18].

When Brophy became president of General Telephone and Electronics, he saw an opportunity to combat the expense of sending a truck and technicians to install telephones. He opened 'Phone Marts' where customers can choose their own phones to plug into jacks at home. 'The phone becomes an impulse item and the cost savings are very substantial', says Brophy. By pioneering such innovations, Brophy has helped raise the company's average return on equity in the telephone business from 9.3 per cent in 1971 to 12 per cent today.

One chief executive has an unfailing test for identifying the entrepreneurial type of leader: 'I throw every candidate in with the alligators. The stable man complains he can't farm alligators in a swamp. The entrepreneur farms 60 per cent of the alligators, markets another 30 per cent for everything but their squeal, drains their part of the swamp, and leases the land for an amusement park overlooking 'Alligatorland'. The other 10 per cent of the alligators? That's his delayed compensation' [3.7].

True leaders are easy to recognise, according to Damroth, former chairman of the Lexington Research and Management Corporation. 'They're not going to talk about comfortable things. They're talking about a meaningful life, adventure, about risk-taking, new ideas and new directions.' According to this executive, true leaders are not the nice ones who are getting along, who look like they're going to be the next department head. 'They're the mavericks.'

Non-conformists

Members of the management team should be reasonably compatible and able to work together without being uniform yes-men. But some companies would rather risk obsolescence than make room for more non-conformists in their midst, and instead follow the Nixon pattern of demanding unconditional loyalty to the organisation and its values from all management personnel.

Such a policy can be a bad mistake, for in every organisation there are marginal people whose contacts and interests keep them at the boundaries of the organisation, between the organisation and the big outside world. As Bennis points out, in *The Unconscious Conspiracy*, such people can be invaluable to the company because they may be the organisation's only link with some better strategy or direction. But often they are seen as disloyal or dismissed as cranks.

The innovative, non-conformist individual is often regarded with suspicion because it is not easy to accept somebody who rejects the *status quo*. Such a leader is ahead or outside of the group to a certain extent, cuts across convention, disrupts the prevailing order – and so may be rejected or branded as a trouble-maker by those responsible for maintaining order, i.e. the administrators.

Yet the need for *more* innovative, expansionist leaders has been underlined by a number of recent forecasts pointing to such trends as the accelerating life-cycles of most new products, increasing foreign competition, and a greater need for home-based industries to penetrate foreign markets. 'I have never been a great one for tradition', says Bulmer's chairman, Prior. 'I have long felt it was at the root of many of our industrial ills. Indeed, in some ways I have felt that non-conformity was almost a positive virtue, one which promoted virtue in industry and, very often, greater productivity.'

Trend-setting

A leader who believes in setting the trend instead of following it is Kubie, chairman of Seligman and Latz, the world's largest operator of beauty salons. Kubie observed his wife's tendency to follow her daughter's advice about hair styles. That experience prompted him to open shops in Cornell University students' union in 1976. 'It's a listening post', Kubie explains. 'The styles will filter up.'

In many industries, leaders must innovate to ensure company survival and growth. In the clothing industry, for instance, innovation is almost a way of life. Dichter, founder of the Institute for Motivational Research explains: 'You have long had a seasonal change of styles. But now you're seeing more and more fashion fads within a single season, such as spearmint belts, the Army look, and so on.' Dichter believes that a way of mobilising companies to deal with rapid and radical change is to bring in younger, more aggressive aspirants to top leadership positions. Lord Ryder, former chairman of the National Enterprise Board, has often criticised elderly directors for clinging to power and refusing to devolve authority to the young Turks down the line with the taste for expansion and innovation.

Leadership on the board

In the chorus of complaints about lack of leadership at board level, there are as many suggestions for reform as there are voices. Change the membership of boards. Make boards smaller. Make boards bigger. Appoint stronger, better informed directors. Don't allow any one man to sit on more than two or three boards. But perhaps the reform which would command most support would be to make a majority of directors well-paid outsiders, with an independent staff at their disposal to examine corporate affairs. A settlement of a suit between Phillips Petroleum and a reformist shareholders group requires the company to add six new outsiders to the board, states that there shall always be a majority of outsiders over insiders, and that all future board additions shall be selected by a nominating committee consisting of outside directors, not management. Clearly, this kind of reform provides an important safeguard against corporate malpractice. In the interests of stronger leadership, some observers advocate a new breed of professional directors who serve on the board as a full-time job. These people would be able to study corporate affairs in far greater depth than directors whose occupations are not principally their directorships.

Texas Instruments found a way of making directors more independent. Three directors – two of them outsiders – were charged with studying the company's operations in depth and making recommendations about long-term goals. The directors were empowered to look at any aspect of the business and to talk to any employee. Later, the three directors made full reports to the board, which thus got the benefit of wide-ranging and reliable advice for establishing corporate priorities.

What qualities are required for board membership? According to one observer, they include:

> Analytical intelligence; the capacity to evaluate strategy; awareness of the social, political and economic environment; the ability to size up the CEO's chief subordinates; and an understanding of the company's strengths and weaknesses [1.17].

The managing director of an electronics equipment company told Copeman: 'The best board is one in which there is an independent outside chairman, a full-time managing director as his opposite number, also full-time functional directors, with each of these matched by an outside critical or consultant director with similar experience. . . . Everyone should have a sparring partner. There should always be two views on any expert matter – one of them the detailed inside view, and the other the wider, external view – perhaps the more objective view' [1.6].

Information challenge

It is naive to expect leadership and sound decisions from the board unless they are well informed. This is the thinking at the Harte-Hanks newspaper group, whose chief executive, Marbut, sends a monthly 'president's report' to the board. This gives the detailed story behind the results. It includes:

1   Production indicators.
2   Current problems.
3   Key elements of revenue, expense and sales.
4   Progress reports on major corporate projects.
5   Key indicators of performance for each division, e.g. production figures, delivery situations, etc.
6   A summary of collective bargaining activities.

Marbut is convinced that his 'directors' information service' has improved the board's decision-making because directors are now fully informed and aware of every occurrence of any consequence.

Ideally, a company should be led by a strong, decisive chief executive whose power is balanced by that of an independent, well informed board. 'The chief executive and his board should be in tune, really reading off the same sheet of music', says Madeline McWhinney, formerly president of the First Women's Bank of New York.

But in practice the board's role varies widely from company to company. Some boards are mere rubber stamps and give the chief executive a completely free reign, his only obligation being to report back once a month on actions taken. Other boards act more like policemen, constantly checking management's actions and involving themselves in many activities such as hiring and firing, approving expenditures, and so on.

Smith, of the management consultancy firm McKinsey and Company, says: 'It would be foolish to say that the board has a logical role. Its role is what the chief executive officer makes it – and there aren't very many who want a strong board.'

One reason why the chief executive so often dominates his board is that directors are the creation of the management they are supposed to supervise. Often directors are appointed as a reward for long and faithful service and become loyal retainers on the board. It is difficult for inside directors to challenge the chief executive or to exercise real leadership.

Continuous reform

Successful business leaders are change-bringers and change-seekers. A survey of 211 chief executives showed that the heads of fast-growing companies are more likely than their counterparts in less successful companies to view new products as the key to growth [3.19].

With rapidly changing technology and markets, many modern organisations are in a state of permanent revolution. Executives in a computer manufacturing firm report four major reorganisations of company structure during the past two years – 'and there's more in the pipeline'. Continuous reform of organisational structure and methods is one way of coping with continuous change. A consumer supplies manufacturer says: 'We have an O&M team permanently reorganising the company, sector by sector. They are more likely to cut staff than to increase it.'

Leadership is needed to initiate change and maintain the pace of innovation: change has to be *made* to happen. Leaders, for example, have to anticipate market trends then act fast to meet them. This is the thinking at YKK Zippers in Georgia where, one night a month, the chief executive officer meets the entire executive team, specifically to listen to any ideas they have for new products, new opportunities, market trends.

Another company stimulates innovation by insisting that senior managers spend a proportion of their time planning and controlling innovative projects. There are weekly meetings of the management group to discuss all matters relating to change and opportunity.

Honda promotes regular contests among employees to stimulate creative thinking which might, with further thought, lead to new product ideas. Prizes, for instance, were offered for the most original new vehicle using Honda engines. Prizes included a flying balloon and a one-wheeled motor bike.

The chief executive of a highly successful medium-sized company says he spends a lot of his time trying to identify new products and potential new businesses that are sprouting within the company. He tries to make sure that these innovations are not stifled or neglected at an early stage by such factors as budgetary limitations or too much concern for core product lines. When this leader spots a new opportunity, he will as often as not develop it as a separate profit centre – occasionally as a new division – and exempt it from the traditional planning and budgeting processes.

Stimulating innovation

International Telephone and Telegraph encourages leaders to innovate by putting financial pressure on profit centres. Each one has to put three per cent of its earnings into a central research fund and gets it back only for successful projects of general interest. Aeroject-General Corporation also uses financial pressures. For instance, it has set up a New Concept Fund to support the development of promising ideas which cannot be anticipated in ordinary budget projections. Each plant manager is allocated a sum to support personnel with promising new projects. Allocations are renewed if, after investigations, the idea appears worthwhile.

Innovations stem from new ideas, and the Institute of Life Insurance keeps on top of new ideas by giving to more than a hundred people from member companies a particular publication to monitor. Abstracts of important articles are made, and a committee meets every two months to consider them. Trend reports about such areas as 'Transportation' and 'Employees' are issued three times a year, each one discussing the implications of the trends for life insurance companies.

The chairman of another company keeps up-to-date by inviting important customers to lunch and discussing their future development plans. This helps him to keep in touch with changes and trends in the market. It also helps him to shape his own company's expansion with more assurance.

Losing market-grip

If a company fails to introduce necessary changes fast enough it can easily lose its market grip. When Mitsubishi Aircraft International decided to install heated windshields on one of its planes, the idea was kicked around for so long that several competitors beat the company to the actual change.

Fast action is needed to deal with market changes. Back in the sixties, Proctor and Gamble was hit by the success of Colgate's Ajax laundry detergent. To recoup the lost sales, Proctor and Gamble's top leadership decided to skip several stages in the product development process. They accelerated test marketing of a new detergent, Bold, and gave it a very high priority on marketing schedules. As a result of decisive leadership, the company was able to launch a counterattack in record time and win back lost sales. The company followed up by forming three teams with an advertising man, a sales executive and an R&D man in each. The teams were set against each other in competition and given just six weeks to throw off new product ideas. As a result of this move a wide range of profitable new products was born.

Innovative changes should, of course, always be followed by a careful appraisal of results. All aspects of the situation, including timing, costs, resources and bottlenecks, should then be compared carefully with the original plan. Why did things go wrong? Where were the weak links? A new projects manager in a rapidly expanding chemical company says: 'This kind of follow-up exercise gives valuable clues about how to plan and how to implement plans more effectively in the future'.

At Texas Instruments, top management grapples with the innovation challenge by turning the problem over to the shopfloor. Seventy-three per cent of manufacturing employees are organised in teams of between four and ten members each. Each team tries to produce a method improvement. For instance, in a warehouse a team worked out a new way of handling, inspecting and recording incoming material. Flow time from the receiving dock to the warehouse was cut from three weeks to three days; the value of material tied up in the flow was cut from $960,000 to $430,000; and the group's productivity shot up by 25 per cent. In 1976, more than 2000 innovations of this kind saved the company nearly $8 millions.

'Doomed to failure'

The history of innovation is full of opposition and scepticism. In 1906, three years after the Wright brothers had first flown, the engineering editor of *The Times* was saying that 'all attempts at artificial aviation are not only dangerous to human life but doomed to failure from an engineering point of view'. In every company, there are managers whose reaction to new work methods, new systems, new products and new participation schemes is 'It's dangerous. It's doomed to failure.' The leader's job is to convince these conservatives that the company's sales and earnings will respond with alacrity to innovative projects which are carefully selected and subject to stringent financial controls throughout the development and launch stages.

Professor Revans has said that 'when events move fast adjustment must move even faster. Whole organisations, not only selected individuals within them, must learn to adjust.' Consider, for instance, the constant stream of new products that many industries must spawn to stay alive, because of the shortening duration of products' primary life cycle (often no more than two or three years).

These are some of the reasons that have prompted Kinney, General Mills' president, to make innovation a way of life. Nearly a quarter of the company's sales come from products that did not exist five years ago. As Kinney says, 'I wouldn't be here today if I weren't a risk-taker'.

Creating a favourable climate

One of the leader's primary duties is to create a favourable organisational climate for innovators and creative people. There is much evidence, for instance, that creative people work most effectively in a 'free', informal environment. The innovator, says Fiedler, 'requires the freedom provided by a non-threatening environment in which one can explore ideas which may seem off-beat even, after further thought, foolish' [3.20]. In 1962, Likert found that research scientists worked most effectively when they had considerable self-determination in their work combined with free access to someone in authority.

Innovators must venture and fail – they must be encouraged by knowing that their mistakes will be tolerated by top management, for most innovators are exposed to formidable odds against success: for instance, about four-fifths of new products fail. Yet it is a mistake for management to permit innovators to pursue only the relatively safe ideas for such items generally make little impact on sales, earnings or prestige.

The pace and quality of innovation can be stimulated by:

1   Reducing the number of administrative checks, reviews, constraints.
2   Deliberately trying to create a 'free', open atmosphere, in which non-conformist ideas are welcomed and non-conformist behaviour tolerated.
3   Bringing regular new blood into R&D, advertising, marketing and other 'creative' departments.
4   Taking risks with projects and people, backing the high-flyers. Innovation is all about risk-taking and there is no way of avoiding risk. When introducing a new product or service it is impossible, even with exhaustive market and motivational research, to determine in advance exactly how the market will react. As Drucker has said: 'The things one worries about seldom happen, while objections and difficulties no one thought about turn out to be almost imponderable obstacles'. Generally, low-risk policies bring low rewards.

The innovative organisation

When management philosophy stresses creativity as an organisational
goal and encourages it at all levels, this greatly improves the chances
of its occurring, and has the effect of accelerating the pace of innovation.
Creative, innovative organisations generally possess some or all of the
following characteristics:

1   More 'leaders' than 'administrators' at senior levels.
2   A policy of appointing and promoting creative, innovative people.
3   Creative personnel, such as some advertising and marketing men,
     research scientists, and so on, have high status and pay.
4   The organisation is committed to change and innovation in con-
     stantly reviewing its procedures, structure and strategy; takes risks
     with new projects and products; welcomes and carefully assesses all
     new ideas.
5   A free, informal atmosphere; non-conformity and dissent tolerated.
6   Participative decision-making.
7   Individuals fairly free in their choice of problems and methods.
8   Many contacts with outside sources; an outward-looking manage-
     ment.

Controls over projects

A new-products manager makes the point: 'It is necessary to ensure that
innovative projects and new products are likely to contribute to company earnings if they are successful. It must be made clear to the R&D
men, for instance, that they are in business not to produce the fanciest
hardware but to produce profits.' This executive reckons that pressure
should be put on R&D people – in the R&D committee, perhaps – to
produce hard evidence that the new product will eventually sell, and
that it will pay off by a particular time.

The company, moreover, must exercise financial control over R&D
projects instead of relying on the auditors and accountants. A financial
director says: 'We do an awful lot of R&D. But I don't recall that our
auditors look at any but the most expensive projects. There is never any
follow-up to see if the company actually ends up with the patents that
should follow the research.' Neglecting to do this kind of follow-up can
cost the company a lot of money.

An economist has pointed to the great number of 'technically inappropriate' R&D projects. 'Even up to present times, according to
American research data, from 60 to 90 per cent of such corporate pro-

jects turned out to be either inappropriate or completely ineffective' [3.21].

Thus any company should ask itself a lot of questions before putting its full backing behind new product developments, such as: What is the size of the potential market? How will we reach it with our message and the goods? Are similar products already on the market? Who are the competitors? What advantages will we have over them? Will seasonal or other fluctuations affect patterns of demand? Will the sales force have to be expanded or trained? What is the best time to launch?

Marketing arrangements

The risks involved in innovating are often considerable. Innovation is usually capital-intensive, especially in the crucial phases of development and launching of the new product, and many new products fail because of inadequate financial resources to carry the schemes through periods of unexpected difficulty or expense. That explains why so many companies drastically limit the number of new products: they lack the capital (or think they do). A way of boosting the small company's chance of success with new products is to make a marketing arrangement with a big company which has the resources to put the new product on the market. Even if the small company can do this for itself its coverage must be very limited, and it usually lacks the prestige and reputation which will encourage a retailer or wholesaler to say yes.

Small companies are often short of capital; large companies, on the other hand, tend to be instinctively cautious and conservative in their approach to innovation, with vested interests protecting themselves fiercely against currents of change and against leaders with radical new ideas. In large companies, the leader is confronted with over-cautious managers and committees. 'There are so many people to be consulted and so many committees to be convinced', says an executive in a large chemical company, 'and such a tremendous effort is required to get a proposal accepted that it is easier simply to forget it.'

Big-company lethargy helps to explain why it is that small companies have such a powerful track record in pioneering new techniques. The Wankel engine, for instance, was developed by a small German organisation and perfected by a small Japanese car maker who saw the commercial value of innovative leadership. While this was happening, the big American car makers were busy not listening to those mavericks who were predicting a big domestic upsurge in demand for small cars.

Small companies can be more flexible, can move quickly and concentrate on smaller sections of the market, or even change to different markets. During the oil crisis of 1973-4, it was the smaller specialist car makers such as Volvo and Mercedes that did well at a time when the American giants were firing or laying off tens of thousands.

Not surprisingly, about three-quarters of all technical innovations

originate in small companies, for instance, air conditioning, automatic
transmission, stereophonic sound systems. A way of encouraging innovators in large companies is to flatten the organisation, so reducing the
number of delays, hurdles and relay posts through which new ideas have
to pass.

The cautious approach

Large companies often have huge sums of capital tied up in existing
plant and methods, and the natural temptation is to preserve the *status
quo* for as long as possible. Philip Morris is second only to Reynolds in
the US tobacco industry and its approach to innovation is typical of
that of many large companies. The company has deliberately not
pioneered a single cigarette category. Instead, it waits patiently for other
companies to establish categories – then moves in to capitalise on their
mistakes and successes.

Compared to Polaroid, Kodak's pace in the instant camera market
seems definitely lethargic. Kodak cuts the risks by planning and developing new products in an orderly sequence; manages their life cycles in a
way that maximises returns and cuts the risk of disruption. 'We try to
keep things in balance', says Kodak's chief executive, Fallon. 'We try to
avoid crash programmes. We bring things on in an orderly way. And we
sleep well.'

Another company which believes in making sure is the Hanes Corporation, which does extensive research into what consumers don't like
about existing products. The company may then try to come up with a
new product to match their demands. The product is submitted to a
consumer test panel and often redesigned to meet their objections. A
marketing programme is then developed – and again subjected to consumer criticism.

Shortage of investment capital

Cash shortage checks the amount of innovation that is possible in many
companies. The trouble with new ideas is not so much the concepts
themselves as the cost of putting them into effect. Some quoted figures
are $6 millions for the development of nylon and £4 millions for Tery-
lene. Innovation depends largely on the availability of capital. But many
companies are short of money for innovation in R&D, design, new plant
and equipment – all essential for technological innovation.

It is with innovative but cash-starved companies that the National
Enterprise Board feels that it can be most effective. Such companies find
it difficult to get financial backing from conventional sources such as
banks. What attracted the NEB to put £650,000 behind Sinclair
Radionics is the work it is doing on the next generation of television

tubes. 'This could have far-reaching implications for the whole UK television tube industry, it could well put us back on top', says an NEB spokesman.

A recent Government report suggests closer contact between universities and industry as a way of stimulating a cross-fertilisation of ideas and greater innovation [3.22]. The report also suggests that more scientists should be promoted to top levels in companies – where they could apply pressures for more innovation.

Control of time

Some years ago, the Machine Tool Industry Research Association found that in four selected machine shops only about 40 per cent of the time available was being used productively. In how many other companies would inefficient use of time turn out to be a major problem if the truth were known? One way of boosting productivity without committing the company to raise more capital or take on more staff is to train executive leaders in the efficient use of time.

Most executives are short of time. They are overloaded with work. They have too many things to do, too many meetings to attend, too many people to see. Many executives have a steady stream of callers throughout the day. They are constantly being interrupted by subordinates, colleagues, telephone calls. Because of the overload, their impact on policy-making and long-term planning is often negligible. They may put in long hours of work, but often find that most of them have to be spent on many small, routine administrative chores.

Many executive leaders feel themselves to be the victims of all the pressures on them. College presidents, for instance, report that there are 'too many people asking too much too often. Too many trivial activities that had to be engaged in. No time for thinking or reading or initiating action' [1.4]. The executive becomes an administrator rather than a leader in order to cope with the day-to-day pressures.

So much is happening on the operating front that it is easy to become immersed in the detail so that no time is left for more important leadership functions such as planning and innovating. One chief executive reports: 'I'm continually being pummelled by immediate problems. I have to be observant and quickly responsive. There is not enough time to be deep-thinking or conceptual.' Administrative chores take priority. Many executives, indeed, admit that they feel efficient when they are 'busy' dealing with phone calls, letters and other daily chores and that they feel least efficient when spending time on longer-term, more diffuse activities such as discussions of corporate objectives, or strategic planning, or special projects. Such an approach to their roles makes for efficient administrators but ineffective leaders.

Drucker's *The Effective Executive* is largely about the importance for leaders of making good use of their time. Several diary studies, notably those by Stewart and Carlson, give clues about why so many executive leaders have difficulties in this area. They show that the manager's job is characterised by brevity, variety and fragmentation of activities. Every few minutes the manager has to switch attention to another person or problem.

One study of retail store managers found that 40 per cent of activities took less than 1 min and that the average length of activities was 6 min. Rosemary Stewart found that top managers worked for 30 min or more without interruption only once every two days.

The result is that for many managers it is hard to settle to jobs such as planning and target-setting which require long bursts of work or concentrated attention. As soon as they get involved in something, something else crops up which demands their attention. The style is management by reaction, not management by objectives. As Mintzberg has said: 'The manager is a real-time responder to stimuli, an individual who is conditioned by his job to prefer live to delayed action' [3.23].

Creating time

How can the executive leader create more time for such important activities as planning and opportunity-spotting? One approach is to plan one's personal timetable to ensure that it is not cluttered with too many trivial, routine activities. For instance, extra thinking and planning time can be created by cramming lots of appointments or callers into a 2 or 3-hr slot during the week, so that the stream of visitors chase each other along. This simple ploy can prevent the entire week being disrupted.

Similarly, general discussions with colleagues or subordinates during working hours could be limited to 10 min or so. After this time the discussion could be tactfully concluded by summarising the points covered and any agreement or understanding reached. One senior executive insists that if a subordinate wants to see him to discuss a new idea or proposal, he should first submit a brief written statement of objectives, methods and costs so that the discussion will be about specific issues and items rather than long-winded general chat.

One consultant has suggested that time is a more limited resource than capital in many companies and that in deciding which projects to pursue, the leadership might find return-on-time a more effective indicator of efficiency than the traditional return-on-investment. If the return-on-investment criterion is used the project may run into severe trouble when the organisation runs out of executive time to manage the project. Thus mergers frequently miscarry because the acquiring company under-estimates the new time demands on executives [3.24].

One chief executive employs a consultant to do a periodic assessment of the way he spends his time at work : he reckons to have saved a day a week by this method. Another consultant will sit down with a client and together they will work out :

1   How much per hour the executive's time is worth.
2   The cash returns being achieved on this time.
3   How these returns can be improved.

Improvement is possible because this executive, like most others, has a considerable amount of discretion over the way in which he spends his time and over the arrangement of his personal timetable.

Delegation

Executive leaders don't *have* to be administrators or mere responders to stimuli. For instance, they can free themselves from a lot of the detail by delegating routine work to subordinates. One sales manager created a lot of extra thinking and planning time for himself by delegating immediate dealings with customers and salesmen to an assistant. A general manager sends his assistant to take his place in all except the most important committee meetings.

The leader who masters the art of delegation is in a very strong position because he can give extra time to important issues such as planning and decision-making. Thus, he gets more and more involved in key issues and, consequently, his responsibility and powers are constantly expanding. Because he has the time, he can gradually master selected key areas, such as finance or resource allocation, and so becomes a key figure in the organisation.

It is always possible to control the amount of time at work that is spent in socialising which, if not controlled, can absorb a large proportion of the working week. A useful device is to make a practice of converting social chat in working hours into pointed, business-like discussion after the first 5 min or so.

It is also useful to make a practice of killing two birds with one stone. For instance, if you have to walk to the other side of the plant to pick up a document, why not take the opportunity to call into a colleague's office to discuss a common problem, or go by a route which allows you to check deliveries in the machine shop or despatch department? When you go to a committee meeting, why not use this as an opportunity to improve relations with people from other departments in pre- and post-meeting conflabs?

Daimler-Benz chairman, Zahn, disciplines himself to use every minute of his working day to positive effect. 'When I'm kept waiting to see somebody, I'm not angry. The delay gives me a chance to dive into my little black bag in which I always keep a number of things I would like to look over in a leisure moment.'

4

When you have hard and fast rules and leave no room for exceptions, you lock everybody in a mould. You destroy initiative and you destroy imagination.

**Fletcher Byrom,
Chief Executive of Koppers Company**

Strengthening the leader's hand

When earnings lagged at International Harvesters in the early 1970s, chief executive McCormick decided that recovery was going to depend on stronger leadership. Managers would have to be held more truly responsible for performance and profits – and this would involve pushing decision-making into the hands of a lot of executives whose experience in this area was strictly limited. But, says McCormick, 'I'd rather run the risk of a little anarchy than be stultified, ossified, mummified'.

In a short time, scores of managers found themselves raised to new levels of responsibility and authority – and the results soon began to show. For instance, the newly liberated leaders of the truck division decided to stop making light trucks (except for a few lines). This meant losing $300 millions in annual sales but it also freed $65 millions in assets for more profitable use. Regional managers started to make more and more of the decisions that previously they had had to refer to headquarters. 'The district managers used to be salesmen basically. Now they handle their own financing and inventory, among other things. They're entrepreneurs now.'

As a result of strengthening the company's executive leadership by giving them more decisions to make, profits rose, and top management were freed from getting tied up in a lot of the detailed argument and analysis.

To operate with strength and confidence, the individual leader must have clear-cut authority and be allowed to work independently with only occasional checks from above. One of the major checks on the efficiency of leaders in many large companies is the absence of clear authority and the necessity of referring decisions up the line. Often a manager knows what changes are needed and what decisions need to be made, but he has insufficient authority to take action. He is hemmed in by a formal web of procedures, precedents and protocol, and finds it extremely difficult, under these circumstances, to operate with confidence or to strike out in bold new directions. Red-tape kills initiative. Selznik has shown that leadership declines as formal structure increases [4.1].

Mistakes allowed

'When you have hard and fast rules', says Byrom, chief executive of Koppers Company, 'and leave no room for exceptions, you lock every-body in a mould. You destroy initiative and you destroy imagination.' When Byrom was production chief of the Koppers tar-products division, he decided to encourage initiative by giving plant superintendents a lot more authority than they had ever had before. But the superintendents had been used to highly centralised control 'and when I set them loose they were totally bewildered'.

Of twenty-five superintendents, says Byrom, only one or two rose to the challenge and started to take decisions on their own authority; and Byrom had to spend 'a lot of time out at the plants, holding their hands', until they developed some confidence.

Today, throughout the company, managers are encouraged to take on as much responsibility as they think they can handle. Mistakes are tolerated – up to a point. 'I tell subordinates that whatever they do, they have to be able to convince me later that what they did was reasonable. If they're not sure they'll be able to convince me, then they should come to me first.'

His subordinates, in turn, are expected to delegate authority to their own subordinates and so on down the line. Not surprisingly, problems crop up at lower levels. 'Lower down, the supervisors are less willing to believe that they are really allowed to make mistakes' [4.2].

The leader is strengthened by an organisational climate which supports him by giving him clear-cut authority and responsibilities. A personnel director in a large pottery-making group reports : 'Every manager should know the precise areas in which he is authorised to act and make decisions, and those in which he should consult his boss'.

Making leaders feel strong

Almost by definition, a strong leader is one who makes his subordinates feel strong, independent and responsible, and thus prepares *them* for leadership too. For instance, a rapidly growing chain retailer was making heavy losses in a particular region. So the CEO picked out a promising executive and told him he had complete confidence in his leadership ability, and thought that he could put the region back in profit. The executive accepted the challenging assignment – and pulled the region round in a year.

Plastow, managing director of Rolls Royce Motors, is another strong believer in developing leaders by means of challenging assignments. 'My own experience of all people in British industry is that they respond well to encouragement and responsibility.'

Plastow believes that if a man has got the basic training and leadership potential, and you say to him when you hand him a tough assignment: 'I think you can make it a success – prove it', he will do a lot better than anyone would have dreamt. But, says Plastow, 'if you say, "I think you might, and by the way you do it this way and that way", he will just be an ordinary guy'.

In preparing people for leadership responsibility, the knack required is to provide opportunities for them to score successes. The leader must keep having success so that his followers can maintain their respect for him.

Strong new direction

After years of drifting, a light engineering company found a strong new direction – up. The change of course came after the old managing director left and a new man was appointed.

This man possessed both business acumen and a flair for man-management – a rarer combination than we sometimes like to think – and accordingly he began by increasing the responsibility and authority of each department head with the idea of 'giving management enough support and authority to stand on their own feet and exercise vigorous leadership'. The new approach worked. 'It occurred to us for the first time', one manager reports, 'that *we* were running the company and responsible for results'.

The vigour and strength of a company depends on strong leadership at all levels. There must always be, at each part of the organisation, somebody who is in charge and empowered to take necessary decisions. Each department head should be able to point to his own desk and say, 'The buck stops here'.

Strong leaders are made strong by the organisation. It is the organisation that gives them the power to take necessary decisions and actions, gives them clear-cut responsibilities and authority. This kind of organisational support helps the leader to knit individuals into effective teams or units. If leadership is weak, however, the unit may split into its component parts with individual managers and specialists pursuing purely personal instead of corporate goals. Moreover, weak leaders spawn weak leaders: researchers at the International Harvester Company found that supervisors tended to behave in the same way as their bosses did.

In the absence of clear-cut authority and responsibilities, fumbling leadership occurs. For instance, managers in a large tile-making company told an investigator that they found it difficult to be effective leaders because they simply didn't know what decisions they could take or what areas they were held responsible for. For instance, they were not sure how much they could spend without higher authority or how much personal initiative they could use in settling employee grievances. Very few of the managers even knew who they were responsible to in specific functional areas such as personnel or quality control. Generally speaking, the managers felt lost in the swamp of big-company structures.

Leaders must be allowed to act and to think for themselves otherwise they are unable to exercise their leadership qualities, says the chief executive of a road haulage firm. This executive grew tired of managers asking his advice about the simplest projects and decisions. So now he insists on every manager with an idea for an innovation or project preparing a written brief containing a thorough analysis of the situation and specific recommendations. 'They were wasting my time and their own', he says. 'Now I expect them to come not just with problems or requests for advice but with positive proposals and solutions.'

Structural reforms

'Everything that goes to increase the importance of the subordinate's role is decentralisation', says Fayol. 'Everything which goes to reduce it is centralisation.' But when a company decentralises its operations in an effort to improve efficiency and strengthen the local leadership, it hands extra power and responsibility to at least a few men who are unable to carry it. There are always some of the newly liberated divisional managers who make mistakes along the way which more centralised controls could have prevented. But in the experience of many companies, they also make countless and profitable innovations which headquarters executives would never have conceived.

That is one of the reasons why Dow Chemicals has decentralised operations into autonomous units – covering the US, Canada, Europe, Latin America and the Pacific – each with its own president and area headquarters. Dow, which is near the top of the earnings league for the industry, has found that when local leaders are relatively free from bureaucratic trammels, they can respond quickly and decisively to the environment, and that even managers well down the line become much more sensitive to the needs of the marketplace. The geographic structure, which is unique to Dow among chemical companies, prevents managers from being inhibited by masses of red-tape emanating from the central headquarters and develops their entrepreneurial talents.

A similar effect was noted by Sunmark Industries when it eliminated two layers of management completely, and converted a complex, centralised management structure into an easier-to-manage five divisions. According to chairman Sharbaugh, the divisions are given certain guidelines, such as capital spending limits 'but we ask them to develop their own business strategy'. As a result of the re-structuring, managers in the divisions are able to act with entrepreneurial gusto and freedom – 'really lead their divisions'. In 1972, Volvo went through a major reorganisation. Headquarters staff was cut from 1800 to 100. Each major product group became an independent division. All major market units became independent profit centres. These changes greatly strengthened the hands of the local leaders who were consequently able to mark up notable increases in volumes and exports.

The experience of Sunmark Industries, Volvo and many other companies suggests that one of the best structural patterns for developing and strengthening leaders is the small strategic headquarters controlling autonomous divisions based on manufacturing plants or geographical regions.

Building strong leaders via decentralisation

A quarter of a century ago, General Electric turned its back on the cosy paternalistic world of management theory where top management carries total responsibility for all decisions. It decided to decentralise to make the company as nimble and manageable as hundreds of smaller competitors. This meant allowing men close to the market to make as many day-to-day business decisions as possible. To accomplish this, the company split its operations into 113 departments, each one tailored to be run as a separate business.

Significantly, GE's sales continued to rise after decentralisation and the chairman at that time, Cordiner, made the point: 'We consider decentralisation a great source of strength which builds high-quality leaders'. To be sure, department managers had a lot of leadership responsibility thrust upon them including authority to hire, fire, set prices and decide on which products they wished to push. Thus, in all departments there were soon more people with a much better understanding of how to run a business. Headquarter executives were freed from detailed operational activity and were able to concentrate on broad strategic issues and long-range planning.

One long-serving GE executive says: 'Under centralisation, managers appointed are usually the type who'll go along with the system; it's conformity, so to speak'; whereas decentralisation has led to the emergence of many leaders who are 'highly unorthodox yet still very successful'.

Some of the pitfalls of a centralised system are pointed out by a secret 1977 report from a committee set up by the British Broadcasting Corporation. The report criticises the BBC's dictatorial, over-elaborate bureaucracy for causing much frustration and inefficiency and argues that many centrally administered services need to be devolved to programme heads.

One executive said he was made to feel like a crook every time he indented for an india-rubber. Another executive was allowed to spend £10,000 on his own authority in commissioning a film or play, but if he wanted to hire a secretary at £3000 a year he was subjected to an insulting inquisition, apparently checking that he wasn't simply creating a post for a mistress.

The report reveals much concern over the complex, centrally-administered system of job grading and evaluation. The Corporation was obsessed with minute distinctions among grades. The report recommended that the elaborate appointments system should be simplified and that department heads should have more say over appointing and fixing the pay levels of their staff.

Centralisation and control

One of the problems of decentralisation is the risk of overmanning, with each department clamouring for all the services and tools available to an independent company. Thus, each department or division finishes up paying its own advertising, marketing, accounting and other staff. Perhaps an answer to this particular problem is for the departments to share a number of central services such as sales and marketing.

The best balance between centralisation and decentralisation may well vary at different stages in a firm's growth. Thus, General Electric, with some quarter-million employees and 200,000 different products, was over-ripe for decentralisation, whereas in a new company, or in a company created by a merger, a greater degree of centralised leadership is needed so that common policies and procedures can be established. Again, if middle management is mediocre, complete decentralisation could bring chaos.

When the coal and electricity industries were formed by amalgamating a lot of separate organisations, they had a highly centralised structure at first because of the need for common policies.

Arguably, operations should be centralised when the main priority is for strong management control and there is a need for standardised policies and procedures; but decentralisation is needed when the priorities are : to encourage initiative in local managers and to strengthen local leadership; to make managers' jobs more interesting; and to ensure faster decisions and a more sensitive response to the business environment.

In *The Reality of Management*, Rosemary Stewart argues that leaders will favour centralisation if they believe that order is essential to a well-run business; that people work best when closely supervised; that managers should conform to organisational methods and objectives; and that only top management can be trusted to make many decisions. Conversely, managers tend to favour decentralisation if they believe that initiative at all levels is essential; that people work best without detailed supervision; and that results are what matter – how they are achieved is up to the individual manager.

Keeping track of the money

Admittedly, decentralisation can exact a high price in dilution of authority, lack of direction and duplication of effort. With each division doing its own purchasing and its own monthly reporting it is much harder to keep track of the money. But Rolls-Royce Motors has found a way round this particular danger by combining the decentralisation of day-to-day operations with strong centralised financial controls. Capital expenditure, for instance, must be approved centrally. Managing director Plastow has said that if he saw a business with a £2-3 million turnover with reasonable control over manufacturing and marketing, he would rake it off and appoint separate chairmen and managing directors so that he would get the decision-making right down the line.

'Giganticism' in modern industry creates problems of leadership and control which defy those who believe that management can be reduced to anything like a science. As an organisation grows, it becomes set in its ways, bureaucracy increases, leadership frequently wanes. Success leads to efforts to hold onto what has been accomplished. Vested interests often predominate. 'Administrators' have more influence than 'leaders'. Moreover, great size requires 'system', and 'system, once established, may easily become an end in itself' [4.3].

As a firm grows in size the leader's problems multiply, and a point is reached (at around 300 employees, according to Argenti) where the leader's problems begin to increase explosively. At such a size the leader begins to lose his hold on the reins of control. He has to create formal systems so that he knows what is going on.

In a small organisation, the leader can go and see for himself whether operatives are fully occupied, whether deliveries are leaving on time, and so on. But in a large company he no longer knows all his employees personally and has to rely on formal reports from others for a glimpse of shopfloor problems. When personal contact between the two sides is no longer possible, mutual distrust appears and the company is wide open to militants.

These are some of the reasons why relatively small companies in the £30-300 million size range out-perform giant competitors, even in times of recession. They can do so, according to Clifford, 'through disciplined control over the economics of the business, intensive development of the right market niches and products and, underlying the rest, a leadership style that sustains entrepreneurial drive and commitment among its key managers' [4.4]. Often, leaders feel stronger and keener in relatively small companies.

A way of increasing the commitment of leaders in the mega-corporation involves combining centralised control of policy with decentralised management. This means setting up a number of small, flexible, relatively independent units, headed by relatively independent leaders who must, however, ensure that the unit follows overall corporate policies.

Stay-small strategy

Marks and Spencer chairman, Sir Marcus Sieff, has said that when a company grows very quickly because of a merger or takeover, 'the well established human relations of the original firm are sometimes overwhelmed by the very size of the new undertakings. Sometimes, bad traditional practices of one of the merged firms become the standard for all. In such cases, trouble-makers thrive.'

This is one of the considerations that encourages some companies to pursue a stay-small strategy even when they are expanding. Italy's Industrie Merloni (Fabriano) is one of them. For thirty years the company, which employs about 3000 workers, has always created a new factory somewhere else rather than expand an existing factory. Management believes that small factories are easier to handle and that employees are happier, and so makes sure that no factory has more than 300 employees.

Large organisations are potentially more effective than small ones because of economies of scale and bigger funds of resources. But in practice, communication and organisational problems abound in large companies and drastically reduce efficiency. Because it is easier to find managers who can handle 200 employees efficiently than to find leaders capable of handling a huge workforce, the advantages of small size include :
1   Better human relations.
2   Shorter chain of command.
3   More positive leadership is possible.
4   Better industrial relations.
5   More efficient leaders.

Production cells

France's Telemécanique has expanded through the creation of numerous small prodution cells. The shortened hierarchy such an arrangement creates allows management to create an atmosphere in which workers have a real sense of identification with the firm – which helps to explain why the company has not had a single strike in the last twenty-five years.

Plant size is also kept small at Edison Electric – there are only a few hundred employees at most Edison factories. Each plant operates as if it were a separate business. And to emphasise the individuality of each plant its products carry the plant name – Rigid Tools or US Motors – not Edison Electric. The company believes that managers have scope to exercise strong personal leadership in conditions like these.

Merloni, head of Merloni Industrie, says there are three reasons why small-scale strategy is not more widespread:

1   It flies in the face of traditional advantages of scale, which are particularly important in chemicals, steel and other heavy industries.
2   It is much easier to expand an existing factory if you already own the adjacent ground rather than move to a fresh site.
3   Setting up small units means extra short-term costs.

These are some of the reasons why the large holding company wishing to gain some of the advantages of smaller companies might consider administering appropriate surgery to itself. For instance, it might set up four or five subsidiary companies of, say, 200 employees, rather than two subsidiaries of 500 employees. Pressure could then be put on each subsidiary to aim at increasing margins rather than size. Similarly, the outsize department or division might be split into several small, relatively autonomous units thus encouraging more managers to exercise strong, personal leadership.

Self-control possible

According to one expert, communication problems in large firms are so severe that 'the best course for larger businesses seems to be to cast themselves structurally and operationally more in the mould of smaller businesses' [4.5]. Sir David Nicholson, former chairman of Reed International, reckons that the British Steel Corporation should be split into four companies because it is far too big to manage itself properly.

In many large companies, intricacies of organisation and production create a skein of relationships almost too complicated to untangle. Standard procedures have to be adopted as a means of controlling complex work processes and a large workforce, whereas in very small companies the workers themselves often control the communication and production systems [4.6]. In small companies, there is direct and continuous contact between management and the work force: this becomes the main method of control and creates favourable conditions for the exercise of personal leadership. In the small firms studied by Ingham, all employees reported direct contact with the department head.

In small units, instead of formal work rules and discipline procedures, unofficial shop customs develop. Entirely self-operating, these customs become the basis for the organisation of work and are, in a sense, the functional equivalent to bureaucratic rules and control procedures. The group itself allocates duties and sets standards for individual workers.

The disadvantages of scale are enormous – vulnerability to stoppages by just a few workers is one of them. The smaller the plant, the less vulnerable it is. Sir Frederick Catherwood makes the point : 'The giant plant employing 10,000 workers is already an industrial dinosaur. Its head cannot communicate with its body. It cannot react to danger and it can be knocked out by a very small blow.' Moreover, the human relations in a small plant and the existence of *personal* leadership make the exercise of naked shopfloor power more difficult. Not surprisingly, statistics show a direct relation between size of plant and hours lost per worker.

Another massive problem is that inside a large company, the individual often feels lost, unimportant among all the machines and systems. Volvo's president Gyllenhammar, points out : 'Employees react to inhuman conditions in very human ways : by job-hopping, absenteeism, apathetic attitudes, antagonism, and even malicious mischief'. But Gyllenhammar believes that such effects can be overcome by organising employees in small, autonomous work-groups : 'Each unit should be free to develop independently, without detailed control or interference from headquarters – headquarters is most effective when its role is sanctioning investments for new approaches and challenging local leaders to take more radical initiatives and risks'.

Volvo's practice supports the theory. The company's Kalmar plant, for instance, is designed so that small working groups of twenty or so can work in quiet, pleasant surroundings. Work is organised so that each group is responsible for a particular, identifiable portion of a car – a gear box, an electrical system, and so on. Moreover, leadership responsibility is shared by members of the group. Each team elects its own spokesman and negotiator, does its own inspection, paces itself as it wishes, and organises work inside its own area so that operatives work individually or in sub-groups to suit themselves.

Flexible leaders

Splitting the outsize company into a number of small, relatively independent operations can lead to faster decisions, stronger leadership – and an improvement in the industrial relations climate.

The leadership in small companies can be more flexible, can move quickly and concentrate on smaller sections of the market, or even change markets. During the oil crisis, it was the smaller, specialist car makers such as Mercedes and Volvo who did well at a time when the American giants were firing or laying off tens of thousands of workers. Leaders in small companies can adjust quickly to changes in the business environment. Big companies, by contrast, are burdened with a frozen mosaic of procedures, fixed methods and protocol. Moreover, there may be vast sums of capital tied up in existing production processes, and

this creates strong pressures to limit the number of innovations that are
introduced. Deliberately adopting a stay-small strategy – i.e. a small
strategic headquarters with a number of small operating companies –
can be a successful way of overcoming these problems.

Among the problems facing leaders in big companies are :

1 Lack of coordination and control.
2 Poor use of time.
3 Lack of initiative amongst individual managers because of fixed
   procedures and red tape.
4 Frequent communication breakdowns because of numerous gaps
   between specialists, levels and departments.

A manager in a large ceramics factory says : 'One problem is that you
don't know where to go for information. There are too many bosses
because of the cumbrous structure.'

One way of making a wider distribution of leadership responsibility
in the big-league company is to push decision-making as far down the
organisation as it will go so that lower levels of management know what
is going on and feel involved in formulating policy.

5

'We have no management development chief at Volvo. The task is too important to be put into a specialist department. Instead I consider it one of my most important duties.'

Pehr Gyllenhammar, President of Volvo

Developing
executive leaders

The development and training of leaders at all levels is essential for survival and growth. Another good reason for developing leaders is to prevent frustrated managers leaving the company. Hale, a vice-president of Shell Oil, points out : 'We have to think a great deal harder than we used to about the manager who comes to work for the company, consciously help him to progress and develop his leadership potential, plan ahead for him as an individual and make opportunities for him consistent with his potential'.

When this kind of planning happens, the company benefits. For instance, one senior executive says : 'We are never limited by ideas or money but by the ability to develop strong management. If we grow beyond a certain rate we have a rocky time. But even at a time of rapid expansion, few leadership positions should have to be filled from the outside.'

But many companies do regularly appoint outsiders to leadership positions. International Telephone and Telegraph, for instance, fills about a third of all management positions from outside. This company, like many others, finds that insiders who lose out when outsiders move in often bounce straight into other companies. Such exercises in management musical chairs make a mockery of internal management development, the idea of which is surely to supply the company's leadership requirements *from within*. That, incidentally, is why it is important to coordinate the management development programme with the strategic plan. For instance, a company which is planning to decentralise operations is going to need more managers with general management experience, more accountants, and so on.

The concept of 'human resources accounting' places a monetary value on personnel when measuring the value of a company's assets. This encourages leadership development because it means that costs incurred in training and developing leaders are treated as an investment to be amortised rather than as a current expense.

Boosting self-confidence

Gulliver, former Fine Fare chairman, believes that one of the best ways of developing leadership potential is to give a manager special projects and responsibilities, because 'people don't learn to be leaders by being unsuccessful. In the last resort, people follow not the man who happens to have been put in authority. They follow the man who seems likely to achieve success.'

Self-confidence is an important element of leadership. A manager's is bolstered when he feels that he is an important member of his organisation and that his responsibilities are growing. Managers learn to be leaders by grappling with problems and being successful. This boosts their confidence and therefore their leadership ability.

How strongly an executive develops depends largely on the relationship he has with his boss. Several studies have found a link between the confidence and self-esteem of supervisors and the degree of support they have had from their managers. House has argued that effective leadership involves:

1   Rewarding subordinates for achieving required standards.
2   Reducing work pressures and frustrations.
3   Supporting them in difficult work assignments, thus improving their chances of success and strengthening *their* leadership ability [5.1].

'It is the individual's self-picture and his perceptions of what his attributes are which seem finally to determine success or failure,' says Lathrope [5.2].

When a relatively inexperienced manager is given a tough assignment, he may not know *how* to handle it, and he probably has less authority than his boss to enlist help. For success, the manager needs tactful guidance and support from his boss and the freedom to make mistakes, otherwise there is a risk of failure and loss of self-confidence. When University of Michigan researchers studied C & O Railroad, they found that high-performing work-groups typically had tolerant leaders who corrected subordinates without destroying the atmosphere of approval. Subordinates were allowed to make mistakes. The effect was to boost their independence and confidence – both important attributes of leadership.

Do you give your own subordinates sufficient support? Find out by answering the following questions :

How much support do you give your subordinates when they are carrying out assignments?

Do you demonstrate that you have confidence and trust in them?

Do you make sure that they are properly briefed and provided with adequate information before starting?

Do you make sure that other people will cooperate with them – for instance, by phoning or calling on other managers and enlisting their support?

Will the individual require close supervision and constant support, or only occasional checks?

More general questions to ask oneself about subordinates' long-term development, are :

What are the strong points and qualities of each subordinate? Sometimes it is possible to build jobs and responsibilities round these qualities.

How can these qualities be strengthened and given scope?

What responsibilities and assignments should be given to each man?

What plans exist for each man's long-term development? A planned rotation of jobs can be a highly effective way of preparing a man for a senior leadership position.

Every manager and every supervisor should be quite clear about his present role and responsibilities so that he can act decisively and confidently within his own area. But he should also realise that this role is not fixed, that his leadership responsibilities will continue to change and grow, and that his boss is interested in and helpful to his future growth.

Thus arguably the development and training of leaders should be the responsibility of the line manager, with the training officer playing an advisory and supportive role. This means that the manager should make it clear to his immediate subordinates that he intends to develop their leadership potential and say how he intends to carry out his plans – by means of job-rotation, perhaps, or membership of committees, or challenging assignments.

Wrestling with real problems

In the field of leadership development an ounce of application is worth a ton of abstraction. The manager learns about his own strengths and weaknesses and develops skills in managing people by wrestling with real business problems, by commanding people in real situations. According to Lloyd, a director of Urwick Orr and Partners, the management consultancy firm, the main way in which leadership abilities are strengthened is through 'response to the challenge of difficult and demanding tasks, expressed, wherever possible, as objectives (something to "achieve") rather than as duties (something to "do")'. Thus the manager's boss, rather than the training manager, should have the primary responsibility for the manager's development, and his aim should be to create a number of carefully graded learning situations with the emphasis on learning, not teaching.

When Bell and Howell's CEO, Frey, was a young engineer with Babcock and Wilcox, he was assigned to deal with a customer who had complained that the company's tubing cracked under normal stress. Frey was pleased to be handed the assignment, even happier when he solved the problem. 'In the education of a young man', he says, 'an experience like that is of enormous importance – to learn how you go about learning to get things done in the commercial world'.

Frey believes that the trick in developing an executive's leadership performance is to give the executive a problem big enough to stretch him but not big enough to break him. This, too, is the approach at W. R. Grace, an American company which makes rocket motors, where promising young managers understudy top executives and so get a top-management view of the company. They also gain valuable experience in analysing 'whole management' problems which, the company thinks, prepares them for top positions.

General management jobs

When Lord Ryder headed Reed International he introduced the 'chairman's cadre' method of advanced management training. This is a project-based method for developing future top leaders, the idea being to give promising executives problems to solve which normally are dealt with at much higher levels.

Consultant Hague suggests providing more general management jobs at relatively low levels as a way of preparing promising young managers for senior leadership positions : in most companies there are few junior positions that carry responsibility for both production and sales and therefore for a real profit and loss. 'The ideal is for each manager to have his own profit and loss account, with a water-tight internal costing system so that his energy is directed to selling and cutting his real costs.'

This kind of approach trains leaders to be highly adaptable so that they are able to cope with a wide range of different situations. In Hague's experience, such general management positions, no matter how small, 'are better training situations than staff positions or functional coordinators' [5.3]. If Hague is right, it follows that centralised structures are less effective for developing future industrial leaders than decentralised patterns of organisaion.

An institution which prepares its students for leadership by requiring them to demonstrate it is the management school at the Buckinghamshire College of Higher Education. Post-graduate students are required, as part of a two-year course, to operate Scanmark, a service dedicated to helping small firms sell their goods overseas. Each year's course starts with the same amount of money and must decide for itself how to use it to attract clients.

The students travel abroad when necessary on clients' business. For instance, they have done market research in Germany and Holland for Apex Packaging of Swansea. Apex chairman Jenkins says: 'As a result of their report we are doing business in those countries'.

Remarkably, this is one of the few courses of its kind in the UK. Course director Bill Anson reports: 'We are turning out export marketing executives who do not need any further training except product familiarisation when they join a firm'.

Another leader in leader-development is the Chicago-based Jewel Companies, a grocery chain. The company attracts bright young business school talent with lures of responsibility and rapid advancement. Financial officer Lunding makes the point: 'Young people today want in on the action. They don't want to sit around for six months trimming lettuce. They want responsibility – so we give it them'.

At Jewel, the divisions are separate profit-centres and division heads make almost all operating decisions barring big-money deals. As far as Lunding is concerned, decentralised organisation and liberal delegation of authority is 'the only way to bring back the entrepreneurial spirit that this business must have if it is to continue to grow'.

Ways and means

Leaders can be developed by many different methods, including:

– participation in task forces, working parties, committees and junior
      management boards;
– special assignments and projects;
– job rotation;
– systematic coaching by the boss;
– performance appraisal programmes;
– formal management training programmes;
– advanced training programmes, such as those offered by the business
      schools, and the inter-company programmes developed by Revans.

The value of inter-company programmes, where executives from different companies work on special assignments in each other's companies, is that the executive learns something about the wider business environment and meets a wider range of people and problems. In-company programmes, Revans has found, may lead to conformist, inward-looking management.

At McCormick and Company in Baltimore, committees have been formed from managers at verious levels in the organisation. One is a junior version of the board of directors. Others deal with functional areas such as sales and manufacturing. The membership of the committees changes every six months so that the entire management team participates and gets valuable experience of decision-making.

Experience-based development

Given the right conditions (such as freedom to make mistakes and continous feedback on performance), learning on the job can be an extremely effective way of preparing young managers and functional specialists for future leadership roles. For instance, a survey by Brookes, former dean of the Sloan School of Management at the MIT, shows that managers who had been members of project teams, or who had had the opportunity to run a small but integrated operation, or who had moved round a number of functional areas, had developed leadership qualities more rapidly than associates who had not had such experiences. Brookes concludes that leadership qualities are developed fastest in a context of work and experience. Brookes also believes that such experience is most valuable when it requires a manager to cross functional lines or to coordinate the contributions of diverse specialists. Moreover, in carrying out assignments, managers learn the valuable lesson that poor performance often stems from faulty job design or badly organised work systems.

It is not surprising that many chief executives insist that their key managers prepare annual goals and development plans for themselves and their most promising people, and that these plans include on-the-job experience as well as formal training.

Executive interchange

Revans believes that managers learn leadership skills in a context of work and experience. As long ago as 1968 he set up a programme to allow Belgian managers to work for several months in each other's companies, tackling tough, top-level problems of a kind they had never encountered before. Each man acted as a kind of top-level consultant. For instance, one man, an advisor to a world oil company, went to one of Belgium's leading banks to clarify its changing relations with the economy as a whole. A research manager helped a large steel company to determine conditions necessary for success in product innovation.

The role of the trainees was not merely diagnostic. They were also

expected to develop action programmes: 'half their time was devoted
to getting something done about their findings'. The role of the trainees'
tutors at the university was confined to suggesting which analytical tools
and operational tactics might be employed.

In the company, the usual method of getting something done was to
set up a work-group to introduce the trainee's proposals, and to continue
the task after the departure of the trainee. Thus what the manager had
learnt was submitted to direct test. In Revans' words the trainees learnt
'how a fundamental problem is both perceived and attacked by the top
management; how it first emerges; what system can be built up for
dealing with it; how objectives can be worked out in detail' [5.4].

A somewhat similar programme has been developed in the US. This
is the Executive Interchange programme, a federal experiment, that
takes promising executives from government and business and gives them
one or two-year assignments in the opposite sector. Each man finds
himself wrestling with completely new problems in a completely new
environment, and the effect is to stretch his leadership capabilities to
the full.

A noise abatement officer in the Federal Aviation Administration in
Washington worked for Mobil Oil in New York for a year as a product
line manager. This meant handling everything from research to the
marketing of hydraulic fluids and synthetic turbine oils. When he went
back to the Federal Aviation Administration he was able to take up a
new, more senior job in systems and research development.

More than thirty large companies have supported the programme,
including American Telephone and Telegraph, Motorola, Bendix and
Consolidated Edison. According to consultant McCullen, who helped to
organise the programme, the participants are high-talent, high-potential
people and, partly as a result of the programme, many should become
future company presidents and, perhaps, cabinet secretaries.

New style MBO

Another method of accelerating the development of future leaders is
management by objectives. This involves a senior and a subordinate
manager sitting down and jointly deciding on specific, measurable
objectives for the subordinate covering the next few months. 'The very
discipline of having to devise a plan and set measurable targets for
yourself makes you keen to carry it out', reports a production manager
with experience of MBO. 'After all, it is your *own* plan.' Another
advantage of MBO is that it provides a yardstick for performance
appraisal.

Generally speaking, MBO focuses attention on how *task* targets can
be achieved. But Corning Glass have given the method a new twist so
that when subordinate managers are discussing progress with their bosses
they learn what *behaviour* they must modify to increase their leadership

effectiveness. A senior Corning executive points out that a manager may fail to achieve cost-reduction targets because he is failing to provide leadership or to motivate his own staff, or because he is not getting on well with other managers. Executives at Corning are trained to give this kind of feedback in a tactful and acceptable manner.

The 'performance management system' at Corning includes a questionnaire listing seventy-six aspects of behaviour identified as important components of effective leadership. They include such aspects as 'Takes the initiative in group meetings', 'Offers constructive ideas', and 'Objects to ideas before they are explained'. These are sent to the person's immediate boss for evaluation. The idea is that potential leaders have a lot to gain from knowing about their behavioural weak areas so that they can work on them – or avoid situations and jobs where those weak spots are bound to be exposed [5.5].

Some companies have found that asking subordinates to complete questionnaires about themselves (including behavioural and relationship aspects) encourages open, unembarrassed discussion of their performance. Each aspect can be discussed 'objectively', starting with the subordinate's own impressions. By using methods such as these it is possible to give a leader insight into his own leadership style. This knowledge helps him to assess any particular assignment, situation, or job and decide if it fits his particular style. Fiedler even suggests changing the work situation when a mismatch between situation and style occurs: 'We can then instruct the leader in making the necessary modifications in the leadership situation so that the situation will match his style' [5.6]. As Fiedler points out, executive job specifications *can* be changed; and many organisations do this regularly to attract the kind of executive they want to attract.

Adaptable leaders

In those cases – the great majority – where a change of job specification is not possible, an alternative approach is to train the leader by means of sensitivity courses, or the kinds of devices discussed above, to be more flexible and adaptive.

Adair thinks that managers should be selected and trained for 'the general work environment' rather than for specific jobs, so that they can respond to the shifting needs of the situation. With such training the leaders concerned could learn to change the situations themselves, and not wait for someone else to change them for them' [5.7].

Adair belives that leadership training is most successful when fully integrated into an organisation. This implies that top management should be fully involved in any leadership programme from the start, either as course members, tutors or administrators. Such an approach to leadership training also implies that managers from all levels and all functional areas should eventually participate in the programme.

Organisations which have arranged for this to happen often discover
that one of the advantages is that a common 'language' of management
develops throughout the organisation, reflecting a shared vision of the
functions and responsibilities of leadership. A more tangible effect of
involving all levels of management is that the concepts and skills presented in the programme will be absorbed and applied throughout the
organisation rather than in isolated pockets. It is not surprising that so
many large companies which have run leadership training programmes,
such as Rolls Royce and Rio Tinto Zinc, report the benefits of a multi-
level strategy being adopted at the outset.

Top-level involvement

Top managers must assume most of the responsibility for training those
who will succeed them. Psychologically, it is not easy to do this. It may
mean preparing others to destroy one's own operational vision. Nevertheless, the success of any development programme depends on top
management's involvement and support. At 3M (UK) the managing
director takes a leading role in organising the training of senior managers, and enthusiastically participates in leadership exercises which
bring together managers from all sectors of the company.

'We have no management development chief at Volvo', says president
Gyllenhammer. 'The task is too important to put into a specialist
department. Instead, I consider it one of my most important duties.
This view is increasingly shared by line managers throughout the company. Their foremen, supervisors, managers and employees are resources
for which they are accountable, just as they are accountable for investments in buildings and machines.'

At Bulmers, the cider-making firm, directors, managers, foremen and
shop stewards go on courses on personal leadership. More than sixty
other organisations have so admired Bulmers' way of developing leadership qualities at all levels of management that they have joined the
Leadership Trust. This body, which was set up by Bulmers, has a
permanent staff running courses for managers from any organisation.
Bulmers chairman, Prior, points out: 'We have never claimed to teach
leadership, but rather to strengthen the individual's belief that he possesses this quality'.

Leadership Trust courses are based on learning-by-doing. Everyone
has a chance to lead in a variety of highly testing indoor and outdoor
situations – most of them totally new situations for the trainees, such as
mountain rescue, rock climbing and underwater swimming. Thus, all
develop the personal qualities of leadership and of caring for men. As
Prior says: 'Leaders must have the self-confidence of achievement, it
doesn't matter much in what field. With that they can develop the
common touch.'

The idea is that mastering some new skill gives an individual new confidence, and that when he goes back to his company it brushes off on his work.

Gilbert-Smith, who heads the leadership department at Bulmers and who organises the course (which has been listed in the best six courses in the Management Courses Index), explains his approach to leadership development in these words : 'It is one's strengths that should be studied to see how they can be capitalised on. Only then will one really start to climb the ladder of leadership.'

Undoubtedly, this approach works. One managing director says that the course has 'the greatest impact of any I know for developing practical, competent leaders'. Another manager comments : 'This training is excellent for developing good working relationships and really effective management teams'.

Action-centred leadership

What Drucker calls the management boom began after the Second World War. This greatly extended the science of management and management education, and led to the emergence of the 'professional manager', fully conversant with management techniques and sophisticated concepts. But it is easy for the manager to become over-sophisticated, to know a lot of sophisticated techniques and theories and not enough about basic skills of leadership. Action-centred leadership tries to correct the balance.

The great thing about ACL is that it is very simple. So simple, in fact, that it can be learnt and applied at all levels from the board to the shop-floor. As in the Bulmers programme, trainees learn leadership skills by actually analysing and exercising command and from the reactions of fellow trainees to their efforts.

The Industrial Society introduced ACL to industry in 1969 – it was modelled on Functional Leadership programmes in the armed services. Since then, nearly three thousand organisations have sent delegates to ACL courses in Britain. It has also been used in the US, South Africa and many countries in Europe, Asia and South America.

ACL courses, which are both simple and practical, are led by line managers as part of their overall responsibility for leadership development, with training specialists in advisory roles. Throughout, the emphasis is on what needs to be *done* to lead effectively. The South East Metropolitan Hospital Board ran a two-day course and found that more than 85 per cent of the trainees gave it top rating with an extremely high application value. Senior officers noted dramatic improvements in the performance of some of those who had attended. One nursing officer reported :

After the module on Action-Centred Leadership I asked myself why I had never thought of myself as a positive leader of staff and

patients . . . I resolved that when I got back things would be
different. A week after my return I forced myself to define my
task. I now saw it as a home provider for my patients and being
responsible for providing a stimulating environment as far as I
could. This led me to set up a meeting to put these ideas to staff . . .
At the end of the meeting I had three groups of staff working on
three different areas of activity . . . These activities have trans-
formed the environment of the hospital [5.7].

Learning-by-doing

Action-Centred Leadership courses get quick results. A bank in Sweden
also believes in learning-by-doing. It runs a mock bank with special
rooms as a kind of leadership training laboratory. Once a week, young
staff members carry out all the tasks done by a bank, from high-level
investment and loans to dealings with members of the public. This helps
the young executives to get wide and varied experience very rapidly.

The Colorado-based Coors Company used Outward Bound as a
leadership development tool – with excellent results. Half of the company's management team have been through the school's rigorous outdoor course. The Outward Bound experience, in the words of Coors
chairman Bill Coors, 'makes a person aware that, in problem-solving,
you have to rely on someone other than yourself. It's people working
together on a common problem'.

Each management group of ten takes off for an isolated spot for a
ten-day expedition which involves climbing, planning a course through
rapids, and so on. Teamwork as well as individual effort is required and,
ideally, the participants return with renewed self-confidence and a fresh
outlook on the importance of teamwork. For instance, one raft trip
foundered because a senior executive wasn't bothering to paddle.

One participant in an Outward Bound trip, reflecting afterwards,
realised that his raft had flipped over because he and another man had
been unhappy having a woman as helmsperson : they had 'subcon-
sciously, by habit, proceeded to undermine the woman' and sabotaged her
efforts of leadership [5.8]. Insights such as this are invaluable at a time
when more and more women are being appointed to leadership positions
in business.

Leaders are grown

An important factor in a manager's development is the kind of relationship that he has with his boss and the boss's ability as a 'coach'. As
McGregor has said, 'Managers are grown, not manufactured', and the
ability to grow good leaders is a key management skill. This process
usually takes the form of on-the-job coaching in the form of discussing

job problems with the subordinate, and offering advice, guidance and friendly and informal instruction.

In *The Human Side of Enterprise,* McGregor argues that a young manager develops leadership qualities largely by identification with more capable people and, in particular, with his boss whose ideas, methods and values the young comer unconsciously assimilates. After interviewing twenty-four presidents of major US companies, Bailey concludes that in most cases an older executive has taught them all they know about management and leadership, i.e. at an earlier stage in their careers, they have been successfully coached, with the boss acting as a mentor and model (or even, possibly, an anti-model – showing them how *not* to do things and handle people) [1.18].

According to Zaleznik leaders typically develop through forming a close one-to-one relationship with a mentor during a formative part of their careers:

> Psychological biographies of gifted people repeatedly demonstrate the important part a mentor plays in developing an individual. Andrew Carnegie owed much to his senior, Thomas A. Scott. As head of the Western Division of the Pennsylvania Railroad, Scott recognized talent and the desire to learn in the young telegrapher assigned to him. By giving Carnegie increasing responsibility and by providing him with the opportunity to learn through close personal observation, Scott added to Carnegie's self-confidence and sense of achievement. Because of his own personal strength and achievement, Scott did not fear Carnegie's aggressiveness. Rather, he gave it full play in encouraging Carnegie's initiative [5.9].

McClelland and Burnham found that 63 per cent of the better managers in large US corporations (i.e. those whose subordinates had high morale) scored higher on the coaching or democratic styles of management compared with only 22 per cent of the poorer managers [1.15]. Evidence such as this suggests that successful leaders spend much time coaching their subordinates, thereby increasing their leadership skills.

Key factors in a leader's development

Many leaders have found that an effective coaching method is to identify subordinates' strong areas and concentrate on developing these rather than attempting to build up weak areas. Thus, the leader may strengthen his subordinate's political awareness by taking him to meetings and in a post-meeting review, discussing the various tactics used by participants and the way that decisions were reached, or by making a practice of analysing with the subordinate a particular kind of job problem and jointly agreeing ways in which it could be solved.

As consultant Hague points out, 'Coaching is a matter for daily contact and it should be part of everyday management'. It consists largely of sitting down with one's subordinate and helping him to analyse his methods and style, discussing the various alternatives, and assessing the actions he has taken in terms of the results achieved. This develops the man's confidence, his decision-making ability and his qualities of leadership.

Jewel Companies of Chicago are so sure that the boss-subordinate relationship is the key factor in leadership development that they have worked out a 'first assistant' practice whereby the senior man acts as the junior's assistant. A senior executive, Lunding, says: 'Each of our executives is first assistant to the person in line below him. He is charged not so much with directing and supervising but with offering assistance to those reporting to him'. Each senior manager is required to be a 'coach' – even if this involves turning the organisational chart upside down.

Another Jewel executive recalls Lewin's idea that instead of groups being objects for the leader to manipulate, leaders should be the means of helping groups to solve problems. And he adds: 'We don't really care if a department manager wants to wrap his lettuce in plastic or not. What we care about is developing his full leadership potential. If that isn't done our whole house of cards falls apart'. In any company, such a total commitment to coaching and developing subordinates means that senior executives should drop many of the day-to-day operational details to provide the extra time.

Changing specialists into generalists

Lyndall Urwick, of the consultancy firm of Urwick, Orr and Partners, says that business has not got an adequate conception of the role of 'assistant to', which should be a device for training leaders and for transforming them from specialists to generalists. A young manager appointed as personal assistant to a senior executive gets a very broad picture of company activities at an early stage in his career, partly as a result of checking and chasing up matters initiated by his boss.

According to Johnson, chief executive at Supreme Life, young comers must have a successful model. 'For instance, our vice-president of sales of cosmetics had never worked in this field before. He didn't know how to go into a store like Marshall Field or Bonwit Teller. So I took him with me, and he and I together opened accounts in about twenty stores. He listened to what I said, he watched when I backed off, he watched when I went forward. And he learned.'

A large oil company develops leadership through the direct influence of senior managers on juniors. For instance, the chief executive regularly appoints a promising young manager as a special assistant for a year. During this time, the young executive works closely with the CEO and thus gets first-hand knowledge of administrative problems and the uses of power. After the assignment ends, the young executive, leadership qualities duly strengthened, is assigned to a responsible line job in one of the operating divisions.

Formal training

Managers today must know more than their predecessors did about marketing, production, international business and finance, and attending a well-selected course is one of the quickest ways of catching up on the latest concepts and buzz-words. L. M. Ericsson, the big Swedish tele-communications company, has become a keen supporter of management education and sends dozens of the company's young engineers to European management centres and business schools. A senior executive in the company says: 'There is no doubt that it broadens their view and makes them more at home discussing economic and financial subjects. Instead of being just engineers they become business managers in outlook.'

Another strong advocate of formal training programmes is Perbos, marketing director of CEGEDUR, Europe's largest aluminium products maker, who claims that 'two years at the Harvard Business School gave me as much experience as working for ten years in industry'. And the majority of CEOs in Burck's survey said they would have benefited from additional formal training – mainly in business administration, accounting, finance and law [1.1].

The performance of a man with natural leadership qualities may be hamstrung if areas of fundamental knowledge or skill are neglected, and attending a course may be the quickest and most efficient method of mastering them. With the explosive growth of knowledge, information and techniques, the need for part-time management education is likely to increase rather than diminish in the future.

New perspectives

One of the advantages of attending a course with other managers stems simply from the fact that you are away from it all with other executives and so gain a new perspective, a kind of detachment. This allows the executive to stand back, as it were, from company problems to try to gain a fresh outlook. Goldston, chief executive of Eastern Gas and Fuel Associates, believes that senior executives should be encouraged, even required, to take sabbatical leaves. 'Corporations are great on sending middle managers to business school or foremen to sensitivity training sessions. But there is seldom an opportunity for the boss, who may need a pause more than anyone.'

Carefully selected outside courses are effective at bolstering managers in certain weak areas. Whether or not they can make a lasting impact problems is that it is not easy to measure the effectiveness of a general management course. The manager's job requires a longer time-perspective than most jobs, and it may be months or even years before the effects really show.

Fleishman and his colleagues (1955) found no evidence that formal leadership training for foremen increased the effectiveness of their departments. Newport (1963) surveyed a large number of organisations in the US which had executive development programmes for middle managers and found no objective evidence that the programmes increased leadership performance. Fiedler and his colleagues compared groups in the Belgian Navy led by untrained petty officers and by petty officers who had received two years' training. The groups led by the untrained petty officers did their tasks as well as the other groups.

Widespread cynicism

Findings such as these have added to the widespread cynicism that already exists in industry about college-based management training programmes. Whitehead once said, 'the second-handedness of the learned world is the secret of its mediocrity', and this is a sentiment that many managers would echo. One of the problems is that colleges are staffed largely by specialists, many of whom have an academic approach to business matters. They use traditional lectures and seminars – though evidence continues to pile up about the limitations of this method.

Copeman feels that any management training courses are almost bound to have a disappointing effect: 'Training courses for people who do not have an element of ownership (in the firm) are to some extent a waste of time. It is like giving someone a ship with a good rudder but no chart or destination' [1.6].

Some of these problems might be overcome if a senior manager rather than an academic were responsible for monitoring the overall progress of executives on formal courses. Alternatively, some companies prefer to bring outside experts into the company to run in-company courses. Lloyd, a director of Urwick Orr and Partners, makes the point: 'An outside catalyst is invariably involved in the design and conduct of effective in-company management training.'

The multi-national company, with a multiplicity of cross-cultural and cross-legal problems, requires techniques and solutions not found in most formal management courses. This has prompted the Ford Foundation and several European governments to set up the European Institute for Advanced Studies in Management in Brussels.

Smith, Professor of Marketing at Manchester University, believes that there is too much slack in many management courses and that more pressure should be applied: 'I think the idea of having managers wandering round quadrangles and Oxford colleges because it will in some way improve their minds is absolute bunkum'. Smith reckons that attending a course should be one part of an overall plan for the executive's development.

Lathrope points out that training must start where the manager is – relate to what he wants and needs. According to Lathrope :

1   People learn by doing rather than by listening to lectures and writing essays.
2   Success promotes learning : thus, trainees should be given assignments and problems to solve.
3   Social and technical skills are best developed together. This happens automatically if trainees are given actual job-problems to solve [5.2].

A training manager at International Computers believes that it is naive to expect a manager with strong views and, perhaps, a set management style to be changed permanently by attending a course. 'For one thing, most managers disliked being talked at – they prefer to do the talking themselves. And they are interested in theories only if they point straight at practical solutions.'

Other disadvantages with outside courses are :
– People tend to forget most of what they hear in days or even hours.
– When the executive returns to his organisation he may find it impossible to put what he has learnt into practice.
– Management courses are usually general in emphasis whereas the manager's needs are individual and specific.

Useful courses

Many companies today feel disillusioned about the value of formal management education – partly because the performance of so many university management graduates has failed to match their high expectations. Moreover, management theory is a gelatinous thing that shifts and changes form according to the fashions of the moment, so that by the time the executive returns to his company, what he has learnt may already be out of fashion. But undoubtedly, a well planned formal programme enables the executive to learn the skills of leadership faster than he otherwise would.

A programme which has been used successfully in France to develop creativity in leaders is based on planning a factory in an undeveloped area. A table is laid out with a river, roads, railway, woods and other basic features. Trainees form syndicates and, using models of buildings and plant, lay out a new factory with ancillary services. Some groups concentrate on arranging the factory for communications advantages, others think in terms of what is convenient for management, and so on. The groups' efforts are then discussed, with a psychologist joining in. What were the priorities and objectives of each group – and why? The group dynamics aspect is analysed.

Mico, president of Social Dynamics Incorporated, believes that since a leader's effectiveness is more bound up with attitudes and personality than with mastery of specific techniques, an executive's leadership qualities can be developed by attending sensitivity training courses. 'They learn how to be effective in groups and how to influence the decision-making'.

Mico believes that when sensitivity training is used at all levels throughout a company it can help the organisation to break down autocratic hierarchies to democratic organisations of effective and creative teams. 'Managers are consultants, not bosses', he says. 'Motivation now goes beyond money. People's creativity has to be tapped.'

Sensitivity training

Sensitivity training can make a leader aware of the kind of situations where he can perform well and those where he is likely to fail. In a T-group, for instance, he can experiment with changing relationships and with methods of winning more influence or control in the group, and so on. Bunker described behaviour changes as a result of T-group training, including :
1   More effort to understand and listen to others.
2   More tact and tolerance.
3   Less willingness to make snap judgements.

But, careful screening of applicants for sensitivity training courses is needed. It has been found that only 30-40 per cent of trainees actually improve their interpersonal skills as a result of attending. And changes effected may not be lasting – when the individual returns to his organisation he naturally begins to adjust to the same old pressures again.

Role-playing is an effective technique for improving human relations skills : the trainee practises the skill in an appropriate training set-up. For instance, a simple, four-stage session is usually found effective :
1   The role-playing is preceded by a film or lecture dealing with interviews, briefing sessions or whatever skill is to be practised.
2   The particular situation which is the subject of the role-play is defined and discussed.
3   Typically, two of the trainees perform the role-play, observed by the other trainees, and the proceedings are recorded on audio or video recorder.
4   The videocassette is replayed. The trainees study their own performance 'from the outside', as it were, and the observers offer comments.

When a series of sessions of this kind is arranged, the trainees gradually build competence in a given area. A big problem remains, however. This is the problem of transferring the learnt skills to their own workplace. From my own experience as a training consultant, it is clear that some do this far more successfully than others.

Like many large companies, Xerox is convinced of the value of role-playing in management development. At the company's training centre thirty miles from Washington, trainees – as many as a thousand are there at any one time – spend a lot of their time role-playing. By this means they learn how to deal with tough customers and situations – and they then have to face up to equally tough criticism from other trainees. As a senior Xerox executive points out: 'It's intimidating – but not nearly as tough as the actual situation can be'.

Role-playing is a simple but valuable training method. When the executive role-plays the union boss or the angry employee, he begins to experience how these people feel and think. Thus a new kind of sensitivity and understanding is created. According to the National Training Laboratory, role-playing exercises should have the following qualities:

1   The scenes which are played should deal with valid problems in human relations.
2   The problem should be clear, single, specific.
3   The problem should be such that the trainees can understand how the characters actually feel.
4   The problem should mean something to the players and observers.

Case studies and business games are also valuable. Trainees learn the important lesson that there is more than one way to run a business, that there are always a number of possible decisions that can be taken, and that different decisions have very different kinds of impact on the organisation.

Many successful formal programmes for developing leadership qualities have been developed including Blake's Grid, Adair's Action-Centred Leadership, Coverdale's group training courses and Rackham's techniques for developing interactive skills.

Part 2
THE LEADER'S
ROLE

6

'Business leaders are people who can achieve results through groups. Otherwise, they'd strike out on their own and wouldn't put up with all the frustrations and difficulties of leadership in a company.'

**Brian Webster, Managing Director,
Bulmers Cider Limited**

Team-builder

Rough, tough leadership can be highly effective – for instance, in some small groups, such as construction gangs or combat crews, where threats, punishment and energetic man-to-man influence may be needed to prevent disruption of the group by disorderly individuals. But most large groups and organisations depend on subtler, more socialised forms of influence and control. Task force or project management, for instance, has grown out of the inadequacy of traditional leadership methods within the modern business context.

Project management achieves results by forming separate teams with people 'borrowed' from different functional areas and returned after completion of the project. A major deterrent to its use is the disruption of normal schedules that is often caused in setting up the teams, together with the difficulties of winning the agreement and cooperation of functional heads. But if these problems can be overcome, project management can be an extremely effective way of tackling organisational problems.

Wilkinson Match uses task forces internationally – for instance, as a way of effecting mergers more smoothly. The teams, which are usually hand-picked by chief executive Lewinton, are given access to any information they require and to any executive's time for the duration of the project. 'It blows routines and is very exciting', says Lewinton.

Task force projects at Wilkinson are usually restricted to thirty days and aim to study a business problem in depth, bringing a wide range of skills and experience to bear on it. They also provide an accelerated way of broadening management experience. One task force studied the possibility of the company acquiring a disposable lighter company, and recommended against it. The company agreed and, since then, the soundness of their decision has been proved, with two giants increasingly dominating the market.

Training-ground for leaders

Decision-making committees are another way of bringing a wide range of skills and experience to bear on business problems. This is the thinking at the Coors Company, where committee work has become almost a way of life. Chairman Coors says: 'Committees pinpoint responsibility and gather the best talent to solve a problem'. And, he adds, they act as a training ground for potential leaders. Coors reckons that the participation of 'just about the entire management team in decision-making' by means of committees helps to explain why management turnover at Coors is almost non-existent. 'They become so strongly identified not only with the Coors philosophy but with the Coors product that you couldn't get them away from here.'

In *The New Industrial State*, Galbraith argues that large organisations are run by a *technostructure*, a team leadership, comprising everybody in the organisation who shares in the decision-making, and that the real achievements of these organisations depend on a massive coordination of the efforts of many people. According to Galbraith, *teams* of managers define organisational goals and ultimately determine the allocation of resources – by contrast, directors and shareholders have little say in these matters. Thus team-handling skills are an essential attribute of leadership.

One of the reasons why team-building is so important is that for most employees the organisation as a whole is too big and complex to identify with. One investigator discovered that Swedish brewery workers were much less concerned about the success of the company as a whole than about the success of their own work-teams.

People will often work harder for the work-team than they will for themselves: it is easy to identify with the team and to grasp its goals. A management consultant makes the point: 'A sales executive should be first a member of the management team and only secondly a sales executive'.

Collective leadership

Wallenberg seemed a monolithic and permanent figure – until he stepped down in 1975 from the chairmanship of the Skandinaviska Enskilda Bank, the sprawling financial group that controls 30 per cent of Swedish industry. He resigned, he says, to make way for a team of four managing directors who meet once a week with a rotating chairman, and whose function is to keep a close watch on the group's individual companies.

'Collective leadership is a sign of the times', says Wallenberg. 'A great modern company can only be run on the basis of absolute authority, and the job can no longer be carried out by a single leader. The old idea of a strong leader as being somebody who overrode all opposition is dead. Leaders still need to act decisively. But that doesn't relieve them of the responsibility to consult with their colleagues.'

In industry 'partnership' generally refers to management-worker relations, but, as Wallenberg's words imply, it is just as important among managers. An efficient management team can achieve better results – and perhaps better leadership – than any of its members could on his own. This is so especially at times of crisis in the organisation when widespread discussion and collaboration are needed to ensure maximum awareness of problems and the range of possibilities.

Without the support of an effective executive team, the top-level leader's authority may be challenged by ambitious individuals and cliques and he may be unable to carry out his decisions. In the absence of a central power group, cliques may form and fight each other for control and influence.

As Drucker has pointed out, there are some forty-five key areas of decision-making in a typical large organisation – that fact alone calls the whole concept of one-man leadership into question, and explains why, to function effectively in a large organisation, the leader needs the support of a team of key assistants. To be sure, team management means more consensus-seeking, more caucuses, more committees, more delay. But it often works out better in the end because there is no one neck for a single sword-stroke to sever, no over-commitment to any one approach or policy.

Managers are team leaders

In Japan, managers are seen to be essentially team leaders. They are expected to communicate constantly with members of their team, to build relationships and team spirit. A manager who recently returned from that country says that the Japanese manager is encouraged to discuss job problems with his executive team and to develop a consensus view of how they should be handled. 'If they fail to do this they won't get very high in management.'

Honda's chief executive, Kawashima, encourages his executives to think of themselves as a united team by sharing a single large office with them – an arrangement that also facilitates the exchange of ideas and information. At Honda plants, distinctions between management and workers are deliberately blurred by having everyone wear identical white overalls. Such an approach stimulates team spirit and cooperative attitudes. For instance, machinery trouble causing a brief lull in production is seen by employees as an opportunity to grab brooms and tidy up the shop.

Matsushita promotes team management through a monthly meeting attended by 200 senior executives. The meeting, preceded by a coffee hour to promote group harmony, is considered an essential forum for discussing new plans for letting each part of the organisation know what the other parts are doing and for promoting 'company-consciousness'.

In the West, too, many leaders achieve excellent results by encouraging their managers to organise themselves in effective teams and by inspiring them to reach for ambitious goals. When William Hewitt became chief executive at Deere and Company, he worked hard to instill a sense of corporate pride and self-confidence in his executives – he knew that if the company was going to reach higher ground it was the management team which would have to lead it there. One manager reports: 'Before he came we were just a bunch of good old country boys. We knew we could make good farm equipment. But we never really looked at ourselves as in the big league. We knew we could make it in Moline but we didn't know that we could make it in New York. Bill showed us that we could. Bill made us realise just how strong a team we were.'

Upward movement

In setting goals for a team, the trick is to ensure that they are ambitious but attainable and also to make it quite clear that the goals *must* be reached. Unrealistically high goals inevitably lead to failure and loss of morale.

For members of the team, a sense of expansion and upward movement is an important part of the challenge. Once a group gets the impression that it is moving to higher ground all marginal problems begin to fade. General Marshall has pointed out that, when a team starts moving upwards, standards of courtesy and discipline automatically improve because pride has been restored: 'Malingering and failure to maintain proper inspection standards become minimal through a renewed confidence and an upgrading of interpersonal relationships . . . When the group gets the feeling of new motion it centrifugally influences anyone who tries to stand still.' High performance improves team spirit and so leads to still higher performance.

In the successful groups studied by Zander team spirit was very high [6.7]. And these groups set themselves – and achieved – very ambitious targets. By contrast, workers in groups where team spirit and morale were low (perhaps because of inadequate leadership), enjoyed work less, had less pride in the organisation and in their own work and consoled themselves by arguing that success is unimportant.

Results through people

Johnson, chief executive at Supreme Life, pulls his management team together by a simple organisational device: 'In most large companies the board are so far removed that they'll have maybe only three people reporting to them. In my case, I have the heads of every department reporting directly to me.' As Johnson says : 'If you fail to establish direct contact with your management team your isolation increases. You may think you're doing all right but you don't know. That's dangerous.' Johnson asserts that leadership means achieving results through people – and that the superior leader achieves such results in many different situations, year after year.

A department head in an electronics firm is careful not to intervene too quickly when there is friction among staff : he thinks that members of the same team must take the responsibility for working out inter-personal difficulties in their own way. But if the conflict escalates, he steps in to ensure that it doesn't get out of hand. Clearly, this kind of tactful leadership requires a sensitive knack for dealing with people – and not all managers possess it.

The leader must be able to deal with people's problems as well as technical problems because, as many investigators have pointed out, he occupies a position in his group analogous to that of the parent in the family. Zaleznik has said : 'He is at the nucleus of a political structure whose prototype is the family in which jealousy, envy, love and hate find original impetus and expression'. The leader is the central figure to whom others in the team make emotional attachments.

The manager's efficiency depends largely on his ability to work in teams. Diary studies by Rosemary Stewart and other investigators show that managers spend, on average, 70-80 per cent of their time in meetings, discussions and other kinds of group activity. In *New Patterns of Management*, Likert states that individuals function best as members of highly efficient groups. 'Consequently, management should deliberately build these effective groups, linking them into an overall organisation by means of people who hold overlapping group membership. The superior in one group is a subordinate in the next group, and so on through the organisation.'

When people are organised in teams they begin to speak the same language – or at least to understand each other's argot – and they learn about each other's aims and problems. Elton Corporation's president, Loynd, points out : 'It's no good just telling people they must think company-wise. One must have deliberate machinery to make them do so'. A useful piece of machinery set up by Loynd himself is the monthly meeting attended by 15 or so of his staff. Membership rotates so that everybody attends a few times a year. There is no agenda. The meetings are simply a chance to talk shop and discuss current problems and for people to get to know each other so that they start to feel they are all members of the same team.

At United Biscuits, the elaborate communications network includes structured briefing and discussion groups from the top down. According to chairman Laing, the system helps to tie the entire organisation together and helps to explain its success.

When a team is struggling to carry out a task people get hurt : they lose struggles for power and influence, get involved in damaging conflicts, lose arguments, and so on. Their emotions are roused and seek expression. The harder the group drives towards its goal, the greater the amount of heat that is generated; the faster the progress the greater the tensions. The pressures of working together cause stresses and tensions that build up, break through and disrupt the work. These tensions have constantly to be dissipated so that the work can continue smoothly and efficiently.

Thus the leader of the group, ideally, should not only be a task leader, who knows how to control the group and impose appropriate structure and discipline, but also a 'maintenance' leader with the necessary social skills to soothe people and motivate them and to maintain morale.

Maintenance leadership means giving warmth, support and encouragement to members of the team, thus strengthening their ability to cope with the pressures generated by work. It means smoothing with one hand the feathers you ruffled with the other in driving towards the goal.

Often the designated leader finds it impossible to be both task and maintenance leader (in a sense, the two roles are contradictory) and instead concentrates on task leadership. During the Second World War coalition government, Churchill gave hope, identity, morale, and made people happy (maintenance) while Attlee, the controller, the numbers man, made the machine work (task).

In groups, there is little chance of the task leaders being able to exercise maintenance leadership too. According to Bales, there is a one in two chance of the task leader being the most liked man after the first meeting of the group. At the end of the second meeting the chances are reduced to one in four; at the end of the third meeting, to one in six, and so on. People resent direction and control. Thus, when the executive in charge of a group concentrates on task leadership, one of the members may emerge spontaneously as maintenance leader. Be sure to identify this person and to treat him as an ally in controlling the group and satisfying its leadership needs : make sure that you and he or she form a mutually supportive pair.

Maintenance skills

In highly effective groups, the entire membership may handle maintenance with considerable aplomb. The skills of maintenance leadership include : *praising* employees for work done well; *complimenting* employees on a particular job or contribution; *conciliating* when there is open conflict between members of the team; *encouraging* individuals during periods of despondency – for instance, by constantly making positive and enthusiastic comments about their work and by showing interest;

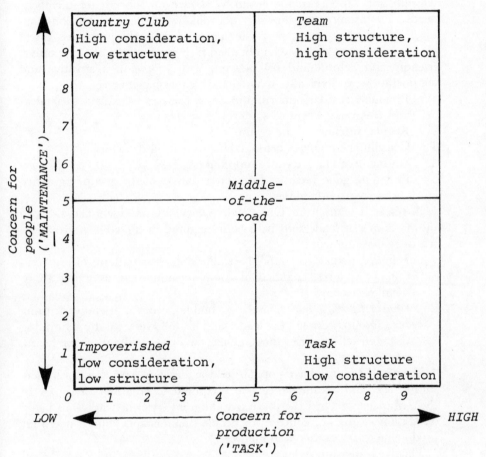

Figure 4 The managerial grid - showing the five different styles of leadership. Blake and Mouton have developed training programmes to change managers towards a 'Team' (9-9) style of leadership

soothing individuals' ruffled feelings when their ideas are rejected or when they have been criticised. This kind of intervention by the leader can prevent psychological withdrawal by his followers.

Maintenance leadership is important because the group needs to be maintained as a cohesive social unity. The maintenance leader builds warmth and rapport in the group by showing a concern for members' needs – for instance, by allowing subordinates to share in decision-making, by being supportive and listening to individuals' problems. Likert (1959) found that leaders who obtained high productivity are supportive, friendly and helpful and try to work with people in a sensitive and considerate way. Typically, maintenance leadership involves:

1 Providing regular opportunities for employees to explain their ideas and feelings.
2 Regular briefings of the group.
3 Consulting employees before taking important decisions.
4 Setting up a fair grievance procedure.
5 Providing good facilities for representatives of the group, e.g. office and secretarial facilities.

A research team from Ohio State University has identified the two distinct kinds of leadership behaviour required in directing a group towards goal attainment:

1 *Initiating structure ('task')* establishing clear patterns of organisation, procedures, channels of communication, e.g. assigning group members to particular tasks.
2 *Consideration ('maintenance')* building warm, friendly, trusting relationships between the leader and his followers, e.g. by arbitrating disputes, settling grievances, giving minorities a chance to be heard, etc.

Blake and Mouton have popularised the idea that *both* kinds of leadership – 'task' and 'maintenance' – are required in organisations [6.2]. In their Managerial Grid there are five different styles of leadership based on varying degrees of concern for people (maintenance) and concern for production (task), as shown in Figure 4.

The five leadership styles are:

1 *Impoverished* minimum effort is made by the leader both in 'people' and 'production' areas.
2 *Country Club* much concern for people, building a friendly atmosphere and comfortable work tempo.
3 *Task* the leader is much concerned with organisation and structure, with the human element playing little part.
4 *Team* highly effective team-leadership, with high output being achieved by happy, committed people.
5 *Middle-of-the-road* leader maintains group morale and work-efficiency at adequate levels.

From the Managerial Grid, it appears that highly effective leaders are essentially *team*-leaders, with maximum concern both for people *and* for production.

Ideally, the executive in charge of a unit or department is both a task and maintenance leader (although the double role is an extremely difficult one to sustain). The leader who successfully combines these roles will keep swinging from concern for productivity to concern for people, and back again. Ideally, the leader is neither production-centred nor people-oriented, but people- and production-oriented. Repeatedly, research studies have shown that highly productive groups have leaders who are considerate and supportive as well as efficient. For instance, Bowers and Seashore (1966) studied 40 agencies of a life assurance company and found that the basic qualities of effective leadership were, first, giving support to employees and providing interaction facilities (maintenance leadership) and, secondly, emphasising goals and facilitating work (task leadership). In practice, the group goal is often best achieved by having *two* leaders – a task leader whose main responsibility is to get the task itself done; and a maintenance leader whose job is to get the other members of the team to interact and work together happily and efficiently. The task leader, e.g. the chief executive, is often the more extrovert.

Maintenance leadership is concerned with good interpersonal relations in the group, with providing support and helping individuals to build their sense of self-esteem. The effect is to reduce stress and anxiety within the group so that it can perform its task more effectively. Task leadership, on the other hand, increases stress by emphasising the successful completion of the task. Task leadership means:

1 Being clear what the task actually is and how it relates to the organisation's objectives.
2 Planning how to accomplish the task.
3 Defining the task so that individuals know what has to be done.
4 Providing necessary resources.

When the organisation is unclear about its task, methods and role systems, the organisation is prey to confusion, inaction and a sense of futility and frustration. As Rice says: 'In this condition an individual who can define some positive goal can exert powerful leadership' [3.16].

Team-building

The managing director of a motor components factory builds team spirit at top level by holding daily meetings with his key functional heads – personnel, materials, sales, and so on. 'Provided the heads of these key functions work together as a team, the company to a large extent manages itself.' When appointing a new executive, this man takes great pains to ensure that he will fit into the existing management team. Even after a manager has been with them for a couple of years, if he's not coping one should be able to say, 'I'm sorry, but we did agree that if you didn't get on well with your colleagues you would have to leave'.

For this man, the secret of a happy, productive team is good personal relations and he personally intervenes at the first signs of feuding, quarreling, or victimisation. 'Whenever I come across any abuse of good personal relationships I make an immediate personal investigation to get all the facts so that I can expose and rebuke the person who is being unfair.'

William Whyte has shown the dangers of conformity. But at least Organisation Man realises the importance of fitting into the team.

At Supreme Life, chief executive Johnson believes that the ability to weld employees into happy and effective work-teams is a key management skill. He tries to keep Supreme Life's work-teams happy and healthy by catering for the needs of their members. 'I try to think of all the things I can do to keep the team happy and well satisfied with their work here. This often involves more than salary. It involves an upgrading in title, maybe occasional trips, recognition of things well done, like a little note thanking them for it, calling attention to an outstanding job.'

Avoiding paternalism

Friendly, direct communication can build team spirit, but it is important to avoid any trace of paternalism. When one general manager offered to arrange management courses for shop stewards, the unions countered with an offer to put on management courses for the foremen.

A manager who gets close to the workforce is Prior, Bulmer's chairman. Prior makes a point of getting out of the office as often as he can and involving himself at shop-floor level – he believes this boosts team spirit at lower levels. 'Generally, it's acting as a driver's mate. I go out and spend the complete day with the driver and then with the drivers at the depot. I give them the opportunity to talk to me and I talk to them about things that are going on in the company.'

Andreassenn, managing director of Denmark's International Service System which cleans offices in 15 countries and is the biggest operation of its kind in the world, builds team spirit in his employees through intensive training programmes. These show employees not only the most effective methods of cleaning offices, but also give them an understanding of the work being done by the company throughout Europe. 'This gives them pride in themselves and in the company.' Why bother building team spirit in charladies? 'Research shows that the stronger the group, the more the individual worker strives to achieve its goals. People often work harder for their groups than they do for themselves.'

Cases like these show that an essential dimension of leadership is the ability to create cohesive and successful teams. This involves helping them to achieve ambitious targets through encouragement and the provision of appropriate information and organisational back-up. This kind of leadership means knowing when to step forward to take control and when to step back and let them do it for themselves. The huge size of organisations today and the overload mean that it is impossible for top leaders to function effectively without congenial and trustworthy key assistants. But Bennis found that leaders select key assistants who resemble them not only in ideas and attitudes but down to such details as height, build, dress – even the cigarettes they smoke [1.12]. But there are dangers when team-building, in focusing too narrowly on the preferred type. If all immediate subordinates are cast in the leader's mould there will be nobody to check his actions or question his decision and the information he sees may be very selective and one-sided. Notice how, in the Watergate hearings, Nixon's aides were difficult to distinguish from each other. They all looked the same and spoke in the same way – and they had all made the same kind of mistakes.

Autonomous work-groups

Team leadership can put the company on a faster track of productive growth by producing policies that really work – because people enthusiastically support and implement decisions that they have helped to make. That is why Enid Mumford, a lecturer at the Manchester Business School, thinks that a transfer of leadership responsibility to the work-group itself could boost both productivity and morale: 'This could be achieved by the group setting its own targets and monitoring them. Management could give the work-group a budget and allow it to buy its own materials and even organise the selling of its own products to customers. Thus, the group would act almost as a company within a company.'

Inside large organisations, individual employees often feel lost and unimportant in the general scheme of things. A way to overcome this effect, according to Volvo's president, Gyllenhammar, is to organise employees in small, autonomous work-groups: 'Groups that have money to spend on their own facilities and a mandate to list their own problems seem to achieve cohesion and cooperation most rapidly'. Citing Volvo's experience in this area, Gyllenhammar adds: 'It need not cost the corporation more money to apportion facilities or safety budgets to the groups themselves than to experts'.

Gyllenhammer says that Volvo have also found that 'the fastest way to get ideas flowing seems to be to set up discussion groups in each working area'.

Shared leadership does work

If a company can flourish when its industry is in distress, it is usually a sign of strong leadership. In the past few years, against a background of stagnant sales and output in the furniture industry, Christie-Tyler, UK's leading maker of domestic upholstered furniture, has opened nine new factories, increased its workforce by 500, and boosted annual sales by 80 per cent.

Chairman Williams attributes the company's success to its 'cell' system of production. 'The system has enabled us to achieve productivity which is three times the average for the industry.'

In the late sixties, when the company was making losses and had trimmed its workforce as the quickest way of paring costs, eight redundant workers asked Williams to back a workers' cooperative plan. He refused but said that if the workers would try to produce three-piece suites themselves in an old barn near the factory, the company would buy the suites from them at an agreed rate.

Six months later the eight workers were producing three times as many suites per man as employees in the factory. This was the beginning of the 'cell' system.

Spontaneous action

Over the next four years, workers in the factories formed their own cells. 'It happened quite spontaneously', says Williams. 'They approached us and suggested it and, of course, we encouraged it.' Today the system operates in all but two of the group's 21 subsidiaries.

Each cell of upholsterers, springers and service-man (who fetches and carries the materials) elects its own leader. His main job is to agree with the works director how many suites will be upholstered each week, and how much the cell will be paid for each suite. Generally, the rates are uniform between the cells. The cash received by the cell is generally split evenly among the members, except for very young members who are allotted a smaller share.

Each cell of between five and ten members is largely self-organised, with the cell itself allocating specific duties. The leader acts as a communication centre within the group and with other parts of the company, and he is responsible for output and quality.

The cell administers its own discipline. A young upholsterer in one factory slept in for two mornings running, so the cell disciplined him by leaving him off work rosters for two days. He lost two days' wages and didn't sleep in again.

The simplicity of the system encourages high output and wages. Christie-Tyler's financial director, O'Sullivan, explains: 'Having agreed to a rate for the job, the cells work on a direct production basis. There is no conflict of interest because the men want high output as much as management do. If management can keep on producing the orders and the materials, they'll do the rest – very quickly. There are no barriers, no hassles. Anything they can do to speed up productivity, they will.'

It sounds idealistic but it works. There have been no strikes at the company since the cells were introduced. There is better discipline than before because the workers themselves exert it. Orders are completed

much more quickly and work-in-progress has been reduced. Absenteeism
and labour turnover have shrunk to negligible levels.

At Dominion Upholstery's factory in Cardiff, the cell's responsibilities have been widened, with the cell taking over all management functions except for sales.

The cell orders most of its own materials direct from the suppliers – polyether foam from Dunlop and timber frames from Dinas Furniture, another C-T subsidiary. The cell makes its own arrangements for loading finished goods, hires its own transport, and so on.

Everything is paid for out of the cash it receives from the company for the finished suites.

But can workers do management's job as well as management? 'We do it better', says Dominion cell leader, Coates. 'We get the organisational details right – such as quantities to be ordered and times of collections – because we know exactly what the production situation is. It's our responsibility – not management's – to get the organisational aspects right. We know that if we walk out on a problem today it's there waiting for us tomorrow.'

Problem-solvers

Throughout the company, each cell specialises in producing a particular suite and so its members become specialists, adept at finding ever-better methods of doing the job. As O'Sullivan says: 'We don't have to keep going to the men and telling them how the job should be done. The men themselves have got the expertise, and they always find ways of solving production problems.'

O'Sullivan reckons that this production system, which eliminates the role of the supervisor and intermediate manager, largely explains the company's impressive output levels, currently running at 5000 suites a week.

There are, of course, snags in any system. According to upholsterer Clemmett, the worst problem that crops up is 'when management can't keep us going with work because the orders have dried up'. This has happened at Glamorgan Upholstery, and at most of the other factories, several times in the last six months.

There are human problems too. 'We want maximum output so we've decided in most cells that everybody should do one particular operation, such as padding the arms or fitting the springs', says Clemmett. 'It means good wages but the work gets very boring. We're working so fast that we've no time to talk to each other.'

Another problem is fatigue. 'It gets very tiring because everybody is working flat out.' At Glamorgan Upholstery the work tempo is unrelenting with men driving themselves hard. What will happen when these young workers grow older and find the pace too hot?

I put this question to Phillips, chief shop steward at Bridgend Timber Products, another subsidiary. 'I don't know the answer', he admits. 'The cells will have to find their own answers. They may decide to give the older members the easiest jobs. Work-groups are very good at solving that sort of problem.'

The Furniture, Timber and Allied Trades Union, to which 90 per cent of production employees in the company belong, accepts the cell system somewhat grudgingly. 'The union doesn't really approve', says Phillips. 'It sees the system as encouraging greed and setting man against man. 'But it accepts the system because it's popular.'

Productivity rates

The system is understandably popular-because of the excellent wages. These stem from the extremely impressive productivity levels. The average worker at Christie-Tyler used to make five suites a week. Today the average is 15, with some cells averaging more than 20 per man.

One of management's basic ideas is that a large company is best able to detect and respond to changing trends in fashion if it is split into small factory units – the largest factory unit has 200 employees – each one concentrating on a specific market sector.

Thus, for years, Christie-Tyler's management has always created a new factory unit somewhere else – or acquired another small company – rather than expand an existing factory above a certain size.

As Williams points out : 'It is much easier to find someone who can efficiently manage 100 people than somebody to manage a thousand'. It is even easier when the factory consists of four or five self-organising cells.

Managing directors of the subsidiaries are freed of bureaucratic trammels. They can take most of the day-to-day business decisions without being inhibited by masses of red tape emanating from headquarters.

Sticking to essentials

The main board has ultimate power, but it is free from the myriad details of day-to-day operations. This enables it to concentrate on such essentials as giving expert design advice to the companies and maintaining tight financial controls via operating budgets and checks on capital expenditure.

Thus the young managers heading the factories gain profit responsibility and general management experience very early in their careers. Not surprisingly, some of them have enjoyed a meteoric rise.

Williams feels sure that the cell system could help other labour-intensive industries, such as clothing and mining, which are trying to increase their efficiency as an antidote to the recession. But he admits that it would be difficult to introduce the system into an established company because : 'You need to shoot half the managers – the system virtually eliminates middle management. If the cell system spread through industry, the first-line manager could become redundant. In most companies foremen are in an impossible position anyway. They are often paid less than operatives and not fully accepted by them; and they are not really accepted by middle management as full members of the management team. They are in a no-man's land, expected to communicate information that they may not fully understand or even have received. The plight of the foreman is one of the main problems of British industry.'

One subsidiary, Dominion Upholstery, owns a factory which consists of cells of workers who are made up almost entirely of former supervisors. 'They realised that their traditional supervisory role was fast disappearing so they decided to form cells of their own and become craftsmen again.'

As Williams points out, the cell system is not suitable for machine-intensive factories, and only the craft and manual workers in the company are organised in cells. Machine-paced workers such as cutters and machinists are organised on traditional lines. About two-fifths of the total workforce is organised in cells.

Linking-pin function

When Donnelly Mirrors reorganised on the team principle, production improved dramatically. The company applied Likert's concept of interlocking work-teams. Chief executive Donnelley explains: 'There's good teamwork and good performance when the leader of one team is also part of a successful work-team at the next higher level and becomes a sort of linking pin between the two teams. This means a steady flow of information and communication in both directions.'

When employees are organised in small teams, says Donnelly, the one-to-one lines of reporting are gone. Members of the team start supporting each other with advice and information instead of running to the boss for help. The boss himself becomes a team leader and expediter of group services rather than the traditional supervisor and controller. 'What we are trying to do is to pay attenion to people on a constant basis. So, in a way, we're having a continuous Hawthorne effect.'

As Donnelly and many other companies have found, thinking of the organisation as a web rather than a pyramid is a neat trick. It reveals how important it is for *everyone* to be involved in setting organisational objectives – and in deciding how they should be achieved. Effective policies and decisions are those that pack in all the resources of the group.

The transfer of responsibility to autonomous work-groups is one means of overcoming the split between management and the workforce. Perhaps this kind of democratisation of the work-place is an essential complement to industrial democracy which makes decisions more democratic but without altering the content of a worker's relation to his job.

Volvo's Gyllenhammar concedes that the new 'group' climate 'demands a different kind of leadership at all levels'. Foremen, who for decades had regarded themselves as disciplinarians, had to be equipped with the new, subtler skills required for team leadership: 'Foremen needed considerable training to regard themselves as information-gatherers, as aides to the employees, as teachers and consultants, rather than as bosses'.

Gyllenhammar reckons that an effective team leader is constantly taking the temperature of his group, 'injecting some of his or her own alertness whenever he or she senses signs of apathy or boredom'. And he adds: 'Instead of giving orders, the manager has to listen, argue, motivate and often compromise. This process takes longer. Decisions are slower. But it works out better in the long run because, once they are made, the decisions are accepted and implemented very rapidly.'

The OD concept

Team-building is an important current concept in organisation development (OD). Team-building focuses on small groups of people who share in making and carrying out organisational decisions. This is based on research evidence that shows that groups reach more creative decisions than do individuals and that members are more motivated to carry out group decisions.

The OD concept holds that organisational change can be accomplished simply by improving the way people work together as teams. In essence, this means allowing people a larger voice in how to do their jobs and ensuring that leaders don't treat employees as impersonal and interchangeable cogs in a machine.

The application of this seemingly simple principle is fraught with difficulties. It often involves the sensitive task of changing basic attitudes both of the leader and followers. When the Saga Administrative Corporation first became interested in OD, they stressed a facet of OD theory called 'team-building'. This involved grouping a leader at any level with some or all of his subordinates into a team of between six and twelve people. A senior executive explains: 'Every leader was involved in two teams – one with his boss and one with his subordinates. In our groups the communication works both ways. The concept of a leader is, after all, to find the needs of one's team and to serve them.'

In this company as in many others, there is little that an isolated leader can achieve. The complexity, size and rapidly changing environment require a multiplicity of objectives that cannot be managed by one person. Thus a first step in boosting performance is to find allies, promote communication between departments and levels and weld individuals into efficient working teams.

The successful team leader is driven not to build or preside over empires but to organise winning teams with the knack of performing in a wards on a group rather than an individual basis. This means less rivalry and conflict within the group, more cooperation and group loyalty. Bulmers managing director Webster makes the point: 'Business leaders are people who can achieve results through groups. Otherwise they'd strike out on their own and wouldn't put up with all the frustrations and difficulties of leadership in a company.'

The well led team

Generally, a well led team can be identified by the following characteristics:
1   The team has clear and ambitious objectives.
2   The role and responsibilities of each member are clear to himself and to others.
3   Members of the team share the same basic values and goals.
4   Communication is continuous and two-way.
5   Members have diverse skills and experience, thus making the group flexible in its functioning and versatile in the range of problems it can tackle.
6   Few grievances and labour turnover is low.
7   The leader stresses successful completion of the task.
   Groups, of course, fluctuate in their needs. When they are working efficiently, little direction and control are needed from the leader. But when crises or disputes erupt, or when the nature of the task changes, or there is a change of personnel, the leader may have to step in, exert his authority and impose structure and procedure until the group finds its feet again. Thus, group and leader are tied together in an eternal three-legged race that allows neither to out-pace the other too far.

Advantages of small teams

One of the skills of team building is to keep the team small so that members can identify themselves with it. Another advantage of keeping the team small is that small teams are easier than large groups to motivate and organise. Absenteeism in a British car factory, for instance, was four times as high in groups of 129 people as in groups of four. Homans thinks that the leader cannot properly control more than twelve people in a group – above that number they can't interact in a reciprocal fashion. In small work teams individuals depend on each other for help and support. All have an interest in good relations. Everybody knows everybody else and so there are few communication problems. These are some of the reasons why it is easier to build team spirit in small groups than in large ones.
   The Cummins Engine group tries to overcome some of the morale

problems that can occur in large units by deliberately trying to preserve a human scale. It has designed a huge new plant so that there is a collection of small units in which employees can feel that they are members of small work-teams.

John Laing Construction tries to keep work-gangs as small as possible because small teams create good relations and give men a sense of loyalty to the gang leader. Several years ago the company had nearly 3,000 construction workers working on the M1 motorway. Chairman Sir Maurice Laing says: 'We had little or no trouble because they were stretched out in small groups over the whole length of motorway'.

Generally small groups are more productive than large groups. Moede observed members of a group who pulled a rope as hard as possible. At intervals, an extra man was added to the team. With each increase in membership there was a decreased average contribution. Likert found that sometimes individuals in factories form themselves into small, unofficial teams, and as a result show consistently higher performance and morale. (Such groups tend to form spontaneously where the nature of the job requires teamwork – among miners or dockers, say.) In a large group, the individual knows that his own efforts will make little difference to the outcome. Seashore concludes that the larger the group the more difficulty it has in becoming an effective and cohesive unit – a finding supported by Gibb and Revans. Kornhauser found strong evidence that working in large organisations damages mental health.

Recruitment

Today companies facing the crunch of competition are having to place a higher value than ever before on the effectiveness of their leaders. Yet the managerial landscape is replete with examples of executives working unhappily and unproductively in jobs to which they should never have been appointed in the first place. Why does it happen? A principal reason is the inept recruitment and placement procedures that characterise many companies. These can have a big impact, for a top-level leader can only do a very limited amount of work himself. His effectiveness depends largely on his ability to recruit an effective team of capable subordinates to do the detailed work and thinking for him.

In assembling an executive team it is important to aim at the right size. If the leader is an empire-builder and recruits too many executives, his own part of the organisation will be top-heavy and inefficient. A department head expresses the point succinctly: 'The more chiefs the more energy is devoted to controls and the less to direct action'. (Wilson, though liked to have five or six 'crown princes' round him when he was Prime Minister because 'I felt safer . . . suppose there'd been three. They might have ganged up'. More than that number might have been difficult to control).

It is important to avoid a number of common errors when appointing people to the 'executive constellation'. Often, for instance, a leader tends to appoint people who are cast in his own image, and this can create the hanger-on syndrome – a group of like-minded proteges who are incapable of adding strength to areas in which the boss is weak. A sure sign of the disease is when the boss moves on, or retires, but without there being any perceptible change in policies. Moreover, making appointments to the inner group on this basis can create a succession crisis when the boss eventually leaves. A consultant who has often seen this happen reports that 'usually an awfully good string of number two guys is left behind but no number one material. The boss's proteges are usually not the best people to step into his shoes.' One reason is that the boss's deputy is often less extrovert and outward-looking than the boss himself (the introverted deputy acts as a kind of anchor for the boss's wayward ebullience).

Research evidence suggests that the leadership qualities needed in any particular situation are not concentrated in any one individual but spread among several. Thus, in filling a top-level vacancy the strengths and weaknesses of the person being appointed should be considered alongside those of the persons he will be working with.

Valuable clues on predicting the future performance of new appointees come from research carried out by Ohio State University. The researchers tried to predict how naval officers would perform in new jobs on the basis of, first, previous job performance and, secondly, performance of their predecessors in the job. They found that the way the man would perform could be forecast almost as well by looking at the behaviour of the previous job holder as by examining the new leader's past performance. One of the researchers concluded that less than half of leadership performance could be ascribed to the person, 'and a little over half to the demands of the particular job'.

Resonance

This is one of the reasons why some firms, when filling top leadership posts, prefer to go outside of the company in their search for talent, or even to retain an executive search firm. Another reason for doing so is that often, when a manager is promoted inside the company, the firm loses an excellent second-level executive and gains an inept third-level leader. Appointing a two-ulcer man to a three-ulcer job can be a disastrous mistake.

Many top executives are understandably reluctant to appoint strong, independent leaders onto the management team. As consultant McMurry has pointed out, 'They may be able to tolerate one, but if they have five of them, that's five guys bucking for their job instead of one'.

New appointees should, of course, be reasonably in tune with their new boss and capable of winning acceptance by the rest of the executive team and by their new subordinates: a liked and accepted leader who disciplines his subordinates may actually raise their morale whereas the rejected leader may trigger off revolt. Thus, it is wise to include some kind of 'resonance' test in the appointment procedures. For instance, appoint the candidate only after he has been approved by several other managers. A senior manager makes the point: 'You quickly see what the person is like if you sit him down with your mixed bag of people and see how he performs'. This kind of screening procedure also ensures that other leaders in the organisation have some sort of personal stake in the new man's future.

Once he has been fully accepted by colleagues and subordinates, the leader needs no signs of rank, 'no organisationally guaranteed powers to get his men to do his bidding . . . This relationship between the leader and his men may become a very strong tie which indeed does resemble the father-son relationship which Freud (1922) described in his psycho-analytic theory of the group process . . . We see this in combat crews where the crew members in many cases cannot admit the faults and weaknesses of their leaders' [3.20].

Screening procedures

Phillipe, sometime chairman of General Motors, has identified the search for executive manpower and the building of the executive team as 'the greatest challenge facing industrial leaders'. As Phillipe points out, the leader exerts control by selecting as members of his executive team men who will perform *their* leadership functions efficiently, and also by influencing by his own leadership style the style and performance of his team. That, arguably, is why the second-level manager should have a say in the selection and placement of the first-level man, the third-level executive should influence the selection of the second-level, and so on. Such an approach may identify the candidates most likely to operate efficiently within a particular organisational context. A potential leader cannot hope to succeed if the organisation fails to identify him in the first place and neglects to place him in a position of leadership and authority.

'Formal, mechanical selection methods often fail to identify the most suitable candidates for leadership positions', says occupational psychologist Pincus. 'It is not easy to assess a man's leadership qualities, or how he's likely to perform in a particular job, by means of formal tests, techniques, or interviews – the failure rate is very high'. But Pincus admits that psychological tests are 'useful for screening out the obviously unsuitable candidates – the very anxious person, say, or the power-loving individual'.

The individual's previous experience and performance can provide valuable clues about a candidate's suitability for a higher position of responsibility, but only if past and present situations are somewhat similar. After research covering post offices workers, meat market workers and others in America and Europe, Fiedler concluded that 'leadership experience appears to have no salutary effect on group or organisational performance'.

Safeguards against mistakes

Corporate planning can aid effective recruitment by showing what executive appointments management should be thinking about *now* – the type of qualities for particular jobs, the kind of management development that is required, the kind of search and recruitment procedures to be used. Thus one company periodically draws up a list of executives showing who will be retiring within the next ten years. A senior executive in the company says : 'In appointing people to key positions you must never be in a hurry. We may want to groom somebody for a particular job over a five-year period. If we decide to go outside the company, we may have to look for as long as two years to find the right person'.

As Texas Instruments have found, an ambitious management development programme means that few executive jobs have to be filled from the outside. And Polaroid reckons that its policy of promotion from within boosts employee morale. On average, there are three upward moves within the company before an outsider is brought in lower down the ladder.

To ensure against mistakes in appointment, why not ask the new person to agree to work on a trial basis for several weeks – perhaps during his or her holiday period – so that both sides can take a longer look at each other? Sometimes a manager performs badly because of inept placement procedures or because he is not getting on with his new colleagues and subordinates : if there are signs of severe conflict, a tactful transfer to another department can work wonders – and employee morale stays intact.

Often the frustration builds up when an executive is placed in a position that is above his head in terms of the communication and social expertise required. The brilliant research chemist may become an incompetent and frustrated R&D manager : as a manager, his job is less to do with chemistry than with leading and inspiring others to be good researchers.

The Eaton Corporation tries to safeguard against future disappointment by inviting job applicants and their spouses in small groups to informal get-togethers where they can chat informally about the company's plans, policies and work methods. Employees take the groups on tours of the plant and encourage the applicants to spend extra time looking round the departments that most interest them.

It often makes sense to appoint a person to a senior executive position because of his or her close knowledge of the industry and the market, or because of close knowledge of the region : this means that the executive is in a good position to attract new customers, suppliers, distribution channels and executives.

The succession problem

An important duty of any top-level leader is to develop a successor – to select an inside candidate then guide and groom him in the nuances of the job and of executive suite diplomacy. It is a technique followed by Ford, General Motors and many other large companies. Ideally, the method operates at lower levels of leadership too.

Massive uncertainty and restlessness throughout the organisation can result when the top executive fails to make plans for his succession. Some chief executives give the impression of being so busy fighting fires and dealing with day-to-day operations that one of their key responsibilities is neglected. Whether they use it as a way to cut costs, realign a top-heavy organisation, or build a younger management team, many companies are turning to early retirement as a way of accomplishing their goals. At IBM all executives must retire at 60, so that everybody knows, years in advance, what vacancies are going to occur. Moreover, the earlier exit of senior executives creates more mobility in the company's middle-management ranks. Consultant Bowen says: 'There is nothing more deadening to a person who has a boss five years older than he is, but who still has ten years to go in his job. Thus early retirement will continue to be a custom-tailored device for companies with a layer of surplus or impatient leadership talent.'

One problem that occurs is the top man who is about to retire but who, even when his successor has been installed in office, still insists on calling all the shots. Companies as different as Genesco and Texaco have seen this happen. It brings confusion about who is in charge and serious conflict and uncertainty about company goals. When Appley prepared to retire from the American Management Association he picked Trowbridge as his successor, but when Trowbridge took over he could never get his own plans and programmes off the ground – Appley's influence, direct and indirect, was too strong. So Trowbridge retired – and became head of the conference board.

For the able woman, there are more opportunities in business today than ever before, but discrimination still exists: it is often said that a woman needs to be much better than a man before she gets a job at the corresponding level. There are many factories with hundreds of female operatives but not a single female manager. The number of women directors in Britain and the US is still ludicrously small. There is not one woman on the CBI's policy-making Grand Council of 400 members. More firms should appoint more women to leadership positions – and not just in women-only factories.

In the experience of many companies, the kind of executive who does well in a senior leadership position is the well rounded generalist who is also a specialist in dealing with people. One study showed that 94 per cent of clergymen who become bishops are not especially good at any single pastoral skill but reasonably good at all of them.

The generalist approach ensures that the executive takes an overall view – not a specialist or departmental view – of company problems. Such an approach, together with communication ability, is more essential for success at top level than competence in a particular functional area.

One way of helping the departmental manager to gain the overview that will equip him for leadership at top level is to give him general assignments which require close liaison with senior executives in the organisation. Another form of preparation is a planned rotation through several departments before promotion to general management. Of the chief executive officers surveyed by *Fortune* in 1976, 62 per cent had gained experience by rotation : 'A "comer" who is skilfully moved through a large company's different departments may well have more breadth than a specialist in, say, finance who has served under the treasurers of three smaller companies' [1.1].

An essential skill at senior levels of management is the ability to simplify business situations – as generalists have to do. The generalist intuitively picks out the most important aspects of a complex situation while the specialist is drowning in detail.

Preparation for leadership

Plastow, managing director of Rolls Royce Motors, thinks that it is almost irrelevant what discipline a person starts with in business because, if he is aiming at top leadership, it is important to move away from it fairly young and 'get proper staff experience on a broader front'. Otherwise, he says, 'you will find it proportionately harder to grasp the many facets of running a business'.

Plastow himself joined Vauxhall as an apprentice and later became a commercial vehicle sales engineer. He joined Rolls Royce in 1958 as a salesman, then set about widening his business experience. Plastow thinks that leadership is not learnt merely from ploughing your own narrow furrow : 'I broke out and got into the general commercial side of things and I got pitched into running a division – I learnt leadership the hard way'.

When functional or department heads are promoted to general management they may take their own narrow functional or departmental perspectives with them and shrug off the larger problems of the company as incomprehensible or irrelevant. Yet as senior executives their most important function is to formulate and implement *general* policy. A way of helping these managers to gain the overall view is to give them wide-ranging general assignments, such as corporate planning activities, or projects which require close liaison with board members and the CEO.

Perhaps the best kind of long-term preparation for top leadership is the kind practised by Lord Robens when he headed the National Coal Board. This involved a planned rotation through several departments before elevation to general management. The idea is that if a man is to be put in charge of several functions he should have had direct experience of all of them.

Moving from job to job within a single large organisation yields a vast amount of experience and is a more powerful training method than any formal programme. It produces a new kind of wide-ranging, wide-thinking leader. Thus, there is a strong case for sending candidates for top leadership positions on administrative courses run by the business schools or by the Administrative Staff College at Henley at an early stage in their careers, so as to wrench them out of a specialist or departmental approach to overall company problems.

Broad perspectives

General Electric's sophisticated management development programme brings executives up through succeeding levels of responsibility while acclimatising them to a wide range of corporate methods and goals. But in many companies, executives are promoted to general management because of their success in a particular function. This has obvious advantages, but it also means that they are ignorant about problems and activities in other functional areas. It also means that they may take an undue interest in their own functional area and somewhat neglect the others. Thus the company should aim at producing properly qualified *general* managers.

Hand, a vice-president at Shell Oil, thinks that top management in the future will include both generalists and specialists. 'I don't think the two are inconsistent. It's foolish to think one can predict a man's area of speciality at the time he graduates from university – or whether he will be a specialist at all.'

Byrom, chief executive of the Koppers Company, believes that top-level managers must have broad perspectives and be aware of what other people are thinking not merely within the company but elsewhere in business and in the world generally. So he leads a bi-weekly seminar for Kopper executives where subjects such as long-range planning, energy and the effects of technology are discussed in depth.

Executives who do not get direct experience as line managers early in their careers often fail to acquire the qualities needed to manage other managers at the top end of the hierarchy. The ability to manage managers is one of the most valuable characteristics of leadership.

7

*'A great leader is not so much clever as lucid
and clear-sighted.'*

Henry Kissinger

Target-setter

A senior executive in an engineering company says: 'It is a mistake to suppose that what you do in office will significantly affect the long-term position of the organisation. The company's success depends more on general economic conditions than it does on leadership or effective planning.' And he adds: 'How many executives are remembered a few years after they've left the firm?'

But perhaps the successful leader is the executive who *does* make a permanent impact on his organisation and whose influence stretches far into the future, as opposed to the *administrator* who is immersed in current operating and administrative problems. For part of the leader's responsibility is to lead the organisation to a changing view of itself; top-level business leaders are goal-setters, concerned essentially with such basic questions as where the company is going and where it should concentrate its resources. Cordiner, a former chairman of General Electric, says: 'The hallmark of leadership is the ability to anticipate the reasonably forseeable needs of tomorrow and beyond tomorrow with at least some clarity and confidence, and to incorporate this in long-term plans'.

Successful leaders seem to have the knack of reassessing past patterns in the light of present events and identifying persistent trends, which they can then write into plans and policies. This keeps the company on-course and provides a measuring rod for gauging long-term progress. When corporate leaders set clear objectives this enables correct policy decisions to be taken in all parts of the organisation so that the company as a whole maintains a realistic balance between stability and change.

Companies with impressive sales records tend to be greatly concerned with goal-setting and strategic planning. In less successful companies this is often not the case. One survey of 211 chief executives found that typically the top-most executives of fast-growing companies show consistent concern with strategic planning, whereas the chief executives of poor-performing companies do not show this concern [3.19]. The company suffers when its leaders are incompetent planners.

Smith, Professor of Marketing at Manchester University, makes the potent point: 'You won't get marketing right unless you have a clear idea of business policy and planning. You really won't get any effectiveness from your marketing until the marketers know what they are expected to work to in the planning and business policy objectives. Business leaders have to do a lot more work in this corporate planning area.' Corporate planning involves, in the first instance, analysing the environment to determine how best to use the existing resources and capabilities of the organisation.

Keeping on-course

Clear objectives spawn consistent manufacturing and marketing policies and prevent a company being blown off-course. When Zahn, Mercedes' chairman, was asked recently if he shouldn't be thinking of buying up a company making small compact cars, he answered: 'We might as well buy a margarine firm. That would no longer be Mercedes and it has nothing to do with us or our objectives'.

In the 1930s, American Telephone and Telegraph failed during four consecutive years to earn the $9 dollar dividend paid to shareholders. The company was tempted to cancel the dividend, but its leaders were quite clear that one of their primary objectives was to maintain a top-grade investment reputation. They held to the goal because future credit, and the financial good name of the company, depended on it.

Hewlett-Packard is another company which has stuck to its guns. Decades ago, management decided to keep to three basic guidelines:
1   To avoid all long-term borrowing.
2   To steer clear of big government contracts that could cause abrupt swings in employment.
3   Never, for the sake of diversification, to enter businesses and markets that it didn't really understand.
The company has kept to these policies. Chairman Packard travels around the country a lot talking to top executives in the company and stressing these and other basic long-term objectives.

Several years ago they were tempted to long-term borrowing so that they could spend more money in developing pocket calculators. But today, with calculators beset by price-cutting, they are glad that they kept to their objectives. Cases such as these remind us of Kissinger's dictum: 'A great leader is not so much clever as lucid and clear-sighted; grandeur is not so much physical power but strength backed by moral purpose.'

A single, simple philosophy guides the huge, Paris-based Societé Bic : the group manufactures and sells only products that can be made cheaply, used for a short time and then thrown away. Instead of inno-vating, the company works on improving products and marketing them world-wide. Chief executive Bic says that the company will finance development of a product 'until we know that we can outdo the com-petition – for instance, we spent £400,000 developing a disposable razor'.

The strategy is simple but extremely effective. Today, the company's disposable pens, lighters, pantyhose, razors and many other products are sold in some 90 countries, ringing up annual sales of around £200 million. Bic makes about nine million disposable pens each day, control-ling a third of the world market.

Bic, like most other top-level leaders, regards the plotting of long-term strategy as one of his main responsibilities. Ideally, this means standing back at frequent and regular intervals and considering where the organ-isation should be heading, what it should be doing. But staying on top of day-to-day operations makes this a luxury for many executives – and perhaps accounts for the high turnover among executive leaders, the many burnt-out cases who have risen to high levels then flopped because of incompetence in the strategic planning area.

Strategic planning is important, quite simply because the strategic plan determines the organisation's total business orientation. From a clear and comprehensive plan flow specific policies concerning costs, prices, distribution and information networks, products, technology used and leadership styles required.

Idea options

According to Anshen, there are three broad strategies or 'idea options' open to companies :
1   All resources devoted to becoming a technological leader, e.g. Pola-roid.
2   Resources mobilised 'around the central idea of becoming an early imitator and adaptor' of the innovations introduced by the techno-logical leaders. An example of the 'early imitator' would be Kodak.
3   Mass production of established products, e.g. Unilever.

As Anshen points out, each strategy implies certain kinds of invest-ment in product and market research, a certain kind of organisation structure, and so on : 'out of each of these idea options can be derived a total scheme for operating a business. This total scheme will be uniquely determined by the central idea' [7.1]. And the company's top leadership is responsible for developing 'the central idea'.

Thus, the manager fails to exercise leadership if he allows himself to be concerned solely with administrative 'efficiency', or if he concentrates too much on ways and means and too little on overall objectives and direction. Yet many managers regard the ultimate objectives and targets of the organisation as 'given' quantities, and the organisation itself as a machine whose goals have somehow been set externally. In certain parts of the organisation which are characterised by narrow function and much routine – the despatch department, say, or the stores – this may well be the case. But 'if a leadership acts as if it had no creative role in the formulation of ends, when in fact the situation demands such a role, it will fail, leaving a history of uncontrolled, opportunistic adaptation behind it' [3.6].

Is planning practical?

Planning involves :
1   Selecting both long- and short-term strategies.
2   Developing specific policies for achieving these strategies.
3   Setting operating standards and specific targets to serve as the basis of control.
4   Revising earlier plans in the light of developing conditions.
For many managers, strategic planning is synonymous with high-minded but impractical intentions – so much verbiage produced to satisfy the corporate office. One manager told me : 'Nobody round here takes the strategic plan seriously. It's simply not practical.'

But the alternative to setting clear long-term strategies is response-or crisis-management – an extremely expensive way of managing corporate resources. Strategic planning is essential because it is a cement which holds together a total structure that otherwise would fall apart. That is why setting targets and moving the organisation towards them must be regarded as one of the main duties of the leader.

The purpose of any strategic or corporate plan is to help managers to manage the actual situation – to guide them in achieving higher growth rates, penetrating new markets, improving efficiency, and so on. Plans are more likely to be practical and usable if the planning group comprises senior line managers rather than numbers men recruited from the universities. When the planning group consists of line managers, this usually ensures that the plan, when it emerges, is practical. In any case, plans should generally be created by the people who will be responsible for implementing them so as to ensure commitment and a full aware-ness of implementation difficulties. Thus, it is a good idea to involve union representatives in the planning discussions from an early stage, for without union support, it may not be possible to achieve many of the key objectives – future manning levels, and so on.

The plan, when it is published, should, first, be simply expressed and presented so that it becomes a usable management tool and, secondly, embody ambitious but realisable goals for all the main functional areas such as production, sales and marketing.

Some companies publish both corporate (long-term) and business (medium-term) plans:

Corporate strategy is broad in scope, affects the entire business and stretches several years into the future. It comprises big investment decisions, such as starting operations in new territories. Generally, its success is measured by such financial indicators as return on investment and capital growth.

Business strategy is less broad in scope and deals largely with the allocation of resources for this project or that product. Capital funds allocated by the board are 'translated into the required input resources' by management [7.2].

Both kinds of strategic planning have been lacking in the cosmetics industry, according to Bergerac, Revlon's chief executive – largely because the industry over-relied on 'charismatic' leadership, or leadership-by-flair. 'Now we need to take a long, hard look at markets, product lines, packaging, distribution and merchandising, and out of them formulate long-range strategies aimed at achieving particular sales, particular profits and market-share objectives'.

Measurable objectives

In both corporate and business plans, clear, specific objectives are necessary for measuring the success of the company's operations. Provided that objectives are stated in specific and measurable terms they can be used to measure results later on. For instance, in a large steel mill, intraplant shipments of metal were often late. Accordingly, management formulated the following objectives: first, to reduce the level of late shipments from 60 to 20 per cent; secondly, to achieve this reduction by the end of the year; thirdly, to take steps to ensure that all managers and foremen were aware of the new objectives and committed to achieving them. These objectives became a spur and a guide to all involved. They focused the attention of personnel on a major problem and quickly led to a general tightening up in efficiency.

When setting objectives:

1. State them in specific and quantitative terms wherever possible. For instance, 'to increase our market share by 20 per cent' is better than 'to expand in this market'.

2   In management meetings, develop *strategies* – ways in which the objectives are to be met – and cost them as precisely as possible. Later, if necessary, revise the strategy to fit the budget. For instance, you may have to cut an advertising campaign or involve fewer people than you first planned.

3   Implement the strategy.

4   Evaluate its effectiveness by measuring results against objectives (which were stated in measurable terms). This enables you to use sales figures, salesmen's reports, enquiries, production data, and so on, to find out if your objectives have been achieved and. if they have not, to decide where you went wrong.

Thus clear and specific objectives increase efficiency and spur management to decisive and coordinated *action*.

Successful strategies

When Cross became managing director of Brent Chemicals International he felt sure that a change of approach was needed in order to boost turnover. So he made a radical reassessment of the company's objectives. Previously, the company had made chemicals then tried to sell them. Cross argued that the company should start to see itself as a marketing organisation serving diverse markets. As a result, the company began to identify specific chemical needs in different sectors, then to meet those needs through a combination of R&D, production and sub-contracting to other companies.

As soon as sales staff were big enough in any territory the teams were divisionalised so that salesmen could really get to know their customers and their precise needs. Brent's results reflect the success of the new strategy: profits have increased twenty-fold over the past five years.

Surprisingly often, success in business is based on extremely simple objectives. As Cullman, chairman of Philip Morris, says: 'We're a marketing organisation. Our success is related to our ability to market and merchandise using consistent and integrated themes aimed at the growth segments of the market.' These simple but sufficient objectives have taken the company from an also-ran place in the tobacco industry to second-largest producer in the US, behind Reynolds.

British Leyland's former chief executive, Park, also recognises the value of clear and simple objectives which can be easily understood and worked towards. 'I'm not interested in projecting the market. My objective is quite simply to produce every car possible. We can sell them all. The trick is knowing whether they are going to be left-hand or right-hand drive. If we can get our output flowing smoothly then we will be making money.'

In some companies, the strategic planning function could be strengthened by setting up a group with specific responsibility for planning activity and manning the group largely with senior line managers (to ensure *practical* plans). Operation research and numbers people could be attached to the group in a consultative or service capacity. Its responsibilities might include refining the budget procedure. According to one expert, planning is 'only a series of budgets added together in time and space' [7.3].

One Swedish company has set up a five-man planning group which reports direct to the chief executive. Each individual is responsible for one aspect of the business. In another company the managing director is responsible for internal efficiency while the chairman is responsible for initiating discussion on new plans and policies : the chairman makes sure that planning actually happens.

The planning group could be made responsible for studying the business environment – customers' preferences, competitors' activities, technological changes, and so on – so that trends and opportunities could be identified and incorporated in the plan. The group could also be given the specific responsibility for analysing data which already exists in reports, financial statements and the like, so that market fluctuations, preference trends, technological breakthroughs, and so on, can be detected and brought to the attention of the top-level leadership.

Minimum financial risks

Often, planners and policy-makers are unduly cautious and unwilling to take what, for the company, would be quite acceptable risks. Planners who are also line managers may tend to put minimum financial risks as a first priority. But if plans need to be realistic in terms of what can be achieved and the resources available, they also may need to be bold – in order to capture a new market, say, or to halt a decline. Cordiner, former chairman of General Electric, once told a consultant : 'My only instruction is to put down what you think is right. Don't you worry about whether we will like this or dislike that. And don't, above all, concern yourself with the compromises that may be needed to make your conclusions acceptable. There is not one executive in this company who does not know how to make every single conceivable compromise without any help from you. But he can't make the *right* compromise unless you first tell him what right is.'

Why not breathe more fire into the planning group by adding to it a number of outside directors? For instance, Osmark Industries makes it clear in a written statement to all outside directors that planning and strategy formation will be among their prime responsibilities. It is not easy for professional managers to free themselves from a certain amount of dependence on the chief executive officer and so to try, unconsciously perhaps, to please him instead of saying what is right. Another problem faced by insiders is time pressure. One executive explains his dilemma in these words: 'I find it very difficult to give sustained attention to strategic matters – I'm under such tremendous pressure to do my job'.

Involving middle levels in planning

Good strategy derives from close scrutiny and questioning of inputs derived from many different parts of the organisation – simply because strategy concerns the entire organisation. Thus it may be dangerous to base plans on a single set of assumptions made by any one group, such as the OR group or a committee of senior executives, not least because a single wrong assumption can wreck the entire plan or indeed the company, as demonstrated by the collapse of many firms during the oil crisis of 1973-4.

It often pays to push leadership responsibility down the line by involving middle and junior managers in planning activity. This brings a wide range of viewpoints and experience to the planning function. It also ensures common agreement throughout the company about where the organisation is heading and how it is going to achieve its objectives. Individual managers and functions get guidelines for future decisions and actions and individual policies have a greater chance of successful implementation because the entire management team has had a hand in setting them and, thus, becomes committed to carrying them out effectively.

When people from the operational level are involved in planning, top management is forced to think about practical implementation details right from the start – realistic time-schedules, a clear understanding of the resources required, and so on.

These are some of the reasons why a food products company formed a committee of middle managers and made them responsible for long-range planning. The company decided that these were the people who were thinking well ahead and who would be at the top of the hierarchy when the planned changes were eventually put into effect. In another company, forward planning starts with meetings of divisional sales managers at which they discuss prospects for the company's products and any changes that are going to be needed over the next few years.

In Japanese companies strategy is developed rather than set. Typically, policy proposals from top management are discussed by junior managers until a consensus view emerges. The developed proposal then goes up to the next level where it is discussed, developed and again sent up the line. It takes a long time for the new policy to take shape, longer still to integrate it into the overall plan. But the payoff is that implementation is swift and decisive. Because they have been involved in the policy decision, junior staff are committed to implementing vigorously and

Practical leaders and ideas

General Motors lessens the danger of a separation between long-term planning and day-to-day operations by arranging regular meetings between divisional heads – Buick, Cadillac, etc. – and the four-man executive committee. The practical men are introduced to new plans and *ideas*. This has the effect of lifting 'the eyes of the divisions from the floors of their factories up to the horizon' [7.4].

A policy committee was set up in a large construction company with two members appointed from each department. Thus the departments, through their representatives, were making company plans and policies. Conversely, policy was being relayed direct to the departments as soon as it was made.

In this company, departments *acted* – not merely reacted – with regard to corporate policy. Each department gained a clear idea of corporate goals and of how all the other departments, in their different ways, were helping to achieve them.

In another company, departments were invited to cooperate in hammering out the corporate master-plan; then, by referring to this blueprint, to devise departmental goals.

A company with an impressive record for involving personnel in planning and policy-making is Donnelly Mirrors. Chief executive Donnelly explains: 'We went to foremen and operators and discussed how they could improve our planning. We got agreement on the principle that when a foreman or an operator accepts the responsibility for producing a certain quantity of a product, he or she is to take it on personally to report any possible variance from the time schedule.'

Donnelly believes that this approach encourages leadership and constitutes the least expensive form of control of plans and schedules. 'It also enhances every job in the company, increases job satisfaction, gets fast action on troubles and improves scheduling.' And when the shop-floor is actually involved in the policy-making and policy-monitoring process, the communication problem disappears.

Updating strategy

Strategy has to be continuously reviewed and reformulated as circumstances change, as new problems crop up, as managers acquire more experience and get a sharper understanding of what is required. Thus as demand fluctuates a decision may have to be taken to push certain lines harder. As return on capital falls below a certain level a decision may have to be taken to trim the product range or to restructure a division. Thus strategy-making should be an on-going process and perhaps a number of policy items of current interest should be included on the agenda of every board meeting for re-assessment.

As Sun Oil realises, policy-making is continuous – you never finish – you have to keep going. In 1975, Sun Oil was a totally integrated oil company. Today, Sun has got rid of the word oil, and set up 14 new companies in industries as diverse as shipbuilding and repairing and the development of coal. Sun chairman Sharbaugh says : 'We shall have a couple of decades of good healthy operation in the oil business. But it won't last forever. One day oil and gas supplies simply won't be there. So we have moved to set up separate and distinct organisations, each capable of developing into free-standing companies.'

Models for accurate planning

Sharbaugh is confident that Sun's strategy is sound. For one thing, the company's information system facilitates very accurate long-term planning. Given an input of data about product prices and volumes, raw material costs and so on, the model can simulate one year's operations using only 14 sec of computer time. The result is accurate forecasts. For instance, net income can be forecast to within 1 per cent of the actual figure.

The model can develop a ten-year projection of net income and cash flow using different investment strategies and different possible conditions. This allows management to assess the impact of alternative strategies. When the diversification strategy looked like being a winner, the company adopted it.

In small companies, strategy formation is less sophisticated. The managing director of a small chemicals company makes the point : 'Brainstorming sessions are better for our purposes than elaborate systems and meticulously planned actions. Generally, a carefully planned action is an obvious one and more likely to be taken up by our big competitors.'

In very small companies, one man – the boss – is responsible for setting and achieving objectives. He personally coordinates the different functions, exacts the required contributions and maintains the performance standards. But in large companies, the complexity, size and rapidly changing environment require a multiplicity of objectives that cannot be managed by one man. Business leadership in these companies, therefore, involves knowing how these multiple objectives can be set and achieved, using appropriate management techniques and communication devices. In large companies, systems management is an important component of leadership because sound systems allow sound planning.

At Bendix, for instance, profits even during the 1974-5 recession were increasing – largely because of the financial early-warning system. The figures showed that car production was outdistancing sales, thus foreshadowing the inventory build-up soon to plague Detroit. Housing starts were not materialising as the company's mobile homes division had expected. Because of warnings like these from a reliable system, the company immediately cut back production and revised its annual financial plan downwards.

Reliable forecasts

What is the real reason behind General Motors' knack for fattening earnings in defiance of the economic principle that the bigger you are the slower you grow? Reliable forecasts. But in spite of all the sophisticated techniques now available, forecasting is still more of an art than a science.

A recent survey by the National Investor Relations Institute shows that 82 per cent of companies could not forecast within 10 per cent of actual earnings. General Electric's president, Jones, has admitted: 'Despite all the computer models that we have of the company, it is extremely difficult to be on-target'. It takes more than techniques to assess the impact of a new product or the way a market is moving: it also requires intuition and business sense – and not everybody has got it.

One company's approach to forecasting has been to set up a separate department to gather and analyse information about technological developments and market conditions and trends by means of market research and other techniques. Armed with the pertinent facts, the forecasters then work with department and divisional heads on questions of policy and strategy, the idea being that the long-range planners should not work in isolation from line management. This forces the planners to think about practical problems and implementation details from an early stage.

In a large oil company, long-range planning is the responsibility of a group which spends most of its time studying data and trying to work out how profits from oil refineries and marketing activities can be optimised over a five-year period.

Good plans depend on sound forecasts. Planning should reach beyond extrapolation of present activities and give special consideration to:

1   Long-term changes in the size and nature of the market.
2   The long-term effect of technological changes on production.
3   The long-term effects of systems innovation on production, distribution, etc.
4   The *timing* of planned changes and the rate at which they should be introduced.

Pace of change

This last consideration is important, for pace is an important factor affecting costs and profits. For instance, crash programmes – implement-ing radical changes as quickly as possible – can be extremely costly opera-tions because of the large number of personnel usually involved and the disruption of normal work schedules. Thus the more the pace is forced the more expensive the change.

A quick and easy way of cutting costs is, first, start planning the change several weeks or months earlier than you had intended and, secondly, involve fewer people than the number you first thought of :

> Fewer people working for longer will always be more productive than more people working faster. This principle is regularly cast aside as the decision-maker needs a quick answer (or thinks he does) and applies the pressure [7.5].

Another advantage of introducing change gradually, little by little, is that no single innovation implies a major disruption. Thus nobody feels threatened and worker resistance evaporates.

Another reason why particular changes need to be planned well in advance and put into effect through an extended period is so that people throughout the organisation – including the administrators with their commitment to preserving the *status quo* – have time to understand and mentally accept the changes.

A new policy cannot be implemented without triggering off effects in other departments, some of which those departments may not be geared to absorb. As Tarr points out :

> There is danger in trying to pull any one part or function of the organisation a long way ahead of the remainder since this can produce strain. The modernisation of the part . . . is likely to be eroded by the links it has with the remainder [7.5].

Thus, effective long-range policy depends on all parts of the organisation having a clear knowledge of the objectives and likely results and a chance to influence the outcome. Policies always have to be implemented in a particular organisational context. As every politician knows, decision-making is the art of the possible and the acceptable. Thus in conservative organisations, leaders should adopt a softly-softly approach to policy-making and introduce change gradually, step-by-step, so that no single piece of new legislation implies a sudden acceleration or a major change of direction.

Visionary leaders

How often is poor management performance throughout a company caused by the board neglecting to set and communicate clear, corporate business strategies? Or by managers ignoring corporate strategy and pursuing individual or departmental goals instead? Perhaps the most telling measure of a department's effectiveness is the extent to which its work contributes to overall company strategy.

Leadership includes a visionary component. The top-level leader must be more interested in what the company is going to become than in what it has been : future survival and growth depend on it. The organisation has to be constantly re-oriented, restructured, renewed. The leader's perspective should include 'not only where the company stands today but, more important, where it should be twenty years' hence. His is a future-oriented role' [7.6].

Arguably, top-level leaders and, in particular, members of the board, should be more involved in planning and strategy than in everyday operations. Indeed, most successful executives say that they take steps deliberately to restrict their involvement in operational problems and decisions. 'If I didn't limit my involvement I'd be literally snowed under – there'd be no time for planning or anything else', one executive told me. 'Anything else' includes such essential activities as studying and planning new products and markets, rates of growth, investment policy, and so on.

It is tempting for managers at all levels to immerse themselves in everyday operations. For one thing, it is easier to get good results from solving everyday problems such as a production bottleneck, a sales boost for a particular product, etc., than to keep the organisation moving towards long-range targets. Another reason is that setting new strategies can create big-scale problems throughout the organisation and trigger off much conflict, simply because strategic decisions have a lot of 'impact', i.e. affect every part of the organisation. Thus, a 'faster growth' decision taken by one division might disrupt quality control's procedures and schedules or force sales to abandon a reorganisation plan or touch off a storm of protest in other divisions which are competing for the same, slender corporate resources.

Avoiding conflict

Thus, the leader may worry about the acceptability – or at least popularity – of his decisions and wonder whether he will damage his own position, or whether it will be possible to implement the decision without stretching resources or creating resistance and resentment. The temptation is to leave things as they are – to neglect the planning area.

It is even more tempting to neglect the objective and target-setting areas when the organisation is prosperous and expanding :

> Once an organisation becomes a 'going concern', with many forces working to keep it alive, the people who run it can readily escape the task of defining its purposes. This evasion stems from the hard intellectual labour involved . . . also, there is the wish to avoid

conflicts with those in and out of the organisation who would be threatened by a sharp definition of purpose, with its attendant claims and responsibilities [3.6].

Yet clear strategy and objectives are essential for long-term success. Back in the twenties, when Sloan headed General Motors, he made it clear to all managers that profit was the ultimate corporate goal. To achieve this he created the classical concept of decentralised operations with coordinated control. The strategy was so successful that it has been at the foundation of GM's success ever since and has been adopted by big companies all over the world.

The board's leadership role

The roles played by the boards of companies vary widely. Some are mere rubber stamps, endorsing management's decisions and actions. Some chief executives deliberately try to restrict the board's powers, avoid policy discussions and limit the monthly boardroom discussions to routine business and such safe issues as training grants and levies, new safety regulations, and so on. The directors of one company were sent no information at all before board meetings on the grounds of 'confidentiality'. Any information which was handed out in the meeting had to be handed back at the end. One chief executive reports: 'The directors don't do a damn thing and they don't give me a bit of trouble'.

This kind of practice makes nonsense of the theory that the chief executive is the servant of the directors, their agent for administering the organisation. It may also threaten the future of the company because of the vacuum which is created in place of clear and consistent strategy. In a successful farm-supply company studied by Fiedler, the chief executive had great freedom of operation and saw himself as the professional working with amateurs – the directors. This manager saw the strongest director as his 'assistant on the board'.

Adequate information is an essential pre-requisite for sound strategy-formation. When Cabot, now chairman of the Federal Reserve Bank of Boston, served on the Penn Central Board his education was fast and brutal. The company was crumbling yet directors were given no clear plan, nor were they given management's true assessment of the situation.

Board meetings were given trivial capital expenditures to approve or shown sketchy financial reports which were rarely discussed in detail. Cabot pleaded with the CEO for the directors to be given an opportunity to review objectives with the management and to be told periodically how actual results were working out compared with short-term targets. What were the shortfalls? What were the reasons? Nothing happened. Penn Central collapsed.

The British Institute of Management has defined the board as 'that part of management that is concerned with determining objectives and policy and with checking overall progress towards their fulfilment'. The board should not, of course, be checking and reviewing policies and management decisions constantly. But as Donnelly, chief executive at Donnelly Mirrors, says: 'The board should be in a position to make recommendation at a formative stage in the decision-making process so that they can keep management tracking towards its long-range goals'.

The board's principal leadership functions are, first, to monitor management's performance and, secondly, to set corporate goals and strategies. But according to Garrett, chairman of the Securities and Exchange Commission in Washington:

> The typical well-orchestrated board meeting with the quick agenda, followed by some report of general interest on the operation of the business, followed by lunch, all on a tight schedule, induces an atmosphere of compliance, of non-inquiry, that may be dangerous.

How many boards concentrate on current activities and let the future look after itself?

In his discerning book, *Directors: myth and reality,* Mace argues that it is:

> *Myth* that boards exist to establish strategy and policy, to ask telling questions, to monitor management's performance.
> *Myth* that outside directors are chosen for their independent, critically inquiring minds.
> *Reality* that they are selected because they are cronies of the chief executive or because their names have prestige value.
> *Reality* that many internal directors never probe or argue in board meetings for fear of upsetting the chief executive officer.

Stronger leadership

When this is the situation, it may be worth considering the following reforms to strengthen the company's top leadership:

1   Bring strong, independent outsiders onto the board. An insider board may not be able to monitor the performance of the CEO effectively.
2   Make all directors subject to re-election every two years. If they are not demonstrating leadership qualities by initiating new policies and probing management's actions, they can be dropped.
3   Put an age limit on directors. Older men are mellower than younger men, less likely to challenge and probe. They often have

old-fashioned ideas about industrial relations and are weaker on financial matters. Lord Ryder, former chairman of the National Enterprise Board, believes that large areas of industry are stagnating because directors have not caught up with the vast changes inside and outside their businesses in recent years. He calls for the appointment of more young directors and says: 'We must find ways of delegating responsibility down the line so that our younger managers have the opportunity to develop and show their potential'.

4   Ensure that the company has a chief executive officer *and* a non-executive chairman, that the former is answerable to the latter and that the latter sees his principal duty as goal-setting and the initiation of policy.

Too many boards have a kind of club atmosphere, where challenging, probing discussions and questions would be seen almost as breaches of etiquette. This is one reason why, according to a senior Xerox executive, 'The board has become in some respects obsolete in large companies. It's partly a legal fiction.' Indeed, in many large companies the real work is done in board committees. Firestone, for instance, has 13 board committees – small, specialised groups that can delve deeply into particular problems and specific policies before making their recommendations to the main board.

Well chosen outside directors – selected on the basis of their expertise or experience – are less likely than insiders to be on crony terms with the chief executives, and not as anxious to avoid upsetting him by challenging his decisions and actions. One long-serving manager was finally rewarded with a seat on the board. In his first board meeting he listened carefully to the discussion then cleared his throat to speak. 'Jones', said the chairman severely, 'If you've anything to say – get out'.

Keith, Pillsbury Company chairman, makes the point: 'I believe the outside must always outweigh the inside. The largest value of the board is to bring in an outside point of view and to question management's decisions and judgments.'

Accelerating growth

It takes fine judgement and a strong sense of direction for a manager to accelerate growth without jeopardising existing strengths. That is why, before taking any particular decision to expand or change direction, the question should be asked: 'Will this change be in line with our long-term policies? Will it increase our strength in the markets we have carved for ourselves?' If the answer is no then the decision is surely wrong. (Alternatively, a negative answer may indicate that the company should review its long-term objectives.)

The alternative to setting *strategic* goals is merely to react to events in a *tactical* way. Yet there is evidence to suggest that many boards are failing to commit themselves to systematic goal-setting, despite all the risks that *ad-hocracy* entail :

> Those companies that could not agree as to corporate direction
> could not define responsibility for decision-making, nor were likely
> to identify changes in the trading environment [7.7].

In the absence of clear strategy, it seems, opportunities and warning
signals alike are bound to be missed. And one can never be sure that the
decisions that are taken are in the best interests of the company as a
whole. In many companies, 'strategy formation is highly diffuse and
political in nature . . . with the personal goals and departmental affilia-
tions of . . . members affecting the directions in which they wish to move
the organisation' [7.8].

Strategic vacuums

During the sixties, Westinghouse seemed to lose sight of long-term
objectives. It entered many new markets in an opportunistic spirit, even
when these moves failed to fit into any kind of overall plan. The result
was a string of loss-making ventures which helps to explain why, today,
the company's profits are shrinking and its operations contracting.

When the company's leaders fail to formulate or to communicate
clear and consistent objectives, individual managers are bound to falter,
like a man shuffling through a maze blind-folded. Other problems which
are created include :

–   low morale;
–   no sense of direction or progress;
–   the pursuit of individual rather than corporate goals;
–   different departments moving in different directions;
–   management by response rather than management by design.

In Britain, many problems in the nationalised industries stem from
uncertainty about long-term objectives. A 1976 report on the nationalised
industries pointed to a 'strategic vacuum' at British Rail, and said that
Electricity Council decisions were often dominated by short-term political
rather than long-term economic considerations [7.9]. Ministers and
senior civil servants rarely last more than two or three years in the same
job. But, as the report points out, nationalised corporations are 'large-
scale industries whose planning cycle must be a minimum of five years
and extend (in the case of Post Office telecommunications, for example)
up to thirty'.

The report suggests that a policy-making council be set up in each
corporation, with members drawn from government, the unions and the
executive board. This would draw up long-term policies and help to keep
the politicians' hands off the corporation.

Lord Ryder, former chairman of the National Enterprise Board, has called for a pact between the political parties on industrial policy to avoid U-turns and policy upheavals: 'The lack of stable industrial policy by successive governments has done untold damage to the country. Policies have been reversed even when the national interest required continuity.' He cites the winding-up of the Industrial Reorganisation Corporation as a case in point.

According to Balfour, chairman of Scottish and Newcastle Breweries, the present low level of investment in Britain is the direct outcome of uncertainties about long-term economic objectives: 'The absence of consistency in political and economic policy shatters corporate planning efforts. The least industry can hope for from governments of any colour is that they will maintain a consistency of monetary and fiscal policy. If you want to have continuity of investment you must have continuity of policy.'

Wagner, senior managing director of the Royal Dutch Shell group, has put forward proposals to safeguard oil companies against policy upheavals in overseas countries where they are operating. Nationalisation is only one such risk. He claims that an international mechanism for risk insurance is needed if the oil and gas resources of the Third World are to be developed. As he says: 'The industry is prepared to accept the commercial risks of exploration and development but the political risks are too great'. Wagner feels that the energy-importing nations should provide the guarantees through an International Resources Bank which would also provide more capital for developing countries.

Another reason for the absence of effective corporate strategies has psychological roots. Managers who are too security- or stability-conscious will usually set unambitious objectives – or even none at all (so that nobody can say they have failed). But managers who seek to *lead* the organisation must develop bold but realistic objectives, sell these to other people in the organisation, then take vigorous administrative action to ensure that these goals are achieved.

Implementation

The board is concerned with setting policies. The next level is responsible for implementing them. Thus the board must ensure that the next level knows exactly what these policies are – and that they intend to implement them. Xerox, for instance, has had a policy of employing more minorities since the sixties and the board makes sure that the policy is implemented. The company makes it clear that managers will be judged on the basis of their performance in implementing this policy, as much as for making machines and money. Some people who failed to implement the policy have lost bonuses, others have lost their jobs. As a result,

the policy has been vigorously implemented throughout the company
and nearly 20 per cent of Xerox's employees in the US are now
minorities.

Pressure is needed to ensure that managers implement company
policies – even the unpopular ones. Gerstenberg, chairman of General
Motors, told all personnel directors:

> The policy of General Motors is that everyone will be given an
> equal opportunity in employment without regard to his or her sex,
> religion or national origin, and every member of management must
> implement that policy. . . . If we have any person at management
> level in any GM facility who cannot function within this policy, or
> is not giving it full attention, then he will simply no longer be able
> to work for General Motors.

Within a division or a department, decisions may be sound in themselves,
as it were, but ultimately damaging because they cut across or fail to
support company strategy. A small instrument company sold most of
its products by direct mail. It had a policy of fast service and low prices
– achieved by cutting costs to the bone. A larger company acquired the
firm and two new policies were introduced: first, to appoint salesmen
to sell the instruments to the retail trade – 'Every firm needs personal
sales representation', an executive declared; secondly, to set up a more
sophisticated accounting system (involving considerable capital expenditure) in the instruments division.

Look at those decisions in the abstract and they seem perfectly sound
and logical. Now look at them *in context*. Both decisions cut clean across
the instrument company's strategy for survival – as later events proved,
for they led to increased costs and prices, and a slump in sales.

Perhaps the most telling measure of a division's success is the extent to
which its work helps to achieve overall company strategy. This, incidentally, raises the problem of how to assess a division's or a department's
efficiency in the absence of any clear *corporate* plans.

8

'It's difficult to lead where there's a sense of failure.'

Peter Parker, Chairman of British Rail

Motivator

Giving employees praise and recognition for a task done well seems so basic that it appears pretentious to label the act a management technique. Yet there are firms which, far from encouraging such an approach, base their whole motivation policy on pitting one man against another, or one department against another. 'But my experience has shown that that's destructive', says Donnelly, chief executive at Donnelly Mirrors. 'If you can get people focused on an achievement rather than on defeating somebody, that's real leadership because it creates a much healthier atmosphere.'

Underlying Donnelly's words is a healthy respect for Skinner's 'positive reinforcement' theory. In essence, Skinnerists motivate people to do better by using praise, recognition and a regular feedback system to tell the person how he's doing. The essential ingredient is to stress the positive. Donnelly himself firmly believes that punishing an employee for poor performance only produces negative results, such as hostility, absenteeism, or poor time-keeping.

Another company with a positive approach to the motivation problem is Michigan Bell Telephones. In one department that was plagued by high absenteeism, supervisors were told to make *positive* comments to operators about their attendance records. Within six weeks the absentee rate had dropped from 11 to 6.5 per cent. *The company is convinced that one of the principal duties of leadership is to maintain an atmosphere of approval at work so that people are not discouraged by failure.*

As many organisations have discovered, problems of motivation increase sharply after a long period of crisis or failure. British Rail chairman, Parker, points out that it is 'difficult to lead where there's a sense of failure. It's terribly demoralising that somehow or other our industry is always associated with rattling a begging bowl. Some railmen are even embarrassed about going into a pub.' But Parker has a plan for getting the railways 'out of the valley of the shadow of deficit'. He wants to negotiate a cash price for the uneconomic lines the government wants to keep open, and BR will then guarantee to fulfil this 'contract'. 'We have got to get rid of that sloppy word "subsidy" so that men who do a damn good job 365 days a year feel some pride.'

Powerful confirmation of the value to leaders of a positive approach comes from a study of school teachers which found that when they expressed confidence in their pupils' abilities and held high expectations for them, this alone was sufficient to cause an increase of 25 points in the pupils' average IQ scores.

Stressing the positive

Webster, managing director at Bulmers, believes that 'business leadership is all about motivating people' and that the secret of motivation is 'to treat everybody as a human being – stress their positive qualities. You get across to people by having trust in them and approaching them on the positive side.' Marks and Spencer chairman, Sir Marcus Sieff, fully supports this view of the leader's responsibilities :

> When management treats employees as responsible people meriting respect, most respond. This results in people working well, less absenteeism, greater staff stability, acceptance of new and more modern methods of production and operation. Under such conditions most people take pride in their work, and this often results in high productivity and good profits.

It is precisely because he respects his subordinates, says the chief executive of a highly successful medium-sized company, that he spends the equivalent of more than a month each year holding interviews with his senior executives. His purpose, he says, is to listen to their ideas, to gain their perspective on problems – and to acquaint himself with potential top leaders.

It is important to employees to feel that they are respected and trusted by their bosses. This came out strongly when a group of managers evaluated management methods at the Eaton Corporation. They summarised their criticisms in the form of a letter written as if by a factory employee to his boss :

> Sir, why must I punch a time clock? Do you think I'd lie about my starting and quitting times? Why must I have buzzers to tell me when I take a break, relieve myself, eat lunch, start working, go

home? Do you really think I can't tell the time or would otherwise rob you of valuable minutes? Why doesn't the rest room I must use provide any privacy? . . . no one has ever really asked me how quality might be better or how my equipment or methods might be improved.

Since that time, Eaton have introduced the following reforms:
1 Factory workers get the same benefits as white collar staff.
2 Time clocks and buzzers are abolished.
3 Management discuss work problems at the employee's work-place as often as possible.
4 Management roundtables are held regularly so that middle and junior managers can express their ideas and make their talents and experience available to the organisation.

In the newer plants, where these positive measures have been introduced, the absenteeism rate ranges from 0.5 to 3 per cent, compared with a 6 to 12 per cent rate at the older plants where traditional methods are still used.

Considerate leaders

According to Supreme Life's CEO, Johnson, employees are motivated by:
1 Showing trust in them; being positive; demonstrating confidence in their integrity and ability.
2 Being friendly and supportive rather than critical or punitive.
3 Treating them as individuals whose feelings and ideas matter.
4 Having high performance expectations – high enough to stretch them but not so high as to break them.

But for Johnson, 'being positive' is very different from being soft. When he became chief executive officer he decided that nobody could be transferred. 'My expectations were high. You had to succeed in your job. You were going to be given an adequate opportunity, but if you didn't succeed in that job you were going to be dismissed. Perhaps that was arrogant, but it was also positive and it turned the company round.'

One survey shows that another important characteristic of successful leaders is that they show consideration for their employees – and that outstanding military and civilian leaders have this characteristic in common [8.1]. Another researcher (Wickert, 1947) reported that a necessary attribute of combat crew leaders was showing consideration for their men. And when hospital researchers studied patients who had considerate, affectionate nurses, and patients with 'regular' nurses, they found that the number of those with post-operative complications was three times as great in the latter category as in the former.

Scholey, chief executive at British Steel, makes the point that 'you can't command loyalty without giving it, and that means knowing your man and, when it comes to the crunch, being prepared to look after him first and yourself second'.

According to a Royal Worcester director, Bullock, considerate behaviour includes:

- recognising and rewarding good work and achievement;
- treating employees as individuals;
- communicating with employees as often as possible, especially about their problems and ideas;
- being sensitive to employees' needs.

Responding to needs

The Granges steel plant in Sweden responded to women employees' needs by inviting two or more women to share one job. Granges' general manager Weichtmeister says: 'We give them the job and then it is up to them how the time is planned out. That way they can make their own arrangements about who looks after the kids.' Result: lower labour turnover, less absenteeism, happier workers.

Faced with an acute shortage of women workers, Reed International opened a day nursery at its Aylesford headquarters – and the response was immediate. This kind of venture is spreading over Europe. In Britain there are over a hundred such nurseries already including those run by the BBC, Barclays Bank and Ronson.

In America and several European countries, strong pushes for flexitime are coming from women's organisations. The freedom to start work at, say, 10 a.m., enabling a mother to drop the children off at school, may be the factor that enables her to work at all. Scores of firms, including Nestle and General Motors, are now using flexitime and finding that it leads to increased productivity and less absenteeism.

After listening to employees' suggestions for improving working conditions, the New York office of Equitable Life compressed the working week into four days. As a result, the error rate of clerical workers dropped dramatically, but without any fall-off in productivity, and employee satisfaction with the job soared.

Single status

Take away from managers and directors the aura of unearned privilege and much of the friction would be taken out of industrial relations. That is the thinking at the Computer Management group in London where all levels have identical desks, the same carpets, the same amount of space. The managing director sits in the middle of a large open-plan office and he is accessible to all – just like the open file which contains details of everyone's salary. A director points out: 'We are like an army with only officers – the computer is our only private soldier'.

Dunlop director, Flaunders, has no doubts about the wisdom of a single-status policy: 'Every sane and sensible human being sees the sense of single status, though of course the staff unions fight hard to keep their differentials.' In fact, as a 1976 British Institute of Management report, *Towards Single Status,* has pointed out, progress towards single status has been remarkably slow, and staff schemes equalising all terms and conditions of employment – pensions, redundancy provisions, sick pay, holiday entitlements – are still rare in the UK.

Yet companies which have introduced single status for manual and white collar employees are characterised, says the report, by good profit and growth records and good labour relations. As one manager reports: 'Single status is not simply about equal fringe benefits and equitable salary structures. It is about the removal of the age-old split between 'works' and 'staff', the them-us syndrome, and as such it is probably the most radical change in terms of personnel policy to be attempted by the company.'

Since 1970, 70 per cent of more than 320 companies surveyed by the BIM have reduced differentials in employment conditions and, in their own estimation, have been rewarded with improved industrial relations and the satisfaction of acting in the mainstream of management practice.

When Kinetic Dispersion first began paying shop-floor workers for days off, many phoney excuses were made. So management and the unions got together and agreed that the man's salary should be docked if management judged that an absence was unnecessary. Since then, the scheme has been working well.

Texas Instruments' non-elitist culture means that in many plants there are no special car parks for managers, one cafeteria for all – and no carpets on office floors, as these might inhibit a factory worker with dirty shoes going into the boss's office.

From losses to profits

The Swedish shipbuilding company, Kockums, has gone from losses of about £7 million in 1969 to profits approaching £50 million in 1978. Order books are full and employee turnover is down from 50 to 18 per cent. An internal report attributes the changes to the top leadership's 'changed perception of the workforce'. The change has led the company to develop a new organisational structure and to introduce monthly pay for all, group bonuses, self-managing groups and a consultative set-up that involves 700 of the 6,000 employees.

At Western Electric, Mayo and his team of researchers found that employees increased their output as a result of the increased interest taken in them by their bosses. By contrast, there is often a drop in morale and productivity when bosses treat employees as if they were mere 'hands'.

This kind of behaviour includes:

-   demanding more than can be done;
-   failing to recognise or reward good work;
-   criticising employees in front of others;
-   attacking employees for making mistakes;
-   refusing to accept suggestions made by the workforce;
-   taking decisions about matters that concern them without prior consultation.

Considerate behaviour includes compensating workers for necessarily poor conditions. Production at United Biscuits' twelve UK factories is highly mechanised and automated and management finds it impossible to make the job less boring so, by way of compensation, it provides a factory radio system with music, talk and news every half-hour. There are many individual loudspeakers so that individuals or groups can control the volume or switch off if they wish. The employees greatly appreciate the service. The case also shows that a concern for employee welfare need not involve massive spending.

Choosing a pay package

An imaginative way of showing concern for individuals is to ask the employee himself to select the components of his pay packet. Each person has different needs and circumstances. Thus some people would take more basic pay, others more holidays, others better pensions. The result would be happier, better-motivated employees – at no extra cost to the company.

Leaders showing concern for their followers brings warmth into the organisation. A Matsushita executive candidly admits: 'We want our employees to spend every day in a peaceful state of mind so that they can concentrate on work'. Thus one of the company's unwritten rules is that the employee is virtually guaranteed a lifetime's employment and welfare. It also provides generous home loans, excellent hospital facilities for all employees and a full range of educational and cultural facilities, such as free language lessons and ikebana (flower-arranging) for female employees.

For the Japanese company Matsushita, people are its most valuable asset. In 1975, profits were the lowest for seven years and 8,000 employees were put on half-days. But they were all paid full wages because the company was prepared to sacrifice profit for the sake of employee welfare and morale. And because nobody was laid off, the workforce were all tuned up ready for a flying start when the recession ended.

Marks and Spencer's method of inducing a peaceful state of mind is to provide elaborate health coverage, worker representatives on management committees, and 750 personnel specialists to look after the individual needs of all employees. Chairman Sir Marcus Sieff makes the point: There's a saying in the company that a senior executive is

treated almost as well as a shop assistant or a warehouseman'. Sir 1
Marcus believes that the top leadership in any large company is honour-bound to provide a strong personnel function and a streamlined grievance procedure so that employees can get a direct and sympathetic hearing on all issues.

At Citroen plants, there is one manager solely concerned with social welfare to every 150 personnel. A senior executive explains: 'He is occupied not with settling complaints but with their prevention. We don't wait for grievances from the workers – we try to find them in advance. It is the job of personnel staff to see that every member of the staff is personally known and has regular contact with somebody who is concerned with his or her well-being and progress.'

The lay-off dilemma

When a company decides to trim its work force as the quickest way to pare costs, the fear of further cuts may damage survivors' morale and efficiency. If heavy lay-offs seriously impair a company's operating strength, each employee may fear not merely for his own job but also for the company's survival. At this point, notes McKinsey consultant Geissler, employees start wondering just how competent the leadership is.

Geissler recalls a textile machinery maker that curtailed its operations by 50 per cent because of its sagging profits. It slashed its budget so deeply that it jeopardised its ability to respond to an upturn in demand. The company's plans for product and market development had to be stretched out three or four more years and morale problems intensified. At one stage, the company's existence seemed to be at stake.

How then should the redundant employee or poor performer be treated? In the words of a personnel director: 'Firing people – even the poor performers – should be the absolute last resort. We can't fight inflation by firing those least able to help themselves.'

For years, Cincinnati Milacrom, America's biggest machine tool maker, has set aside a special reserve from its profits to help keep the workforce intact during economic downturns. The company reckons that it has a big investment in its employees and that laying off is simply a loss of investment capital.

Donnelly Mirrors' approach to the problem is to try to time purchases of labour-saving equipment to coincide with upswings in their employment. They even guarantee workers against redundancy: anybody who loses his job through rationalisation or technology is kept for at least six months at his old pay – though he may be asked to do a different kind of work. The company has now added a guarantee of annual income: 'That increased our people's sense of security', says chief executive Donnelly. 'We get a return to the company in human trust.'

When lay-off is inevitable, the redundant employee's problems can be reduced by giving generous severance pay; by giving the man as much notice as possible so that he has plenty of time to look for a new job while still employed; and by taking positive steps to help him find a new job. When the Bankers' Trust Company was forced to lay-off 400 workers to cut costs it offered all those made redundant the services, free of charge, of an employment consultant. All those who sought his help were successfully placed in other companies.

A senior executive who spent some time in Japan reports: 'Looking after employees is a top priority in Japan. There is none of the kind of thinking natural in Europe and America that the shareholders' rights come first. If jobs have to be cut in a particular department nobody is fired. He just moves to another department.'

Wider distribution of leadership

There are still a surprising number of organisations, including the armed services, which seem to rely on an unimaginative application of simple reward and punishment as a primary means of motivating employees. But in today's climate, subtler methods can be highly effective.

For instance, when glass breakage in a General Motors plant rose to 46 per cent of glass handled, management instinctively fell back on traditional methods in their efforts to cut the loss – tighter controls, cash bonuses, and so on. But it didn't work. Frustrated supervisors walked out in despair. Finally the problem was turned over to the employees themselves, and they promptly began to identify the causes of the breakages. For example, a car's window might break because the car's body was improperly aligned: so the window fitters and body workers would get together and work out a solution.

As a result of handing the problem to the employees themselves, glass breakage in the plant has almost ceased. 'We rely less on managers to solve specific job-related problems', says Warren, a senior GM executive. 'Now the employees participate in problem-solving where they have the best information. And they communicate more among themselves at work.'

As this case illustrates, making a wider distribution of the responsibilities of leadership can be a winning strategy in modern industry. 'Allow the employee to earn his high wages by contributing more to the company', says one personnel manager. He doesn't mean that more time or speed should be squeezed out of workers. He means that leaders should encourage employees to use more of their own judgement and initiative and to contribute more ideas.

But too many leaders still waste their human resources, or may not even know they exist. When Taylor, the founder of 'scientific management', was working in a steel mill, a worker tried to explain his ideas for streamlining a particular machine operation. Taylor cut him short: 'You're not paid to think. Let other people do the thinking.'

Motivation is closely linked with communication. If success is to be continuous, the employee must fully understand his job with relation to group activity. The problem of every leader is to create this kind of understanding, for the wider the perspective that employees have of their work, the better their performance tends to be. An assembly worker may not worry about quality control or output figures – until he learns that he is assembling a vital component for an important order.

An upward flow of communication is just as important a contributor to efficiency. Sun Company chairman, Sharbaugh, says: 'No job in any company is better undersood by anyone than the person who does it – whether floor sweeper, secretary, mechanic, or president – and we must listen carefully to any ideas they've got'. Sharbaugh reckons that telling employees how to do their jobs is usually self-defeating: 'The key to achieving really productive growth in the future lies in more fully and more effectively developing and utilising the creativity and capabilities of people'.

'In the past', he adds, 'we've built jobs in the form of little boxes. The lines of those little boxes signal to the people inside that the scope of their work and responsibility is rather rigidly limited and that involvement beyond those limits is neither encouraged nor welcomed nor rewarded. In doing this we have effectively blocked off real involvement in work.'

Sharbaugh claims that an important part of the leader's job is to erase the lines around those little boxes 'and to develop a new way of thinking about people at work'.

Idea-tapping

An instance of this 'new way of thinking' occurred when the unions in an engineering company demanded a big pay rise. Management pointed out that this would cost the company an extra £130,000 a year – a lot of money when you haven't got it. But management said yes – provided the workers themselves worked out ways of saving that amount. So the employees got together in lunch and tea breaks and drew up a list of possible economies and improvements. They submitted their ideas and subsequently most of them were successfully implemented. Employees got their pay rise and the company saved £300,000.

When Texas Instruments started to lose money on a radar contract management turned the problem over to the ten female assemblers. Time required and costs involved had been under-estimated, so the women were asked to find ways of streamlining operations. They came up with 40 suggestions for more efficient assembly. When implemented, these cut manufacturing time by half.

Groups that participate in setting goals for themselves often make higher demands for themselves than management considers practical.

When this happened in one factory, a furnace-cleaning job was cut from four to two days, service calls were reduced from 1 in 14 to 1 in 21 and repairs per man-day rose by 50 per cent when the employees themselves planned the service. An industrial psychologist has said that groups of workers having instructions carefully explained to them don't significantly increase their output; but those who have both an explanation and a chance to decide how to act on the instructions often increase their output considerably.

Job enrichment

Motives differ. People are complex and different from one another. One man wants responsibility, another security, a third money, because that represents achievement and success. One of the skills of leadership is to respond to employees as individuals so that it is possible to identify each man's driving force and then go on to motivate him effectively.

Some want more independence and freedom. Others need the security of a system that guides their activities. Thus the top leader should agree with each of his immediate subordinates on certain areas – wide or narrow depending on the subordinate's ability and temperament – within which he is free to operate and take action without reference to his boss.

Most shop-floor workers respond well to the opportunity for more group involvement with other workers, for the social aspects of work are what gives the job its meaning. That is why Volvo, like many other companies, has redesigned work in several plants so that each man becomes a member of a small team assembling a complete part of an engine or chassis. Communication between workers is improved, and each worker can use a wider range of skills.

'Boiling with frustration'

Job-enrichment schemes overcome the mind-numbing restrictions of many shop-floor jobs. The need to find new and effective ways of motivating assembly workers and others with boring jobs was underlined by an American survey of 2,460 workers which found that only 13 per cent of unskilled workers were very satisfied with their jobs compared with 38 per cent of managers and 42 per cent of professional and technical people. Studies by Inkson, Porter and Lawler show that those at the top see their jobs as interesting and challenging but that those at the bottom often feel bored, hemmed-in and frustrated and that very little of them is involved in the work. Four-Fifths of the workers surveyed in Kornhauser's study in the US car industry said they were boiling with frustration inside. According to Blauner, the industrial disease of alienation has four main symptoms: boredom, a sense of isolation, a feeling that work is meaningless and a sense of being powerless to alter things [8.2]. *159*

In fighting against boredom and alienation, the leader should remember that people value intrinsically rewarding jobs and hate repetitive fragmented tasks. When a job has an endless rhythm, the worker feels that it has neither beginning or end – or any point. That is why laundry workers work better in small teams with their names attached to newly laundered shirts. When Corning Glass made each employee in one plant responsible for assembling a whole meter instead of one component, employee satisfaction and productivity soared.

Cash incentives

Industrial strife usually appears to be all about money, says ICI chairman Wright, 'but it is invariably the way workers express frustration'. Wright points out that workers become unhappy at work for many reasons – boring jobs, lack of recognition, and so on – but that they express their discontent and frustration in standard, ritualised ways, such as pay disputes. Support for this idea comes from a University of Michigan survey of 1,500 employees, which found that pay came only fifth as a 'satisfier' after:

1   More authority.
2   Better information.
3   Better tools and equipment.
4   More interesting work.

Herzberg found that the people he studied – engineers and accountants – were motivated by the work itself rather than by the tangible rewards from it. They were most satisfied by success and achievement in performing their work and by the opportunity to grow professionally. Money was only a 'hygiene' factor – a preventer of dissatisfaction. This seems to be the case with blue-collar workers too. High wages in the British steel and car industries fail to prevent very high absenteeism rates. In many coal mines the best paid workers have the worst absentee records. General Motors' wages are above average for the industry. But at one plant absenteeism was so bad on Mondays and Fridays that an extra man had to be hired for every ten workers as a standby to keep the line moving when workers were away.

Lupton has argued that payment by results works well only when the circumstances are right:

1   When the work is repetitive and easily measurable.
2   When the job is not subject to frequent changes because of technological developments.
3   When there is an established tradition of incentive payments in the company.
4   When the time study department is efficient.

Generally, group incentives work best when workers are organised in small cohesive work groups, as in the coal mines. A production director reports that in his experience group schemes are less effective than individual incentives in large groups, 'but a group scheme does stop workers quarreling about who should have the easiest timed jobs'.

Doubts were cast on the lasting value of incentive schemes by a 1976 British Institute of Management survey which found that nearly all incentive payment schemes 'soon become an accepted element of pay', thus dissipating the aim of providing motivation. Of 245 companies surveyed, 185 were operating incentive schemes. 42 per cent of the schemes were judged very successful, 53 per cent partially successful and only 5 per cent not successful. The survey concluded that payments-by-results schemes were declining, while profit-sharing and share-ownership schemes were increasing slowly.

Incentive scheme checklist

Before introducing an incentive scheme, top leadership needs to consider if the organisation is capable of coping with the changes which might be brought about :

1   Are there enough experienced and qualified staff to introduce the scheme, review it and effect modifications when required?
2   Is the scheme simple enough for all employees to understand how their pay will be calculated?
3   Will wages staff be able to cope with bonus calculations, etc., without additional help?
4   Has the principle of using work measurement been agreed with the trade unions?
5   Are other parts of the organisation – sales, distribution, production – able to cope with the increased flow of materials and output that may result?
6   Do you intend to introduce the scheme at all levels? If so, what method of measurement will be used for white collar and managerial personnel?

There is considerable evidence to suggest that senior managers are, in fact, more dissatisfied with pay than any other sector – irrespective of how much they get [8.3]. Haggas, managing director of a Keighley firm of worsted spinners, says : 'Government simply doesn't understand about incentives. We only built factories for personal gain and as long as they mess around with taxation, car expenses and things like that our attitude is stuff 'em, I'll have another day's shooting or racing.'

Shared leadership

Often, the solution to a complex problem turns out to require a wider distribution of authority and decision-making than first planned. The sharing of leadership responsibility may indeed be the only practical way of coordinating the many different skills required for large-scale projects and plans. This is the thinking at J. C. Penney where groups of managers were formed, given access to company files and records, and presented with a simple brief : assess the company's future. Gradually the groups began to marshall evidence, collate and compare results – and four months later Penney's new long-term plan dropped out of the participation machine.

J. C. Penney, clearly, have found an effective way of motivating their managerial staff. The difficulty of doing that has been underlined by a report from the American Management Association which points to 'increasing conditions of alienation' among executives, largely because of the 'highly bureaucratic and authoritarian structure' of many modern companies. Alarmingly, three-quarters of the managers polled thought that the situation was worsening.

Modern office machinery and O&M thinking have made many office jobs as routine and boring as life on the assembly line. The arrival of the computer has brought changes in the office comparable in impact to what happened in industry early in the century when the assembly line started – hence the high labour turnover and absenteeism rates in most offices.

One problem is that the work done by many managers and white-collar workers doesn't show. Managers don't make anything. There is nothing they can pick up at the end of the day, look at and admire. All too often there is only a feeling of 'So what !' The leader must find ways of ploughing through this kind of motivational barrier because output and the health of the organisation depend on it.

According to one medical expert, the pressures and frustrations of office life are much greater than we like to pretend and can damage mental health. 'Chronic anxiety about one's future or one's ability to beat inflation can lead to intense politicking and heightened competition in the office.'

Motivating managers

Top leaders must motivate middle management and middle management must motivate the workforce. If the top echelon fails to motivate their immediate subordinates, productivity and morale throughout the organisation must suffer.

The methods used to motivate personnel differ according to level. With middle managers, for instance, opportunity for more responsibility is an important part of the challenge. Professional and managerial personnel respond enthusiastically to increased challenge and responsibility, as Herzberg has shown. People at this level want to be *involved* – in discussions, plans, situations.

In *New Patterns of Management*, Likert points out that the more educated the employee the higher his expectations regarding authority and responsibility. Thus sharing leadership responsibility is a shrewd move because it stimulates individual commitment and effort. An example of sharing responsibility might be to set a challenging assignment or to involve a middle or junior manager in a top-level decision. A managing director told me : 'I've noticed time and time again that when people think a policy is partly their's they have a tremendous interest in carrying it out effectively'.

To boost efficiency in your own department or organisation, why not reach down through two or three layers, pick out promising young managers, and load them with challenging assignments or responsibilities?

That a severe motivational problem exists among executives was shown by a survey of managers carried out by the Chemical Industries Association. This found more job swapping than in the past; more emigration; and a reluctance among foreign-serving staff to return to the UK.

The most difficult jobs to supervise are those that have little routine and so are difficult to monitor and check, such as some sales or research jobs, many managerial and technical jobs, and so on. In *Contrasts in Management,* Rosemary Stewart points out that jobs such as these are not boss-dependent, and that such employees are more likely to respond to the boss's lead if his style is democratic and his authority is based on superior knowledge and experience. The manager of managers needs a much subtler leadership style than, say, the manager of operatives or labourers.

Shared goal-setting

McGregor has pointed out : 'In the recognition of the capacity of human beings to exercise self-control lies the one fruitful opportunity for industrial management to realise the full potential represented by professional resources'. Shared goal-setting is one way of realising the potential. The method improves the performance of management personnel by involving them in decisions about the goals they should be aiming at and the work methods they should be using. A company which has gained a lot of experience of shared goal-setting is Monsanto Chemicals where, for instance, a subordinate manager might discuss with his boss the improved results he wishes to attain and the specific methods he plans to use. After a time, the manager and his boss discuss the manager's performance in detail and corrective action is taken if necessary. The boss keeps on prodding and probing and showing an interest in the manager's progress so that the manager is strongly motivated to keep on trying.

During the initial interview, the trick is to set tough but attainable goals which are as specific and measurable as possible so that progress can be checked and corrective action taken if necessary. The boss makes it quite clear that these goals *must* be achieved. Such an approach, according to Monsanto, pushes the man's – and the company's – development as far and as fast as it will go.

After one such interview between an R&D man and his boss in an engineering company, the following goals were agreed :

1   To present more positive proposals to the R&D committee every month.
2   To develop more new products.
3   To liaise more closely with production and sales.
4   To cut costs on the present development programme by taking a number of agreed steps.

This kind of participative technique gets more out of managerial staff by tapping their talents and experience and winning their total commitment. This in turn touches off production leaps and zippier growth.

Leaning on subordinates

The motivational challenge facing the leader is to channel the in-built aggressions and drives of his subordinates into constructive outlets, for instance, towards achieving ambitious goals. There is evidence that when an organisation demands high performance standards from management trainees in the first year and makes it quite clear that these standards *must* be achieved, the trainees concentrate their efforts and develop more positive attitudes to work that leads to high performance in the future.

Asking for high standards and productivity from employees can be a risky business because of possible resentment and resistance. It is much safer to settle for mediocre performance and to rely on incentive schemes and other impersonal devices for increasing output. But some people *have* to be leaned on in the interests of better productivity. It is the only way to motivate them. National Cash Register president Anderson is well practised in the art of leaning : 'When I became president I looked at each guy through a magnifying glass. Was he a leader? What mistakes had he made? Could he have helped them? I judged each one individually.' Subsequently seven vice-presidents were demoted or had their organisations eliminated. Five senior executives, after receiving the treatment, took early retirement, seven others found themselves new jobs. But Anderson's tactics revived the company. Managers began to set themselves more ambitious targets and productivity and profits climbed [8.4].

Budget or progress meetings are an effective way of putting pressure on specialists or managers to improve their performance. One manager reports : 'I have a monthly budget meeting . . . why aren't sales targets being met? . . . why are expenses over their budgets? I don't worry about figures that are on target' [1.6].

Taking a tough line with management staff right from the start can help a manager to establish himself in a new job. An executive who was appointed managing director of an office equipment company faced resentment and resistance from executives who had been passed over for the job. He dealt with the situation by inviting these executives to have a frank eyeball-to-eyeball talk. During the encounter, he made it quite clear that they had two choices : cooperate or leave. They cooperated.

Stopping the alienation

The social and psychological concepts that shored-up traditional management-employee relations are being eroded. Traditional methods of leadership are no longer as reliable as they used to be. One manager reports : 'I'm saying and doing the same things as I did in the sixties. Then I was applauded as progressive. Now I'm attacked as a stubborn defender of the *status quo*'.

Donnelly, chief executive of Donnelly Mirrors, makes the point : 'More and more companies are finding that to continue to operate they have to have better contact with all their people. You have to stop the alienation.'

He adds the potent point : 'We've got to make it possible for more and more people to share in the enjoyment of success, in the psychic increment of work'. Referring to job enrichment and participation schemes he says : 'People can get satisfaction from a group effort as well as from individual effort. This is a good thing because in an industrial organisation it's group effort that counts.' 'You can't expect your crew to follow orders blindly', says British Steel's chief executive, Scholey. 'You've got to convince every man on the team of the whys and wherefores. That's the way to a committed team, and winning that commitment is the art of leadership.'

In Britain, the swing to more democratic styles of leadership was reflected in the Salmon Report on nursing staff structure. This recommended a change in hospitals from an authoritarian approach where one person, the Matron, had all the authority, to a more democratic structure of delegated responsibility, with authority being shared among nursing staff at many levels. It recommended a scheme of systematic education to prepare nurses and sisters for exercising greater responsibility. Most of the report's recommendations have now been implemented.

Traditional leadership inadequate?

In hospitals and many other organisations, traditional leadership methods are no longer adequate – largely because of the rapid changes in markets, technology and social attitudes during the past two decades. When General Electric adopted a decentralised, more democratic management structure, its president at the time, Cordiner, explained : 'Unless we can put the responsibility and authority for decision-making closer in each case to the scene of the problem, where complete understanding and prompt action are possible, the company will not be able to compete with

The democratic leader adopts a Theory Y approach and gets results
by decentralising authority and decision-making. As Cordiner said, GE
first moved into decentralisation to try to become as nimble as smaller
competitors. It decided it had to let men close to the market – the
managers on the periphery – make as many day-to-day business decisions as possible. In the words of a company manual, each GE department was tailored as a business 'a single manager can get his arms
around'.

An essential feature of the scheme was that the general manager of the
department took over many of the responsibilities and powers formerly
wielded by the mandarins at headquarters. Thus, he was empowered to
hire and fire, set prices, decide on products he wished to push, and so on.
If he was successful, his reward was substantial bonuses to be shared
with his staff. As a result of decentralisation, says Smiddy, a vice-president at the time, GE had 'in all components more people with better
understanding' of how to run a business. 'While many GE managers
have made mistakes along the way, which more centralised controls
might have prevented, they also have made countless and profitable
innovations which central executives never would have conceived.'

Curbing the power of top-level leaders

Decentralised structure and democratic management methods curb the
naked power of top-level leaders by making even the most powerful
individuals answerable, to some extent, to other managers. They prevent
too much power concentrating in any one pair of hands, or in any one
part or level of the organisation. Instead, many managers share leadership responsibility and have a direct interest in the major areas of
corporate activity.

Admittedly, a dictatorship can make quick decisions, but much time
and energy may have to be spent later explaining and winning support
for those decisions, or in persuading people to implement them smoothly.
A decision by an individual strong-man to transfer somebody or to carve
up a department can easily trigger off an emotional storm from which
the manager himself may eventually emerge dishevelled, distraught and
eating his words. But if the same manager can get the same decision
made jointly by his colleagues, there is much less risk of a backlash. For
one thing, it is just not practicable to make a *dozen* heads roll.

The democratic leader consults widely and boosts efficiency by stretching his staff and thrusting on them more and more responsibility and
challenge. He involves his subordinates as closely as possible in the activities and decisions of his department.

Thorsrud, former director of the Work Research Institute in Oslo, has
an answer for all those people who doubt the ability of employees to

share in decision-making. Thorsrud served in the resistance during the war and 'saw in those circumstances how very ordinary people can become leaders and how they can solve apparently complex problems'. This democratic approach has been confirmed in his work – he has been involved with autonomous work-groups, job rotation, job enrichment, creativity teams, and so on.

Democratic ideals

At Tandberg in Norway, democratic ideals have been put into practice. The company is actually owned by employees and all corporate earnings are re-invested. All promotions in the company are made from within, with *employees* selecting their leaders. Once appointed, executives are sent on group dynamics courses to make them more sensitive to the needs and problems of their subordinates.

Support for the validity of this approach comes from the research of Melzer, Pelz and others who have found that freedom to set one's own work methods and work pace is connected with good performance. Tannenbaum and Kahn (1958) found that organisations with greater diffusion of control and influence and wider participation in decisions consistently tend to show better results. In *New Patterns of Management,* Likert produces evidence to show that a manager who uses a participative style is more likely to have a more satisfied group of employees who also produce more than groups with more authoritarian leaders.

As one department head explains : 'The greater the participation, the greater the commitment. This helps you to be a leader because the word gets round that you have a totally involved team.' This manager believes that decision-sharing results in a growth of confidence and competence among employees – which in turn triggers off higher output. T.R. and M. Batten have published case studies showing that people are more likely to act on what they have freely decided to do than on what they have been told to do.

Sometimes, temperamentally submissive people try to push the leader into an autocratic role so that, like children, they can enjoy the security of a dependent relationship. (The insecure man feels happier in the safe role of follower.) When this happens, the leader may fall into the trap and start to provide all the ideas, all the initiative, and make all the decisions. But, people who feel that they are the pawns of a dominating leader 'tend to be passive and useless to the leader who gets his satisfaction from dominating them. Slaves are the most inefficient form of labour ever devised by man' [3.14].

In the interests of productivity, the leader should refuse to accept total responsibility – for instance, by reflecting back all requests for ideas and decisions : 'Do you think we should discuss this problem with the other departments, or simply inform headquarters?'. 'That's a good question – what do you think?'

Another way of overcoming passivity and involving staff in the running of the department is to give each subordinate a particular responsibility, such as dealing with all customers' complaints or liaising with another department, so that each man is forced to play a positive and active role. Thomas (1957) found that by creating a division of labour in which members perform complementary roles, a co-operative relationship is established between them. This encourages maximum participation by each man and maximum communication between individual members of the unit.

Martial law

There is mounting evidence to show that throughout industry there is a swing to more democratic and participative forms of management. 'To the extent that you have to rely on the authority of your position you're a questionable leader', says Donnelly Mirrors' chief executive, Donnelly.

Autocratic leadership styles can produce low levels of accomplishment combined with high levels of frustration among employees. For one thing, any dictator, even the brightest, must be wrong on occasions. When the boss is too dominant he may take wrong turns in face of slashing opposition arguments and evidence; or force subordinates to suppress non-conformist views that the organisation badly needs. As Fiedler says: 'The slave-driving leader is essentially one who cannot get his men to perform in any other way' [5.6].

Consider the case of Polaroid president Land, who took a decision against the advice of most of his colleagues. This was to spend big money developing the SX-70 instant colour camera. A pushing, impatient man, Land insisted on speedy development and as a result problems cropped up which dented the company's profit graph.

Land, though, is unrepentant: 'I represent a framework of ideas. The men who have come with us know this framework and have chosen to live with it.'

A marketing director complains: 'They listen to me too hard. I'll be just speculating that a red can might increase shelf visibility when suddenly the cans *are* red.' Nobody dared to tell this martinet that it was his special brand of iron-heel leadership that was transforming speculation into martial law.

Hard-line hazards

Some leaders show their flair for getting results from subtle, democratic methods. Others falter and fall back on traditional hard-line methods, which carry with them the following dangers:

1 *Potential disruption* Because he works crudely by fear and threat – Theory X without the carrot – the hard-driver triggers off resistance and resentment in his staff and is thus a potential source of disruption. When the group rejects his leadership 'his basic problem is to keep himself from getting knifed', as Fiedler puts it, or from having his plans and projects sabotaged. Witness the case of the managing director who sent a curt memo to all employees threatening the withdrawal of all privileges and possible suspension from duty unless their timekeeping improved forthwith. When the factory went on strike he put it down to the agitation of 'troublemakers'.

2 *Morale may droop* The autocrat dominates his staff and concentrates the decision-making in his own hands. Not surprisingly, morale may droop because the most telling measure of a man's status in the company is his right to have a say in the decision-making. Selvin (1960) found that autocratic leadership in units in the US Army led to high rates of absence without leave, drunkenness, fighting, eating between meals and seeing the chaplain.

3 *Employees' initiative untapped* Autocratic leadership can produce regressive behaviour in employees. For instance, some respond to an over-strong boss by behaving like children and remaining dependent, waiting for the boss to define their role and tell them what to do. Others react like adolescents and become counter-dependent, sniping at the boss at every opportunity. Other people cut themselves off from group involvement and pursue individual rather than organisational goals and in this way try to preserve their self-respect and individuality.

4 *Consant supervision needed* When Lippitt studied leadership styles in boys' clubs he found that groups which were democratically led worked just as hard when the leader was out of the room. The boys who had autocratic leaders stopped working as soon as the boss left the room. In companies, autocratic management methods may stimulate employees to behave like these boys and to get their own back on a hard-line leader by stopping work as soon as his back is turned.

When pressure gets results

But many companies have flourished under dictators. Kircher, former chief executive at Singer, once described his leadership style in one word: fear. Yet over a 17-year period the company grew impressively under his autocratic thumb. Kircher, clearly, was a highly efficient executive, for if the autocrat is inefficient his group is bound to be inefficient and get poor results. For instance, if he drives them hard and efficiently towards the wrong objectives they inevitably fail.

Another efficient dictator is Abboud, chairman of First Chicago Corporation, who has a leadership style that can only be described as no-nonsense tyranny. 'There can only be one ruler here', he told his executives, 'and you're looking at him'. His rule is so harsh that during an 18-month period there was a 12 per cent brain-drain of executive talent – 118 executives left the company, complaining about being driven out by Abboud's harsh, militaristic style. The company, however, is flourishing.

Hard-line leadership works well when times are hard and tough measures have to be taken. After a period of declining profits at the National Cash Register Company, president Anderson decided to shake some lethargy out of the company. He told his employees : 'Complacency and apathy – these are NCR's greatest sins. Until we see a return to profitability, something akin to martial law will be in effect'. After listening to this, one vice-president turned to his colleagues and said, 'Gentleman, we have a leader'.

Anderson was as good as his word. Seven vice-presidents were demoted or had their organisations eliminated. Five senior executives took early retirement. Seven others found new jobs. Anderson took to dressing down staff for such heinous crimes as smoking in meetings or carrying coffee in elevators. In fact, Anderson applied all the autocratic pressures that were needed to pull the company out of its nose-dive [8.4].

A hard-driving style

Autocratic leadership means that painful and unpopular – but also necessary – measures can be taken without argument. For instance, Anderson leaned heavily on poor performers, regarding everyone as guilty until proved innocent : 'When I became president I looked at each guy through a magnifying glass. Was he a leader? What mistakes had he made? Could he have helped them? I judged each one individually.' Executives who failed the inspection were simply squeezed out of the company or demoted. Anderson's tactics worked. Managers began to set themselves higher targets and productivity and profits climbed.

Bry, a vice-president with the Otis Elevator company, is another leader who believes that you have to be cruel to be kind : 'When the Peter Principle takes hold you have to tell them the jig is up. We're not running the Salvation Army here. It's terrible for a leader not to face up to a subordinate's lack of performance. It's pretty tough stuff, but you have to tell it like it is.'

A leader can get good results from a hard-driving style when the task is highly structured. (In the operating theatre people *have* to fit into the system and results there, anyway, don't depend on how people *feel*.) But, even then, the leader needs to be supported by a lot of organisation authority, as in the armed services, so that he can be sure of the compliance of his staff, even if he does not get on well with them. Thus two essential attributes of an autocratic manager are, first, that he has sufficient authority and power, e.g. to give or withhold favours such as bonuses, promotions and, secondly, that he is adept at structuring and controlling the work.

Autocratic leadership is needed in organisations where crises frequently occur and where, by definition, decisions have to be taken quickly and promptly by one man – as with airline crews, fire brigades, and so on. Strong control and structure ensure that the various aspects are dealt with systematically and in the time available.

When times are lean, get tough and mean

Arguably, a 'tough' leader is needed to shake some morale and energy back into a group after a long period of stress or failure. An officer in the Marines reports how he successfully trained a platoon torn by racial and other forms of conflict, by treating them so harshly that they hated him more than they did each other.

A few years ago, Lucky Breweries were deep in money trouble when tycoon Kalmanovitz moved in. Two weeks later, Lucky was minus two-thirds of its sales staff and personnel staff, and its president. The telephone system was replaced with one costing half as much to rent. Packaging was made plainer and cheaper. Managers were told to cut costs or go. There was no argument. All this just happened. Result : the company saved half a million dollars in the next years; operations became lean and efficient; morale soared. At Kaiser Resources Limited, a coal-mining operation in the Canadian Rockies, chief executive Kaiser keeps morale high by driving his men almost as relentlessly as he drives himself. He makes a point of under-staffing, which ensures that all his managers are grossly overworked. Kaiser simply says : 'People are happier when they're over-utilised'.

Leading a new company

It often makes sense to appoint an autocratic type to lead a new company or unit. Roles are uncertain. Staff are not sure what they should be doing or even how they should be talking to each other until somebody tells them. A 'strong' leader imposes structure and overcomes initial uncertainty. Thus, in the short term, the group is helped to overcome the communication and organisation problems that preoccupy its members and can start working together, efficiently and smoothly, without delay.

Autocratic leadership is also effective :

1 *When the work of a department* or unit consists of much routine or relatively low-level work, such as in the general office or the typing pool. Guetzkow found that programmed, repetitive tasks can be most effi-

ciently carried out by imposing structure and using autocratic methods.

2 *When grappling with complex technical problems* Usually, a certain approach is known to get good results – a certain work method or procedure – and this is the method that has to be imposed.

3 *When the group is large* Strong control and structure are needed if clear decisions and actions are to be hammered out of the wide range of approaches, interests and opinions represented.

Structure and centralised control allow speedy solutions to many problems. A structured, organised approach is particularly necessary when a group is working under time-pressure, or in a very competitive environment. But centralised control can also bring problems. Bavelas invented a simple information-exchange game. The performance of each group playing the game varied according to the way it was organised. For instance, when everybody could communicate with everybody else the group took a long time to complete the task, but morale was high – everybody enjoyed the participation. But when the group as a whole was organised and members were allowed to communicate only with one other person – the leader – the task was performed with great speed and efficiency, but the price to be paid was low morale : only the leader, the man at the centre, enjoyed himself.

9

'Industrial leaders must communicate. The gulf must be bridged between what management knows, because they have access to a lot of information, and what employees believe, often in ignorance.'

**Sir Marcus Sieff, Chairman,
Marks and Spencer**

Communicator

Consider this piece of mid-twentieth-century idiocy. In the middle of an industrial dispute at a Liverpool factory, management and workers found a supplementary issue over which to lock horns: where the wages should be handed out. Workers refused to allow management into the factory building to distribute pay there. Management retaliated by refusing to allow workers into the office block. Eventually a compromise was worked out. Wages were dispensed through a side window while the workforce queued in the rain. Needless to say, such bloody-mindedness is hardly conducive to the development of harmonious industrial relations.

Nor is rigid adherence to official union channels sufficient guard against such absurdities. In many industries there is a communication gap between union officials and the rank and file and management may not get a true picture of shop-floor attitudes by talking only to local organisers and elected representatives. In any case, only highly specific issues – usually 'grievances' related to pay and conditions – are normally dealt with through the representative system. Unless management creates extra links with the workforce whole areas of possible concern will inevitably be neglected.

The creation of such links is the responsibility of leaders at all levels. A department or divisional head might, for instance, take the initiative in setting up formal communication machinery. An example of this kind of machinery is General Electric's Employee and Management Co-operation Plan which provides a valuable means of dealing with grievances and disputes as quickly as possible. Initially the employee is interviewed by his foreman. If the foreman is unable to settle, it goes to a review council, consisting of managers, operatives, the worker's supervisor and the personnel manager. If the council fails to find a solution, the manager of employee relations can call in everybody who is involved and sort the matter out. The existence of formal channels means that each grievance can be quickly communicated up to the appropriate level for settlement so that there is less risk of disruption on the shop-floor.

Companies in the US and in a number of European countries have clear-cut ways for management and the unions to communicate – with relatively strike-free results. For instance, at Volvo in Sweden, the communication machinery for consultation already exists : there is a hierarchy of works councils throughout the company with representatives from both management and the workforce. Some of these councils have been required by law since 1948, but others, like the Corporate Works Council, was set up by top leadership to meet their own needs for communication and consultation with the workforce.

Social leader

A works manager in an electronics factory believes that the key to industrial harmony is a good relationship between each employee and his boss. 'A manager should be able to handle grievances informally. My own door's always open. Grievances must be settled promptly, otherwise they become obsessions.' According to this executive, the manager must be a social leader in his own part of the organisation, the figure round whom the unit or department revolves. 'Good social relations mean a lot more to employees than many managers realise.'

Several studies, such as those by Clark (1955), show that the relationship of the leader and his staff determines the degree of morale in the group; and that this relationship deeply affects members' self-esteem and sense of psychological well being. 'To be liked and accepted by a powerful figure represents security'. The leader has a therapeutic role to play and his main method is direct communication.

Thus, for better labour relations, it may be necessary to promote to leadership position the type of executive who mixes easily with employees and gets on with the shop stewards. Contrast the managing director of a motor components factory in Birmingham who sent a curt massage saying he was too busy to see a union official who had called to discuss a dismissed foreman. Next day the official made four phone calls, only to be told each time that the managing director was not available. So every foreman in the factory came out on strike in protest.

When the board of one company was asked what they regarded as essential qualities for business leadership, they placed equal stress on business efficiency and the ability to communicate with staff. In informal groups, such as work cliques, the leader stays leader only as long as his relations with the group remain good. If relations deteriorate, somebody else takes over. Similarly, if an officially appointed leader is unable to

sustain relations with his group, an unofficial leader usually emerges and
may become a focus for resistance or even rebellion.

'Primarily a communicator'

A report published by the British Institute of Management has pointed out that 'the more senior a manager becomes, the less concerned with technology his job becomes, more and more emphasis being given to interpersonal relationships'. At senior levels, the leader is primarily a communicator. The senior executive is constantly in front of people, representing the company to other organisations and in the community. As Drucker has pointed out, the manager manages 'through constant communication, both from the manager to his subordinate and from subordinate to manager'. It is a two-way process.

When communication between the two sides is poor, it is easy to blame the unions, but often the problem begins at the top. For instance, many boards in Britain do not have a single member who has ever worked on the shop-floor – or who even knows anybody with a blue-collar job. Sir Richard Marsh, former British Rail chairman, says: 'There are many problems you get working on the shop-floor which you don't understand unless you've done it'. Parker, former managing director of McKinsey's consultancy operation in London, sees class consciousness as an important factor inhibiting many managers from going down into the factory or office and communicating directly and on equal terms with the workforce. 'Too many managers don't identify themselves with the interests of the managed. They stay aloof – at arm's length from the workers.'

It is not sufficient to rely only on 'machinery' or techniques for improving communication. The ever-open door – the mere mechanics of communication – is less important than the attitudes of the men on either side of it. If there are no points of emotional contact, no mutual respect and sympathy, there can be no real communication. Often the manager is to blame for the psychological gap. According to industrial psychologist Knowles, it is the authoritarian, neurotic personality who often gets himself promoted to management position; and organisations are full of emotionally unstable, non-communicating executives who are unable to exercise leadership because they cannot express their own feelings or listen properly to other people's. Other authorities argue that many managers have unconscious aggressive feelings and lust for power that drastically limits their ability to meet trade union representatives, for example, and talk to them on equal terms.

Gyllenhammar, Volvo's president, says that in his company's experience, 'tight management need not be authoritative. Today's manager must be able to talk to people, and to listen as well. If the manager is alert to every opportunity for improvement and full of zest for his job, this communicates itself to others.'

Some managers are reluctant to talk freely to employees about plans and policies for fear of the consequences. If a manager speaks about a policy or even an intention, he is likely to find himself with a public commitment to action. But, the higher a manager climbs in the hierarchy, the more he is cut off from the details of operational activity and unless he can establish direct communication links with the workforce he is bound to be left in ignorance about a great deal that is happening on the front line. The natural temptation is to interpret no news as good news, but the deathly hush from the shop-floor may only indicate that the communication lines have been cut.

Yet ironically, communication is the major component of the executive's job. Copeman found that senior executives spend 74 per cent of their time with and directly contacting others. Diary studies by Stewart, Carlson and others show that most managers spend 70 to 80 per cent of their time at work on one or another kind of communication activity. Mintzberg (1955) found that chief executives were required to make contacts with an incredibly wide range of people – subordinates, clients, business associates, suppliers, managers in other organisations, government and trade union officials, and so on. Communication is such a vital part of every leader's job that if poor communicators are inadvertently appointed to leadership position efficiency – and financial results – are bound to suffer.

Keeping communication lines open

Keeping lines open undoubtedly consumes time and energy but far more time and energy will be spent settling disputes if these flare up because the communication system is either non-existent or non-functioning. Moreover, the flow of information upward through the organisation is unlikely to be adequate unless there is also a healthy downward flow. Marks and Spencer chairman, Sir Marcus Sieff, says : 'Industrial leaders must communicate. The gulf must be bridged between what management knows, because they have access to a lot of information, and what employees believe, often in ignorance.' As Sieff points out, one of the problems facing business leaders is the large size of many companies today, as a result of which top management may be separated from the shop-floor by five or six intermediate levels. In these circumstances, it is all too easy to lose sight of the information needs of individuals at lower levels.

When Blumenthal headed the Bendix Corporation he personally used to deliver many of the memos he wrote to his managers. 'It's a nice way to stay in touch. I like to see where a manager works – you know, what his or her desk looks like, and so on. It kind of rounds out my picture of the person.' Blumenthal reckons that office efficiency depends, above all, on senior management establishing direct communication links with people at lower levels. But personal contact need not be confined to the ranks of management. According to the chairman of one ballbearing factory, a manager should know every employee by name. 'Of course, in the very large companies this is impossible. But at least two levels of management above the foreman should know the employee by name. It is, after all, impossible not to like somebody who likes *you* enough to stop and chat whenever he sees you.'

Shop-floor leader

Direct communication gives the leader a chance to size up the faces and personalities behind the dozens of reports, requests and proposals that he is faced with every week. It also gives him a chance to iron out grievances before they become obsessions and spoil the industrial relations climate. When Crawfords, the Liverpool biscuits factory, made 15 workers redundant without winning the prior consent of the unions, problems of mistrust were created that took years to heal. Managing director Reed has expedited the healing process by becoming a shop-floor leader. He arrives first thing in the morning and usually leaves after six. 'That way I get to see all the shift workers'.

Another believer in leadership by example is Vernon, chairman of Ash and Lacy, the Midlands-based engineering company. Vernon, always arrives before his staff in the morning and leaves after them at night. 'There are no bad troops', he says, 'only bad officers'. In 1976, Vernon brought workers and shareholders together by holding the annual meeting at the International Exhibition Centre. The entire Midlands workforce were taken there by a coach for a three-course lunch. Vernon says that this sort of involvement makes workers feel more involved in the company.

Ritchie, a senior executive at Texas Instruments, thinks that one of the keys to leadership is the leader's willingness and ability to involve himself with the workers – perhaps to the extent of sitting on the production line and communicating with them on equal terms, getting to know them as people, absorbing their ideas about how the job should be done. 'The subordinate learns too – what the boss's problems are and what's expected of him'.

Bridging the perception gap

Direct communication with employees tells a leader how their minds work and how they see things. As Drucker has pointed out : 'The human mind attempts to fit impressions and stimuli into a frame of expectations. It resists virtually any attempts to make it change its mind, that is, to perceive what it does not expect to perceive . . . Before we can communicate we must therefore know what the recipient expects to see and to hear.'

In *Dynamic Administration,* Mary Parker Follett pointed out: 'A disagreement or conflict is likely not to be about the answers, or indeed about anything ostensible. It is, in most cases, the result of incongruity in perceptions. What A sees so vividly, B does not see at all. And therefore what A argues has no pertinence to B's concern and vice-versa.' This helps to explain why the business leader must be willing and able to get to know his employees as people. A poor communicator not only fails to generate enthusiasm and goodwill among subordinates: he also runs the permanent risk of making poor decisions simply because he is insulated against other people's thinking and criticism.

One of the dangers of power is that the power-holder does not *have* to listen, does not *have* to be sensitive to the ideas of others. Thus, the leader may use his authority to wall himself off from others by means of waiting rooms, outer offices, secretaries, and so on. Another danger is that the leader will surround himself with loyal place-men as the easiest way of eliminating conflict and opposition. It is also the simplest way of guaranteeing that bad decisions will be made, because nobody will ever tell the leader when he is being a fool.

Affable leaders

Some companies do at least make it conscious policy to appoint to senior positions affable, approachable types who mix easily and on equal terms with employees, shop stewards and union officials. Esso is one. Its former chairman, Biggs, says: 'We selected our managers at least as much for their ability in the communication area as for their expertise in their particular field. Anyone who seeks to manage other people's efforts must involve himself in the problems of human relationships.' Many more companies could benefit from this philosophy.

A manager tells the story of a medium-sized company where nine workers, questioned at random, were unable to direct a visitor to the deputy managing director's office: they did not even recognise his name. As he says, 'you can't have contact with 3,000 people, but you can with some. You gain a lot in general morale when ordinary people find that their problems are the concern of top management.'

In achieving his results, it is tempting for a manager to rely on impersonal 'techniques', says Halbrecht, president of Halbrecht Associates. But Halbrecht himself believes that the main priority for any leader must be to be a good communicator. 'Too many executives have the notion that leadership means making the right decisions. They talk about management decisions as being 'optimal'. These are cop-outs by very capable but primarily analytically and quantitatively oriented people who are not really managers of people but of things. These managers are rarely mentioned as inspirational leaders.'

There are many studies which show that workers are generally more productive and co-operative under a communicative, employee-centred boss. Gellerman describes one successful supervisor :

> He believes in allowing the natural dynamics of a group to govern it. His main practical problem at all times is to help that group to be generally successful . . . His style consists of reassuring the discouraged, jollying along the angry, and leaving those who need no help pretty much alone. In brief, he gives as much support as is needed, and only where it is needed [9.1].

There is no doubt that employees prefer to work for a leader who can communicate face-to-face. This not only makes for easier relationships : oral instructions permit opportunities for questions and clarification. So why don't more managers 'walk the job' every day, talk to people, and, if necessary, *tell* them what they should be doing? Certain Japanese companies – Matsushita is an example – encourage the habit of personal communication by insisting that budding executives should work on assembly lines and sell the company's products before being appointed to permanent management positions. They thus take on a common vocabulary with the workforce which facilitates understanding

The same company holds regular 'free talks', as it calls them, between managers and employees, who are encouraged to express opinions about working conditions, company policy and anything else which concerns them. Ideas or grievances which emerge are sent straight to the board for its reaction. The company believes that direct communication, operating as deliberate policy at all levels of leadership, can pull the entire organisation together and unite it behind top managemant's objectives; also that employees will feel their problems and attitudes matter to management if the boss is something considerably more than a photograph in the house journal.

The leader as therapist

Such thinking, of course, is not exactly unknown in the West. Marshall, president of Avis, dismisses the 'theory that the top people should stay in their offices, gather in the information they want and do their thinking there – we disagree with the ivory tower attitude. It's far better to get around.' Marshall himself certainly gets around. His travels, he says, account for about 40 per cent of his working life. He keeps his senior executives moving too. 'All this activity means better understanding, better decisions.'

Communication breakdowns and withdrawals occur in all organisations and dealing with them is one of the challenges facing a leader. In this sense, says Rice, every leader 'has to be a "therapist" of at least sufficient sensitivity to make judgements about when to contain the casualties within his organisation, when to call in specialist help' – an example would be an organisation development expert – 'and when, for the sake of the other members of the organisation, as well as of the organisation itself, to remove the casualties' [3.16]. The leader needs to have a hard streak when required.

In the interests of better communication activity at work, members of the management team might well be encouraged to develop working relationships out of working hours. For example, one senior manager of an electronics group regularly plays tennis with his managers. 'It gives me a terrific opportunity to find out what is on their minds', he says. 'You'd be surprised how much I learn changing in the locker room or sitting round afterwards.' Paradoxically, the same opportunities may not always exist at the work-place. The same manager gets up from his seat and taps on the wall: 'I worry about these. When managers spend a lot of time in offices and call people in, it creates distance between themselves and employees.' So this executive puts steady pressure on his subordinates to communicate constantly with the shop-floor. 'I ask them what problems have cropped up on the shop-floor, what the operatives are thinking and check that they have passed information down the line.'

Roaming the plant

The chief executive of an insurance company insists that executives must get out of their offices regularly and meet people face-to-face. 'People in the departments can feel very isolated, but they feel a lot better if the chief executive looks in now and again and listens to what they have to say.' If this executive wants to see somebody, he doesn't order him upto his own office. 'I go down and see him. I'm all over the building all the time. I know my people, I socialise with them and we're friends.' He tries to think of ways of making his staff feel happy. This involves 'recognition of jobs well done, like a little note thanking them for it, calling attention to an outstanding job'.

One of the reasons why the leader must communicate is so that he can encourage people to keep trying. Several years ago, Byrom, now CEO at the Koppers Company, headed a task force trying to find ways of reviving an ailing plant. He didn't do the job from the comfort of his office. 'I would roam the plant', he recalls. 'I was asking people to do things they didn't think could be done, and sometimes I practically had to hold their hands.

'If a machine had been producing 14 gallons of chemicals a minute, I would have the operator push it to 21. The operators would say, "Mr Byrom, we can't do that", and I would reply, "Maybe we can. Why don't I stay here with you while you try it." Most processes are susceptible to refinements and improvements – little changes here and there.

You should never accept what you're doing as being the best you can do' [4.2].

Another leader with a distinctive communication style is Frey, CEO at Bell and Howell. He recalls that when he worked for Ford he would pry into every corner of the plant. While other senior executives stayed in their offices, he would stand with the men on the production line, listening to their complaints. Or he would drop into people's offices, chat informally and pick their brains. This approach, he says, kept him in close touch with problems at the operating level. 'The pressures on a chief executive are all in the direction of hurry-up, but he's also the last person in the company who should lose his patience or his temper. I think I'm less impatient now than I used to be'. He always finds time to communicate 'because that's extremely important'.

First-line leaders

At lower levels of leadership, too, communication is extremely important: apart from anything else, managers expect their supervisors to be the main channel of communication with the shop-floor. The supervisor is in daily contact with his men and his relationship with them is considered by many to be the most important factor in determining group productivity and morale. This is an important implication of the Hawthorne studies, for instance. The first-line manager is in a key position in the organisation because he links management with the shop-floor and translates the plans and instructions of management into a form that the shop-floor can understand and implement. He also translates the workers' grievances, ideas and requests into a language management can understand. He may be judged primarily by management standards – productivity figures, absenteeism and scrap rates, and so on – but he also needs to be one of the boys. He must communicate with employees, have a genuine interest in them as people, and hear them out when they come to him with problems. Most supervisors are promoted from the shop-floor and so find this kind of relationship easy to establish.

Likert and his associates compared *production-centred* and *employee-centred* supervisors and found that the latter tend to have the highest-producing work-groups. Presumably, some production-centred supervisors create resistance and unfavourable attitudes among employees which ultimately reduce output. There is evidence that highly productive groups tend to have a supervisor who :

1 Has the ability to communicate.
2 Keeps them well informed about what is happening in the company.
3 Tells them how they are doing.
4 Treats them so that they feel free to discuss problems with him.

An effective way of keeping employees informed is by regular supervisors' meetings when the supervisor tells his team about safety, production schedules, plans, and so on, then answers questions and invites discussion.

Useful techniques

One of the simplest ways of involving the entire management team in policy-making is management by objectives (MBO). In its simplest form, this means discussing the job with a subordinate manager and agreeing on goals and targets for the next three or six months. The method has been found to integrate the company's need to clarify and achieve certain goals with the manager's need to develop and gradually increase his responsibilities and improve his results. MBO therefore implies a high standard of leadership at all levels of management.

In training sessions, managers quickly learn to avoid the pitfalls that destroy true communication. There are numbers of common mistakes which are guaranteed to trigger off hostile reactions, yet which are committed very frequently and quite inadvertently. Patent insincerity, of course, must always be avoided. But so should false jocularity, a 'superior' voice or manner suggesting that the speaker is patronising or talking down to his listeners; also a domineering tone and a tendency to express one's feelings too forcefully.

Ultimately, of course, good face-to-face communication is not a matter of 'techniques' but of evidently *wanting* to communicate. A department head in a computer organisation makes the point: 'Nothing irks me more than receiving memos on a hundred different subjects. If they are so important, why doesn't the manager concerned drop in and talk about them once in a while? He'd learn a lot more about the problems and about me if he would sit down and talk.'

Informal networks

Probably a leader's biggest intangible asset – often greater than his specialist skills – is his ability to communicate directly and easily with colleagues and employees. As would be expected, most of the best-known management theorists place enormous importance on face-to-face communication. But so do many notable practitioners. Borel, the brilliant French catering entrepreneur and, until lately, head of Europe's biggest restaurant chain, spent a fortnight every year working as a waiter, mixing with waitresses, cooks, cashiers and customers. Borel argued: 'If one hasn't been in touch with every detail oneself – and it's a sector in which details are supremely important – one is unable to take genuine command'. Spode's former general manager, Bullock, like many others, kept in touch by touring the factory daily. 'It's amazing how often I pick up information this way. It gives me a feeling for what goes on'. Even such brief daily routines, cumulatively, can demand a big slice of a top manager's time, but Bullock reckons that the answer is to make the most of every opportunity presented by the working day. An inspection tour is also an opportunity to talk to employees and discuss problems. An internal meeting is a chance to get on terms with people from different levels, and so on.

Informal communications pervade every organisation, yet are so complex that they can never be charted. Nevertheless, as Eastern Airline's president Borman notes, it is by using the informal network that the leader gets the work done. Incidentally, Borman gets to the office every day at 7 a.m. and breakfasts in the cafeteria with any workers who happen to be there. He also insists that other managers follow his lead, so that those who deal with employees have to attend friendliness classes. 'If you fail to get good face-to-face communication with people your isolation increases,' says Borman. 'You may think you are doing things right, but you don't know.'

Naturally, the formal channels are mainly used for the record. Standard reporting items – production and inventory reports, orders, sales, statistics and so on – generally follow the lines of the organisation chart. But for solving problems, making decisions, and for bringing life and meaning to the organisation, it is the informal network – the face-to-face factor – which really matters.

Pumping information downwards

'A real leader is a thoroughly informed professional', says Gyllenhammar, Volvo's president. 'You can't command respect if your team members have to turn to somebody else to find out what's going on in the minds of higher management.' As his words imply, one of the leader's main priorities is to make sure that employees get as much accurate and timely information as they need to do their jobs efficiently.

It sounds a straight-forward task, but there are many hazards. One of them is the fact that information defies the principles that govern gravity. Information does not 'flow' down the line; it has to be pumped. A survey of managers and supervisors at H. & R. Johnson, the ceramic tile makers, found that 84 per cent of foremen and 62 per cent of managers thought that they received 'too little information about the company's decisions and activities'. And when Ciba-Geigy (UK) surveyed employees, they found that about half felt they knew very little about company operations, or the kind of decisions being made by management.

The survey also revealed that the most common source of good information was certain managers: those who had established good working relationships with their employees. As a result, Ciba-Geigy has recommended all managers to have more contact with subordinates and to make the facts known to them by informal contacts, frank and friendly teach-ins and meetings, and frequent employee information programmes.

An independent survey conducted at British Steel in 1974 found that supervisors relied most heavily on the grapevine for information about what went on in the organisation, with the Corporation's newspaper *Steel News* in second place and their own management lagging fourth below even the press and television. But the Corporation reckons that it has an answer to what it regards as primarily a problem of leadership. In the words of chief executive Scholey, this consists of 'getting more senior managers into shifts'. This, he says, will break down the time barriers that separate many managers from their supervisors. In addition, the Corporation is introducing systematic procedures to keep first line managers informed on matters such as agreements, negotiations, costs, performance and standards.

Information and productivity

One way of improving employee communication is to make it the responsibility of a senior manager with enough leverage to ensure that middle and junior executives will keep the channels open. Another approach is to train managers to assess and satisfy employees' information needs. The primary interest of the great majority of employees is in job-related information in a highly personal sense. They are concerned with *their* jobs, *their* departments, *their* conditions and advancement opportunities, the effect of *their* work, and so on. So every manager should be encouraged to provide feedback in these areas.

There is little doubt that information of this kind can and does boost productivity and morale. To take one small example, instruments were installed in a boiler-house to tell each man how efficiently his boiler was working. Performance figures were collected and announced each week. As a result, the men set out to improve their efficiency, with a saving of £200,000 a year on the fuel bills.

When operating results are broken down and presented in such a way that workers can see figures of their own performance, delegation of responsibilities is greatly simplified. As Copeman has said, 'It is then possible to lean very considerably on the propensity of normal, responsible adults to operate in the black rather than in the red'. When the leadership provides information of this kind, employees can automatically take corrective action when the figures reveal that management controls are beginning to slip out of gear.

Leader's duty

To measure work against company objectives, employees need information – and it is the leader's duty to provide it. Management must convey this information not only because employees want it but also because efficiency requires it. Drucker points out that the great majority of employees may never be reached in spite of management's best efforts, 'but only by trying to get information to every worker can management hope to reach the small group that in every plant, office, or store leads public opinion and moulds communication attitudes'.

Some companies run courses to instruct managers in how to set about communicating with employees. The following instruction might well be suitable for a professional engineer: 'transmissions containing formal gearing require detergent lubricants of high viscosity range'. But if the same information is intended for fitters or mechanics, it would be better expressed more plainly: 'Use green-label oil in the lower gear-box'.

Industrial leadership involves communicating clearly what the organisation as a whole is trying to achieve and how each part – and each individual – fits into the big picture. This means that for top-level managers communication must be a continuous, systematic activity. It means that they must make special efforts to establish good communication and rapport with middle management for they are the people who are responsible for keeping in direct contact with the troops. Laing, United Biscuits' chairman, says: 'Leaders must communicate and to do this effectively they need to get out and be seen. Communications, like friends, have to be cultivated.'

Communicating the plan of campaign

One of the functions of top-level leadership is to communicate clearly where the whole organisation is going and how it is going to get there. Rockwell, a vice-president at the Board State Street Boston Financial Corporation, believes that communication must be systematic and continuous: 'Leadership lies in the manager's ability to keep his people going technically and yet to steer their direction so as to support corporate objectives. The leader has to work constantly at keeping everyone on the same wavelength and thinking positively so that everyone is going in the same direction.' To do this effectively, Rockwell adds, the senior man must sustain a strong and continuous dialogue with middle management personnel.

When company goals are effectively communicated throughout the organisation, people feel that they are important and spur themselves to greater efforts. One of Field Marshal Montgomery's ironclad rules was that the plan of campaign should be communicated to every soldier and discussed by all ranks so that everybody would fight with a will.

When the top leadership fails to communicate the company's major policies and objectives, the company as a whole lacks a clear sense of direction. Decisions are taken on the basis of self-interest, and this can damage the company. For instance, the political assassination of a rival's proposal may mean that the company loses a profitable new product or a new marketing opportunity.

Thus the top echelon should take steps to ensure that all managers are clear about corporate strategy and that the decisions they take actually reflect it. As Jay points out. 'By all means assume that any given manager is always working exclusively for the general good of the whole corporation; but construct the system so that he is penalised if he is not' [9.2].

A large engineering company communicates the big picture downwards by a four-stage process:

1   New policies are explained at a meeting of divisional heads. The financial and strategic implications are fully discussed.

2   Each divisional manager calls a meeting of department heads and leads a discussion on the new policy and how it affects the departments.

3   Department heads inform section heads of the policy and underline its relevance to the particular section.

4   Section heads have details of the policy typed and posted on notice boards. Operatives are invited to discuss or query the policy via section heads.

Going down the chain

Organisations are like kaleidoscopes. You look through the eyepiece and if you're an accountant you see a financial problem, if you're the sales director you see a sales problem, and so on. In one investigation 23 managers were given a case history of a company to study. Eighty-three per cent of the sales executives identified the major problem of the company as a sales problem, 80 per cent of the production managers saw a production problem, and so on.

People from different disciplines and different departments see skewed pictures of reality. Communicating strategy – the 'plan of campaign' – is a way of pulling all the different facets together and achieving an over-view. A sense of the company's overall purpose can lift the eyes of the divisions from the floors of their factories up to the horizon so that they can see where the whole company is heading. They beome more committed to achieving corporate as opposed to merely departmental goals. Problems of coordination are reduced. As one manager says: 'The wider the perspective the better the performance of individual managers. All parts of the organisation must know which way the company is going.'

But employees in many companies *don't* know which way the organisation is going – the necessary leadership is lacking. When Peterfreund did an attitude survey for American Telephone and Telegraph, he found no evidence that management personnel have a consistent awareness of what company goals are, where the company is heading or how they themselves fit into the overall scheme. One manager told him: 'Managers have so little contact with their top executives

that they really don't know what the executives are thinking, what
the plans are'.

One chief executive who makes sure that managers do know what the plans are is Frey of Bell and Howell. He regularly checks that the policy message is being communicated down the line. He says : 'There are times when I'll make a policy decision then, to see how it works out, I'll go eight links down the chain to some lowly clerk and ask him what he's heard about the policy. I may find that he hasn't heard anything. That means I've got to start over again because ultimately he's the one who's got to do what I want done.'

Frey believes that the ultimate responsibility for communicating objectives down the line lies with the chief exective officer and that doing this constitutes an important leadership function.

Gauging information needs

Like a pointilliste painting, like cells under the microscope, the closer you look at an organisation the more it divides into a myriad parts. Each part has its own function, its own characteristics, its own information needs and preferences. Different groups have to be communicated with in different ways. Some people only absorb the information they hear. Some want to see it presented in graphical form. Some want to read it. That is why a close knowledge of the social structure of the organisation and of the people within the structure is a pre-requisite for successful communication. Armed with this kind of knowledge, the leader knows who should receive information and the most suitable method of communicating it. Some people, for instance, want to see the facts on paper. Others prefer an eyeball-to-eyeball meeting with their boss.

Information has to be shaped to suit the recipient. Lower levels often take a rather narrow view and want to know only how they and their departments will be affected. A study in one company showed that on average 44 per cent of the items of information given to employees by management was absorbed by them. But this figure was far higher if the items were specific and relevant to employees' own jobs.

Senior people are usually more interested in long-term, strategic implications. Thus as an item of information passes down the line it may have to be re-shaped and re-presented at every level. More and more detail has to be added. General instructions, for instance, have to be *applied* to more and more situations, level by level, until eventually they reach the man on the shop-floor who wants to know exactly how he should set up his machine, measurements required, tolerances allowed, and so on.

In *The Social Psychology of Organisation*, Katz and Kahn argue that the goals of employee information should include :
1   Specific job instructions.
2   Information about organisational procedures and practices.

3 Information about the rationale of the job (for motivation purposes).
4 Feedback to employees about their job performance.

How to avoid information distortion

Large companies tend to become bureaucratic in the sense meant by Weber – i.e. constantly growing in size and complexity and characterised by specialisation, hierarchy, chains of command and division of labour. Messages must pass through more and more relay points and information gets delayed and distorted by the Chinese-whispers effect.

One way round the problem is to shorten chains of command wherever possible – and where possible to go direct. At Bulmers, for instance, each manager is expected to solve problems and take decisions up to his own level, instead of referring such problems up the line. If a labour dispute crops up, the individual manager is expected to deal with it quickly and decisively if it comes within his terms of reference.

Bulmers is keen on direct contact between management and unions. Personnel manager Sanders says : 'We attempt to negotiate as informally as possible. We create an atmosphere of informality at meetings and conferences. I think it is important to create good personal relations with union officials, give them a feeling of equality and dignity and recognise that they have a job to do'. This approach works. Sanders can recall few cases of communication breakdown with the unions at Bulmers.

Johnson and Johnson's answer to the problem of information distortion is to pass information down the line through a series of meetings at successive levels. These are held in quick succession so that management can pass the information right down the line before rumours start.

One managing director gives important information to the unions personally : 'Negotiating with the unions is one function which no boss should delegate – otherwise he is not the boss any longer in terms of the labour force'. An executive who previously worked for Texaco points out that poor information demoralises : 'The serious error made with me was not giving me a glimpse of the big picture from time to time so that I could go back to my little detail, understanding how it related to the whole'.

Reliable sources

To improve accuracy, the leader must learn to identify and utilise reliable sources of information. For instance, some people will only tell their boss the good news, or what they think he wants to hear. Bennis found that junior officials in the State Department often decided not to tell their bosses what they knew from the field because they thought the boss would not accept it and that the result was distortion of information on a big scale [1.12].

To sustain morale, people must have an interest that goes beyond the mere mechanics of the job. Accurate, reliable information motivates the workforce and encourages them to identify themselves with the company and its products. A management consultant points out that if people feel well informed 'their attitudes on every score tend to be better; their interest starts high and is maintained at a high level'.

To improve employee information, why not arrange an employee attitude survey to find out:

1   How much information is being received?
2   How could presentation be improved?
3   Which aspects of the company's activities interest employees?
4   Which are the preferred channels of communication – e.g. foreman, department head, shop steward?
5   Which people are isolated from communication chains? – e.g. 'staff' managers often receive more information than line management. If certain groups or individuals are under-informed, the problem can be put right by stepping up the volume of information directed at them.
6   Is job performance feedback adequate and effective? Much uncertainty is caused when feedback information is poor. A management accountant says: 'I know how well I'm doing by my own criteria but I don't know how they compare with my boss's'. A works engineer reports: 'I worry quite a bit because the people who judge my performance do so on a subjective basis. I don't know whether they judge me as an engineer or as a manager'.

Presentation methods

Cassette tapes were chosen by Pearl Assurance as a way of keeping staff in 500 district and divisional offices well informed. The method is also used as a way of complementing training courses. A new agent is given basic product knowledge which he can absorb at his own pace. Gestetner is another company which breaches the gap between headquarters and regional offices by using tape cassettes. Each month, general manager Lowry records a tape commenting on the previous month's sales figures, what he expects for the current month, and which products he wants to stress. The tape, lasting between 30 and 60 minutes, also includes comments on the company's market, the economy, social notes and other information. It is played at monthly staff meetings and any comments are reported back by the branch managers. Copies of the master tape are made by a recording firm at a cost of about £50 for each edition.

Marks and Spencer have used slides with taped commentary to communicate company policy to personnel at its 252 stores. Each store has its own cinema projector and library of slides. Shows are given regularly in company time. The slides include information about financial results, dealing with customers and employee options under the company's pension scheme.

United Biscuits' elaborate internal communications network includes a private broadcasting station, a company newspaper, weekly factory newsletters and structured briefing groups from the top down.

Communication is a technique

Areas like these show clearly that communication is above all a technique when applied to leadership. The inevitable social and environmental stresses which crop up in the industrial organisation do not admit social contact between individual leaders and employees in an entirely normal way, for the factory or the office is always an artificial environment in which individuals cannot choose each other's company.

The problem is compounded because of the frustrations and resentments that build up in the workforce as a result of tedium and discipline. Such feelings are not dissolved by cash incentives, unless they are abnormally high.

In large organisations, formal patterns of communication between leaders and followers will always predominate. But the trick is to promote better relations by encouraging informal communication between employees and leaders at all levels.

This is not something that can happen overnight with some magic gesture. It will be the product only of a consistent policy, set and monitored by top leadership, that sets out to win and deserve the confidence of the workforce. To achieve that, top leadership must not only accept the principle of good communication, but get down to the planning of a detailed campaign.

Such a campaign might be spearheaded by the techniques described above. But in any case, it will require the cooperation of the other side as a starting point.

10

'Control consists of verifying whether everything occurs in conformity with the plans adopted.'

Henri Fayol

Controller

When Volkswagen rang up a deficit of 800 million DM one year, business leaders throughout the world were reminded what inadequate control of costs and new products can do to a company, for business leaders are operating in the high-wire area where losses of control can bring sudden disaster. Losses in just a few divisions can suddenly materialise in outsize proportions and, like blood spurting from severed arteries, weaken the entire corporate body.

Sometimes a division or subsidiary is so independent or so remote from head office that top leadership loses control of the total situation. One of the reasons why Penn Central went bankrupt was a lack of control of subsidiaries, a failure to mastermind the detailed system one or two steps down.

To minimise the seemingly infinite risks, firm financial and operational control is essential *and leaders are responsible for applying it.* Yet there is evidence to show that this kind of control is lacking in many companies. A 1976 report by the British Institute of Management reveals that many British factories are so badly controlled that they are achieving shop-floor production efficiency no higher than 30 per cent. Only four out of 186 plants surveyed had been able to achieve 100 per cent delivery of customers' orders on time in 1975. Twenty-five per cent had delivered less than half their customers' orders on time.

In the majority of plants, 70 per cent of the time taken to produce components is simply spent queuing, waiting for the next production process. And far too much money is tied up, says the report, in stocks of work in progress. Bad leadership is one of the reasons for the malaise, according to the report. According to one financial director: 'Effective accounting and management information systems are the key to effective control. To operate efficiently and to remain competitive year after year, a company must have accurate measures of how well it is using its investments in plant and equipment, raw materials, services and human resources.'

Control of money and materials

According to this executive, a high proportion of small and medium-sized companies still do not have adequte accounting and information systems. 'Without overall detailed profitability data, companies can't work out strategies to take advantage of the most profitable items in their product lines.' For most companies, the overwhelming percentage of profits comes from a handful of products but management may not be able to identify this handful because of poor accounting and information systems.

Consider the consequences when accurate measures are lacking. When a large paper company concluded from its internal accounting that its pulp operations were highly profitable, it built two huge new pulp mills. In fact, though, the company's transfer pricing mechanism was badly out of balance. The pulp group got its raw materials at a low internal cost but billed its product to the next company group at a relatively high price.

Once the new mills had been built, the company discovered that the pulp operations were losing money rather than scoring high profits. It had bought itself an enormous chunk of unprofitable excess capacity.

Cases like this help to explain why, at a time of increasing competition, it is essential for the leader to bring basic inventory and financial controls, budgeting and planning to the long-neglected operating side. In many industries there are new pressures – customers are more demanding and less predictable; the regulatory climate is colder, following a plethora of new legislation affecting the way that business minds its own business. It's a different climate now', says one manager, 'and we need to learn to control *ourselves*.'

ABV, a Swedish civil engineering company, has developed an effective way of controlling spending. Many companies overshoot their budgets, but ABV have invented a system which provides information on the way the job is moving *a month in advance* so that they know at any given moment how projects are developing. Production manager Ostman explains: 'The trick is to check out the progress of the operations by the bills for supplies – cubic metres of cement, and so on. The figures for outgoings, which come in the form of bills, after coding, are passed on the following day for processing by the company's central computer. At any point it is now possible for the site management or the staff to recall spending too much on concrete, or racking up more bulldozer hours than appeared on the original estimate.'

Ostman adds : 'Thanks to our direct booking of the bills before they are checked and paid we now gain a clear month in knowing what exactly is going on in each site as far as production is concerned'.

Control of production costs

This continuous control over production costs also allows a much closer assessment of profit margins : 'The new control system makes us masters of the planning instrument'. ABV seems to have benefited from the system, moving from heavy losses in 1970 to healthy profits in the last two years [10.1].

The importance of effective control of materials and supplies was underlined by a British Institute of Management report in 1976 which found that, while more than 50 per cent of factory costs are typically accounted for by materials and brought-out parts, direct labour only accounts for 20 per cent; yet management often appears to concentrate far more on control of labour than on purchasing effectiveness and other kinds of control.

The general manager of a company making control equipment reckons that, for control to be effective, operating results need to be presented in such a way that variances are immediately identified and analysed. He points out : 'It is essential for the report to follow the event quickly. Key operating data – sales, profits, cash balances, and so on – should be on my desk within 24 hours of the close of the period.' *Thus, accurate and timely feedback information is a prequisite of effective control.* Control depends on :

1 Detailed planning.
2 Frequent and prompt feedback of operating results.
3 Quick responses to problems and changes in operating conditions.
The business leader must be able to identify the key areas, to assess the present position in relation to targets being persued, and to plan the next steps to be taken – and the efficiency of the whole cycle depends on accurate and timely information.

Financial nit-picking

Today, in order to survive, management has to wring out the operating side of the business – perhaps by centralising what used to be a one-man show, or by tightening up basic financial and management controls. 'I have to know which parts are doing well', says one managing director. 'If any section is not making satisfactory profits, overheads are very much in question.'

Honda's chief executive, Kawashima, says : 'We're trying to cut production costs partly by tightening management controls, partly by eliminating the wasteful habits we acquired in the era of high growth'. When visiting one factory, Kawashima noticed all the lights ablaze though only part of the plant was being used. So he had more switches installed. This may seem like yen-pinching, but it cuts energy consumption by 20 per cent.

When Borel headed Europe's biggest restaurant chain, he improved margins by becoming a time and motion expert. For instance, he would clock off the time spent by customers on each dish with a stop watch. He would put pedometers in the shoes of waiters as a basis for cutting down time spent carrying dishes. 'I'm not employing people to walk but to work', he said. He went in for portion control to the nearest gramme. 'Management is sordid because it's all about saving and making money.' Borel complained about drivers stopping at restaurants only to use the lavatory : 'They cost me 11c each in paper and hot water'. But he remains convinced that 'if one hadn't looked after the financial details oneself one would have been unable to take general command'.

Control by budget

Emerson Electric aims to be the low-cost producer in every product they make and since it manufactures thousands of products from motors to military electronics, it can only hope to achieve a good return on investment by imposing the most stringent fiscal controls on every overhead expense – including labour. The success of its control methods can be gauged by the fact that its average return on investment has been around 30 per cent in recent years while its growth rate has been averaging nearly 12 per cent annually – much of this being generated internally through cost cutting.

Chief executive Knight reckons that the company's 'ABC budgeting' method explains the company's success in the control area : 'The system breaks down the company's business into individual products and markets. For each product, no matter how small, divisional management must come up with a five-year projection of sales and earnings. Once agreed by top management this is called Budget A.'

Knight explains that Budget B is a contingency plan allowing for a 10 per cent drop in projected sales – but it demands the same operating profit as Budget A. And if sales drop 20 per cent, Budget C goes into effect – but with management still committed to the same profit. With the budget in hand, a plant manager is relatively free to implement his goals by increasing productivity, cutting costs, funding new markets or products, and so on. But he must operate within the controls laid down by the budget.

Budgeting

When a company grows so large that the boss can no longer per-

sonally supervise spending, budgetary control becomes essential. Depart-
ment heads are free to spend within budget limits, but top leadership
keeps overall control by setting the budgets. The leader's control over his
management team 'depends very considerably on his control over capital
expenditure. This is the control which chiefly determines the scope for
promotion of his subordinates, and so largely affects the loyalty they will
give him' [1.6].

Apart from increasing top leadership's control, budgets also give subordinate managers a keener money sense, as Samsonite, the world's largest
luggage-maker, discovered. The company imposed formal budgets on
salesmen and regional sales managers just a few years ago. But they
were also given freedom to operate within these budgets. Thus top management were able to stay at the financial controls – but without hamper-
ing the sales people who were able to make more decisions on their own
operations and who got a clearer reading of their own performance. The
result, according to a senior executive of the company, was that sales
executives started to 'directly relate sales costs to sales volume generated
in a particular store or sales trip' – an admirable outcome in these days
of soaring overheads.

Naturally enough, the most elaborate, carefully worked out systems
that leaders can devise turn out to have serious flaws when applied to a
big organisation. For instance, regaining control of operations at British
Leyland has involved, first, introducing worker participation; secondly,
restructuring the company into four separate businesses for greater speed
and efficiency and, thirdly, making government funds available for investment via the National Enterprise Board. All this has solved many
problems but created others. For instance, the government's involvement
has possibly made it more difficult to introduce product change because
the decision-making process is longer and more exhaustive, and the command chain has more links, with the NEB monitoring Leyland's performance monthly. Then there is the Industry Department sitting at the
top of the pyramid – and the Treasury watching from the wings to see
how the cash is spent.

Keeping systems simple

It is worth struggling to acquire a familiarity with budgets and balance
sheets not least because, simply by checking figures, the leader can share
in the guidance and excitement of a great number of different operations.
One company makes sure that leaders are *au fait* with the financial
realities by encouraging managers to attend each other's budget meetings
– a manager can attend a colleague's meeting and discuss the figures related to his own function.

The head of a food retailing firm increased his control over operations
by spending some time in each department, doing a consulting job in
each and forming the budgets, including the detailed costs. The exercise

took nine months. But it gave him a clear picture – and more control – of what was going on.

The great and obvious virtue of budgeting is that it is easy to understand and simple to apply (whereas over-complicated systems can easily go wrong and waste rather than control resources). Mintzberg found that managers often ignore complicated, formal systems. Today, says Bergerac, Revlon's chief executive, the key to success is planning and control – but the controls must be simple. 'One can end up spending more time trying to create systems to control the job than actually doing it. Moreover, if a manager becomes too systems-oriented, there is a danger that he will start to disregard the personal relationships that make the systems work.'

Control of purchasing can be a simple way of keeping in touch with the activities of subordinate management. As Copeman has pointed out, any changes they make 'are likely to show up in the changed purchasing requirements'. In *The Chief Executive,* Copeman describes the head of a large department store who kept a continuous check on operations by :

1   Seeing all letters that came into the firm, and invoices from every supplier.
2   Getting daily reports on the number of customers, details of invoices sent and accounts received, cash in hand, etc.
3   Getting a twice-weekly report of cash paid to suppliers.
4   Seeing a weekly total of sales and stocks held, and an assessed net profit.
5   Getting a monthly analysis of sales and a list of substantial debts.

Forward budgeting

A powerful new method by which the leader can keep day-to-day control over decentralised operations is forward budgeting. This involves comparing results not with the previous year but with forecasts made for the period in question. When there are any significant deviations from plan, these show up and allow course corrections to be made.

Forward budgeting involves making detailed business forcasts, assessing their financial implication and monitoring progress against the figures derived. A chief executive says : 'You watch the dial to see if the plane deviates off-course and when it does you nudge it back with the controls'.

As Heller points out in *The Once and Future Manager,* an efficient financial director should be able to install a management and financial accounting system into the company without too much disruption; and perhaps the most eagerly demanded leaders of the future will be those who are equipped with enough financial know-how to understand and apply techniques like these. That is one of the reasons why Ford, like many other large companies, insists that managers who are earmarked for senior leadership positions should be properly trained in financial control techniques.

Some banks have offered industrial customers courses in financial management – even to take over their entire financial function. And there are many reputable financial consultants who offer the same service. There is no reason today why any company, no matter how small, should not have an efficient financial control system.

The importance of financial control to corporate survival and growth explains the current strong trend to promote financial men to top leadership jobs. It is becoming increasingly apparent that a financial background is one of the best and fastest routes to the top: the financial men have more information and therefore more power than anyone else. But as an accountant moves up his outlook has to change. The middle-level accountant, for instance, is dealing with specific bookkeeping techniques, particular controls; but the financial director is more involved in risk-taking, gauging markets, allocating resources. It may be that little in his previous experience has prepared him for this new role and advanced management training at a business school or elsewhere may be required.

Prompt information for tighter control

Plastow's method of financial control is his greatest pride. Plastow, managing director of Rolls Royce Motors, says: 'Within four working days of the end of the four-week financial period the group financial director has a view not only of group sales but our snap report on profit. And within ten working days the main operating divisions have their full management accounts. I don't think you'll find many companies of our type that can do that.'

Plastow reckons that his control system explains why Rolls Royce emerged from the oil crisis worried but relatively unscathed. 'We've had the system going for the last five years and thank goodness we did.' *Plastow thinks that the successful leader has to learn to think money – to put a financial value onto objects and activities – because this tightens up his control of operations.* For instance, it tells him whether a particular action will help to achieve a turnover target or a particular percentage return on investment. 'The important thing is to get away from the naive concept that something must be done regardless of cost. Engineers are notoriously bad at finance. They tend to feel there is an intrinsic value in a thing regardless of its market value.'

As Plastow's words imply, divisional or organisational leaders need to combine the warmth of the natural motivator with the steely unsentimentality of the accountant. An eye for accounts is even more important, in a sense, than an eye for sales because a penny saved is pure profit whereas extra sales mean extra costs – or even overall losses. A General Motors executive says: 'The guy who takes a nickel out of a switch around here is a hero'. At du Pont too, hard-nosed cost and profit controls are imposed on each of the firm's operations. The firm now balances its accounts *every day* – president Meyerson insists on having a daily working profit and loss. And for the first time in its history the firm now has an inside auditor who frequently pulls unannounced audits on departments.

Applying the controls

One financial director attributes the success of his company to financial know-how. 'For most companies, cost-cutting is a sometime thing – done aggressively when business is sour, neglected when business turns up. Here, it's almost a religion.' This man reckons that the secret of good financial control is, quite simply, a matter of cutting costs to the bone and ensuring that the company has always got cash in hand to meet its management targets.

He makes the point: 'I can make more money in ten minutes on the telephone than the sales manager can make in ten months on the road, and I cost less'.

One way of making department heads more cost-and-profit conscious is to provide them with regular operating results. In a furniture-making factory, each department head receives a complete breakdown of his product sales figures showing the various cost elements involved. Budget figures are sent to regional sales managers to show them where improvements must be made. In another company, all managers receive a complete breakdown of all the company's activities which shows sales of different products and various costs involved in administrative overheads, maintenance, advertising, and so on.

In some companies the board itself applies the controls, elsewhere the job is delegated to management. In one company all facets of the business, including all purchases and expenditures, come before the board – typically at monthly intervals. At the year end, the board's audit committee can probe whether the hard financial facts square with management's account of progress being made. Budgets and projects can be checked and any improper practices rooted out and exposed.

Technical leaders

The computer and systems analysis have created a different breed of leader – one who adds a technical element to managerial control. Managers are going to have to get used to working with these technical leaders in solving their problems – just as the technical men are having to apply their specialisations to management problems. Arguably, the leader in modern industry must develop his numerical skills so that he can at least understand and make use of such control aids as linear programming, network analysis, forecasting techniques, simulation, and so on.

But the golden rule when setting up any information and control system is to keep it simple and flexible enough to be capable of quick and easy adjustment as the environment changes. For most organisations are in a constant state of flux because of changes in production methods, market conditions, and so on; and large, complicated, unwieldy systems are liable to become obsolete. So :

1   Keep the system simple.
2   Keep it flexible and capable of rapid adjustment.
3   Choke off unnecessary paperwork.

All this adds up to a three-point plan for tightening up your managerial control and improving the quality of your leadership. But in many large companies the control machinery works very slowly. Hacket has pointed to the 'increasing number of cases in which the managements of large well regarded companies face financial emergencies because their control systems detected serious problems only after they had reached crisis proportions' [10.2]. Why does this breakdown of control occur?

Control information

In a very small company the top man can monitor all aspects directly. He looks out of the window and can see for himself that deliveries are going out on time. He walks round the machine shop and sees for himself that the workforce is busy. But in a large company of, say, more than 500 employees, direct control of all aspects becomes impossible and he has to rely on intermediaries and on written reports. Thus in a large company, the *quality* of the information or 'feedback' received by senior management determines the quality of the control which they are able to exercise.

A useful comparison is the study of self-controlled machines in the field of cybernetics. The only way to control the machine is to feed back information about what it has just done and in such a way that this affects what the machine does next. Once the engineers have got this information system right, the machine can control itself, keeping temperatures or speeds within certain limits, homing in on a target, or, in the case of a business enterprise, achieving its objectives.

Leaders rely on accurate information for effective control. The general manager of a large jute mill in Bangladesh told me that in maintaining control of an organisation of 6,000 employees he relies heavily on a comprehensive daily report. Under the old system, he used to receive four reports every day from production, accounts, the labour office and quality control. These contained substantially the same information about man-hours, absenteeism, production, and so on. Departments were collecting some information independently then obtaining the rest from each other, so that they could prepare their daily reports. So the general manager made a management accountant responsible for screening and collating all incoming information and sending a single, condensed and accurate report to the general manager.

At Proctor and Gamble in the sixties, feedback information showed clearly that there were too many products for management to effectively control. The information made it clear that the company was failing to effectively schedule all the brand promotions or to sell all the brands. A grocer, it seemed, simply wouldn't stand a list that long – a fact reflected in the sales graphs of many products which had a depressing droop. Introducing new products was proving equally tough.

The reports told a depressing tale – but they allowed the company to decide on the necessary corrective action. When the group was split into two separate, more manageable units, the increased volume and efficiency more than offset the added cost of having a second sales force.

In assessing the control information that reaches him, the manager should be careful to distinguish between truly accurate facts and figures, and apparently accurate figures. A list of precise, detailed figures purporting to show output levels by department, say, or by product group, may appear accurate enough .But probe the reality behind the figures and you may find that they are based on somebody's subjective assessment or wrong assumptions, or on incorrect data. As one manager sourly remarked : 'People tell bosses the story they think they want to hear'.

Operating reports

Many leaders in large organisations rely heavily on reports to help them check on progress and spot problems. A chief executive reports : 'Every month we have a report on research and development, broken down by project, showing the amount of money spent so far and the total estimated to complete the project'. Another chief executive receives a monthly capital expenditure report. This shows the amount spent and the amount committed compared with the budget.

Like many other large companies, Westinghouse maintains control of numerous varied activities and projects by means of monthly operating reports. These provide a kind of built-in alarm system, the company claims, and allow continual monitoring of all parts of the company by top leadership. An additional measure of control comes from having divisional managers operate within budgets and other constraints prescribed by top management.

The control function is a follow-up to planning and target-setting. It consists of continuous checks on current performance to determine if planned targets are being achieved. Fayol pointed out that control consists of 'verifying whether everything occurs in conformity with the plans adopted, the instructions issued and principles established'. The main purpose of control is to discover errors, lapses and weaknesses as they occur, or as soon as possible, so that they can be corrected and steps can be taken to prevent them recurring.

According to management writers, the fundamental control process consists of :
1 Setting plans or performance standards.
2 Measuring performance against these.
3 Correcting any deviations and establishing further controls to prevent their recurrence.

This three-stage process involves getting information about output levels, quality of products, expenses and costs of materials, overheads and inventories, and so on. It also creates a need for information about worker performance and attitude, cash flow, manning levels, and so on – covering all aspects of the business. Information is the key to effective control.

One problem is that many organisations have a weak data base. In many cases, information about past events and decisions is not retained or, when retained, is difficult to retrieve; thus, information about current activities is scant.

Accuracy essential

Another problem is that information systems tend to become outdated very quickly as the technology, the organisation or markets change. Thus the information received by management may be accurate but largely irrelevant to the present situation and production or industrial relations crises may develop with management unaware that problems even exist. Thus constant reviews are needed. In a large engineering company, department heads are required to define their information needs in detail once a year. This forces the department head to riff through old files, surveying the kind of information he has been sending and receiving, and asking himself and other people in the department : 'Was this information really necessary to me or anyone else? What control problems were caused because of inadequate information – or lack of information? Which information that I received was badly presented?' (Data processed to suit one department may be useless to another : for instance, accounts may require production information in cash terms, while production want the same information in physical units.)

The computer can provide extremely useful control information if this is presented appropriately, e.g. in the form of a selective print-out of key data, or as an image on the screen of a VDU. The key to useful computer-based information is, in many cases, the understanding that exists between the department head and the computer manager : do they understand each other's problems and information needs? Does the department head appreciate that the computer can only give answers to questions that are asked in a certain way? Does the computer manager understand what the operating responsibilities and problems of various departments actually are, and the kind of information required to help solve them? Would the provision of a crash course in basic computer technology help departments to make better use of the computer?

Control and coordination of people

Systems theory teaches that if one of the interlocking elements in the organisational network changes, then effects spread to some or all of the other elements. All parts of an organisation are interdependent. Changes in a manufacturing unit, say, may send shock waves crashing into sales, personnel, R&D and every other part of the organisation. Thus, the ability to control these effects as they spread is an important function of organisational leadership.

Control of this kind means keeping in touch with managers at lower levels, rigorously questioning their proposals and decisions to ensure that these fit in with overall company policy. This ensures that your own part of the organisation is consonant with the rest of the company. Actions by different units should be consistent with each other and should contribute to overall company objectives. Individual actions should serve a purpose, as defined in the company's stated business objectives.

Much of the time in a large company, the leader must act as a kind of chairman in a participatory system, coordinating other people's efforts, bringing them together to solve problems which none of them is capable of solving individually. In this way the leader helps to overcome the instinctive organisational torpor of many large companies. The law of organisational inertia states that anything that requires a coordinated effort of the organisation to get started is unlikely to get started.

In order to get people to solve problems, the leader needs to coordinate and conciliate, to suggest compromise solutions, to encourage people to work with each other. Thus the leader as controller is essentially the man at the centre, co-ordinating and regulating periperal group activity.

Multi-national companies

The large, multi-national company is particularly reliant on this kind of leadership. A former chairman of General Motors has said:

> If the South African assembly operation and its recently added manufacturing facilities are to function smoothly and efficiently, they must today receive a carefully controlled and coordinated flow of vehicle parts and components from West Germany, England, the US and even Australia. These must reach General Motors South Africa in the right volume and at the right time to allow an orderly scheduling of assembly without accumulation of excessive inventories.

Likert has referred to the linking-pin function of the leader. The large organisation can be controlled and coordinated successfully only if there are persons in each sub-group who link it to the larger organisation. When these linking pins function effectively, communication can flow smoothly up the structure – and control can flow down.

At Johnson and Johnson's factory at Camberley, management keeps in touch with production units via a chain of small meetings between, first, managers and foremen, secondly foremen and supervisors and, thirdly, supervisors and operatives. The system has proved its efficacy as a communication and control method time and time again. For instance, several years ago when Britain was working a three-day week because of the Arab oil embargo, it proved easy to keep the workforce posted daily about how things were going and what actions needed to be taken and management were getting feedback on problems almost as soon as they cropped up.

Liaison leadership

The industrial leader has been defined as somebody who maintains internal equilibrium in an organisation, for instance, by setting up shock-absorbing machinery like that created by Philip Morris, the American tobacco company. The company reduces the chances of in-fighting by promoting communication between different divisions. For instance, the New York-based marketing staff fly to Richmond, Virginia, every month to discuss common problems and strategies with production and R&D people. At Philip Morris, each division and each function always knows what the others want and what they are doing. R&D keeps its own liaison team in New York.

Lack of liaison between functions can create chaos. For instance, in a company making high-class tableware, lack of liaison between production and marketing led to order promises being made by the sales force which could not be met on the shop-floor. A manager in the company says: 'The problem was one of leadership, not capacity. The orders could have been met if someone had only thought of bringing the two sides together.'

As Rice points out, leadership is required in an organisation to 'control the internal and confused strivings of its members and to relate them to the external environment' [3.16]. (This important aspect of control is considered more fully in Chapter 8.) Barnard has made substantially the same point: 'Survival depends on two general factors, first, the effectiveness of the system of governance with respect to the external relation of the organisation and, secondly, its internal efficiency' [3.3] (which depends largely on coordination and control).

Sometimes, adopting a multi-plant manufacturing policy encourages firmer control at each plant (besides allowing transport costs to be slashed). Multiple plants make a lot of sense if:

1   The product is heavy or bulky.
2   The markets served are spread out across widely separated regions.
3   The company is too big anyway to allow adequate control by a single management.

The loss of control that can occur when a company expands on a single site was demonstrated when an appliance manufacturer diversified the product range. This meant more work yet, without calculating the effect on material supplies and flow, the company decided not to decentralise operations. But as they expanded, the volume of metal moving through the metal-working increased as did the choas as order processing and deliveries got badly fouled up.

Controlling from a distance

Many successful leaders maintain control over day-to-day operations by involving themselves in operating details on a strictly selective basis. They may involve themselves in certain key activities such as production control or employee communication. But they also know when to stand back and let other people do the controlling.

At General Electric, for instance, department heads are given a lot of responsibility and a lot of freedom to hire, fire, set prices, decide on the products they want to push, and so on. But in return they must account to the top leadership for their stewardship. They are judged largely by profits. High profits bring rewards – fat salaries and bonuses. Failure brings punishment (firing is a frequent penalty). Thus top management uses the management doctrine of accountability as a means of exercising control – from a distance.

At Lanvin, president Schmidt exercises control over the departments by requiring each department head to submit a monthly report on progress and problems and suggested solutions. The managers are required to draw attention to any omissions and explain why they occurred, report on the staff situation, production, and so on. Schmidt finds that by reading these monthly reports he keeps in touch with everything that is going on throughout the company.

Control-selective involvement

As these cases suggest, keeping track of everything does not mean immersing oneself in day-to-day operations – although getting involved in details from time to time is a convenient and easy way of keeping in touch. As one manager puts it : 'If you sit at your desk all the time your glasses fog up'.

The managing director of a food-processing company arranges a series of visits to plants in the period immediately before the Annual General Meeting. Because of this fact-finding tour he is completely *au fait* with problems and progress by the time of the AGM. Some American companies make sure that board members at least know what the factories and their managers look like by rotating board meetings among cities where major plants are located.

Marks and Spencer chairman Sir Marcus Sieff believes that leaders must give meticulous attention to detail when particular problems crop up. Recently, for instance, when a friend noticed that a button popped off his St Michael shirt, Sir Marcus himself traced the cause back to a manufacturer's defective needle. One chief executive says: 'If somebody writes in with a complaint I never leave it till it has been followed right the way through. It is astounding what this method will reveal.' He receives few complaints but says it is vital to act on those few because for every customer who complains there may be hundreds who don't. In another company, every letter of complaint is considered at the weekly executive committee meeting, and the managing director makes a point of seeing personally all retailers who make a complaint.

Control via delegation

When a journalist asked Sir Charles Curran, Director-General of the British Broadcasting Corporation, if the job of controlling an organisation with 25,000 employees was too much for one man, he said: 'If you say 25,000 people, then it sounds impossible. But in fact I am dealing with very many fewer.' Curran believes that the art of controlling a large organisation is to 'reduce to a reasonable minimum the number of people with whom you have to deal directly . . . It is by delegation to a satisfactory number of people that you can run a big organisation.'

As Curran's words imply, delegation allows the manager to keep track of what is going on without having to do the work himself. The general manager of an electronic equipment factory says: 'The trick is to use delegation to reduce demands on your own time yet still keep on top of every job'. But, he adds, the manager cannot keep on top of delegated jobs if he remains a mere onlooker: the manager who turns over a job to a subordinate *carte blanche* is always in danger of losing control of the outcome. 'If the subordinate makes a mess of it, *I'm* responsible – *I've* got to answer to the board.'

When jobs are delegated, some sort of supervision by the boss is essential. In the case of a diffident or inexperienced subordinate, for instance, the boss may have to put pressure on other people in the organisation to ensure that they will cooperate with the junior man and he may have to supervise every phase of the assignment. If the job is given to a more confident and experienced man, supervision might mean making a periodic audit of progress. Whatever the precise circumstances, some degree of supervision and control is essential.

Management consultant Hague has found that it usually pays to delegate duties one by one, as the need arises, instead of together on a sink-or-swim basis. This allows each new assignment to be properly discussed and assessed, so that gradually the subordinate grows in confidence and experience.

Reports on progress

Hague suggests that the leader should list the varied problems in the subordinate's job that are likely to crop up and that these should be classified under three headings:

1   Subordinate to take action as he thinks fit.
2   Subordinate to take action, but to tell boss about it.
3   Subordinate to ask the boss before taking action.

When giving assignments, it is important to agree on a completion date and to fix times – weekly meetings, say – for reporting on progress. This helps to ensure that projects which are enthusiastically started don't just fade away. According to one senior executive, the leader can stay on top of delegated jobs by taking the following actions:

1   Explain the assignment to the subordinate and ask for a report in writing with his plan of action. This forces the subordinate to focus his thinking and to start thinking about ways and means.
2   Ask the subordinate for periodic progress reports, with product performance statistics, detailed costs and expenses, etc.
3   Arrange regular interviews with the subordinate to discuss problems arising and how the subordinate is dealing with them.
4   Make regular personal checks on the work being done. This shows that the boss is genuinely interested and enables him to make constructive hints and comments.

Having to present intentions and results to his boss periodically applies salutary pressure on the complacent subordinate manager to tighten up controls within his *own* area of command. That is why Henry Ford encourages his own boss – the board – to criticise him: 'I have to talk with the board about my performance, whether I'm emphasising the right things. I've always told them quite openly that if the time ever comes when I should step down, they ought to tell me.'

11

*'Effective leaders take the important decisions
and delegate the rest.'*

Henry Ford

Decision-making

Today, problems no longer need to be solved on the basis of hunch, precedent or self-interest, for new tools of prediction and control (statistical analysis, operations research, etc.) are available which are capable of turning problem-solving into a precise science. Even if a leader does not understand the new techniques there is usually somebody in the organisation who does. Clearly, decisions about such matters as stock-control, forecasting, or planning should be taken after consultation with people who have the relevant quantitative skills.

The growing complexity of business problems has coincided with the development of technical tools of handling them. Information can be assembled and processed today on a scale never possible before. The computer can take the guesswork out of decisions by producing masses of information at the right time. By making use of such tools via the appropriate specialists, the leader can make far better decisions. It would sharpen the leader's decision-making skills to attend even a crash course on basic computer technology so that he understands the strengths and weaknesses of this valuable resource and the kind of questions it likes to receive. Before any management information system is installed, the managers for whom it is intended should be trained to use and control it.

Equally, the members of the computer department would benefit from training. A short course on how to assess the information needs of managers would be invaluable and would, no doubt, lead to the provision of more relevant information, and therefore better solutions. As many companies have found, computer departments have to be trained to translate the results of their searches into the language of the executive, i.e. language that sets forth simply and clearly the values, effectiveness and costs of alternative courses of action.

As several studies of managerial work have shown, managers tend to base their decisions on 'soft' information derived from gossip and hearsay in meetings, telephone calls and face-to-face encounters, as opposed to 'hard' information of a more systematic kind that is provided by management information systems. Thus a relatively small investment in training managers to make better use of the MIS could yield big returns in the shape of sounder decisions.

In a factory, expensive labour gets the back-up it needs in the form of efficient machinery, automatic conveyors, and so on. Modern decision-makers need back-up too – management information systems, adequate data, tried and tested decision-making models, competent secretarial and administrative support. There are new management tools for making investment decisions – and executive leaders should be aware of them. For instance, a management information system might give a simulation model of a company which could simulate the effects of making this or that investment policy.

The traditional skills of leadership – the ability to make quick daring decisions, the playing of 'hunches', and so on – are becoming less relevant in modern business as new skills and tools emerge. More and more decisions are being made by rational calculation and the logical assessment of risk-reward ratios. For example, decisions about allocating large sums of capital to various projects can be improved by the use of sophisticated mathematical techniques or models.

Avoiding indecision

While a rational decision-making system may not guarantee good decisions, at least it helps the executive to avoid indecision by telling him where to begin and how to proceed. (It is often tempting to avoid taking a decision because this also means avoiding the possibility of failure.)

Bales has studied hundreds of decision-making meetings and finds that a 'natural' system often evolves, with the group working through three distinct stages of the decision-making process:

1 Clarification (what is the problem?).
2 Evaluation (how do we feel about it?).
3 Decision (what are we going to do about it?).

This is remarkably close to the 'classical' model used by decision-makers everywhere:

1 Define objectives.
2 Collect all the pertinent information.
3 Work out alternative solutions.
4 Screen these alternatives.
5 Decide, and set up controls to prevent failure [11.1].

The broad principles of structured decision-making were set down

with enduring clarity by Dewey as long ago as 1910 in *How We Think*.
Dewey's deceptively simple questions for decision-makers were:
1   What is the problem?
2   What are the alternatives?
3   Which alternative is best?

The four-stage method

Problems facing managers vary according to the extent to which they are
well structured and can be precisely solved:

PROGRAMMABLE   UNPROGRAMMABLE

Inventory   New products
levels   division

However, the outcome of decision-making meetings, even those dealing
with unprogrammable decisions, can be rendered less fortuitous by
developing the 'classical' method and utilising this simple strategy, which
breaks the meeting into four distinct stages:
1   Study the problem.
2   Generate alternatives.
3   Evaluate the alternatives.
4   Make the decision and forecast the outcome.
    When the problem is complex, dealing with each stage in a separate
meeting can add to the tidiness of the discussion. The kind of breakdown
suggested above follows the 'natural' contours of development in a meeting. Several investigators have found that in most meetings there is a
natural progression from much information in the first third to much
opinion in the middle third and to many suggested solutions in the final
third.
    The four-stage approach is useful because the four stages involve quite
different kinds of intellectual activity:
1   Analysis (studying the problem).
2   Imagination and creativity (generating alternatives).
3   Criticism (evaluating alternatives).
4   Judgement (making the decision).
All four activities enter into every decision-making meeting but, usually
in a confused and tangled way. The idea of the four-stage strategy is to
disentangle the separate activities, to pick out and focus on each one in
turn and in a logical sequence. Perhaps such 'rational' procedures should
be applied more systematically and with greater care in major matters
than in minor ones.
    Clearly, the first stage of problem-definition is critical to the success
of the whole process. This stage involves collecting information from

records, the experience of individuals, and so on, and evaluating the true nature of the problem in the light of this information. Maier (1962) has shown that better decisions are often produced if the discussion moves away from conflict about alternatives and moves towards a careful assessment of what the problem actually is.

Jury-of-executive-opinion

The 'Delphic technique', or jury-of-executive-opinion, is a quick and simple method of making sound decisions concerning very uncertain events – such as the likely demand for completely new products or services. Many elements in the projection of future developments are difficult or impossible to quantify, and elaborate statistical or mathematical forecasting techniques can be expensive and inaccurate.

The method, originally developed by the Rand Corporation, consists of bringing together executives from a variety of functional areas and levels so as to ensure a wide spectrum of experience and opinion, and combining and averaging their views about the item to be forecast.

Shortly before Forsythe's book, *The Shepherd,* was published in 1975, Hutchinsons asked a panel of carefully chosen 'experts' (booksellers, critics, readers, publishing and sales executives), to forecast likely demand. They were given copies of the manuscript and the proposed cover design. The publishers themselves had been considering a print order of 35,000, but as a result of the panel's more optimistic forecasts they increased the print-run to 55,000. As it turned out, the panel was right: over 50,000 copies were sold in the first six months. The total expenses of the exercise – £400 – were easily justified by the results.

Inter-related decisions

In his role as resource allocator, the leader must authorise the important decisions of his unit before they can be implemented. By retaining this power the leader ensures that decisions are inter-related and support each other. The alternative to co-ordinated decision-making is disjoined organisation.

In a sense, the leader cannot make effective decisions unless he knows what the overriding *objectives* of decisions taken in the organisation actually are. Thus, decisions may be taken with the aim of cutting costs, boosting profits, increasing volumes or margins, achieving 'cost-effectiveness', and so on. *But over and above each individual decision there should be some controlling strategy. Without it, how can the effectiveness of decisions be measured?*

It is the leader's responsibility to ensure that specialised decisions do not weaken or confuse the distinctive identity and purpose of the organisation. A way of co-ordinating decisions made in different parts of the organisation is to hold frequent inter-departmental meetings. These can help to ensure that all departments move in the same direction, i.e. towards corporate goals. Think of the range and variety of ideas that can be brought to bear on company problems when people from different departments sit round the same table. The enticing possibilities prompt one company to hold weekly meetings of department heads to review sales figures. The meetings provide guidelines for each department's activities in the following week : each meeting produces an action-set of minutes with the department that is required to take action named in the margin.

A case could even be made out for allowing managers from other parts of the organisation to share in the decision-making in your own department, for major decisions taken by the department will probably affect all the others. For instance, a decision about advertising policy will affect the basic demand and supply pattern in the company and this, in turn, affects all the other departments. Thus, departmental decisions need to be in harmony with the rest of the organisation.

The 'impact' of decisions

You can't take action to eliminate a problem in one department without triggering off effects in other departments, some of which those departments may not be geared to absorb.

> There is danger in trying to pull any one part or function of an organisation a long way ahead of the remainder, since this can produce strain. The modernisation of the part . . . is likely to be eroded by the links it has with the remainder [7.5].

Effective departmental decisions imply having a clear understanding of what all the other departments are thinking. In a conservative organisation, the leader may have to adopt the softly-softly approach to decision-making and introduce change gradually, piece-by-piece, so that no single decision implies a sudden acceleration or change of direction.

The leader has to know which decisions it is *possible* to make. How much money is available? Will the decision be acceptable to the people who will be affected by it? Will the decision be acceptable to the organisation? By taking account of such matters, the leader helps to ensure that decisions which are taken are successfully implemented.

The time-span of decisions

One of the basic skills of decision-making is to involve people from the levels most appropriate to deal with the problem. Generally, the level should vary according to the time-span of the decisions to be made.

1   *Long-term strategic decisions,* such as whether to diversify or to break into new markets, should be made by senior executives, because only senior men would have the experience and the over-view to grasp the financial implications and to overcome the inherent uncertainty of this type of decision-making.

2   *Medium-term managerial decisions,* such as what kind of machinery to purchase or how to restructure a department. Middle managers should be involved in this kind of decision. They involve less uncertainty and risk; less is at stake as far as the company is concerned; more attention to technical or administrative detail is required.

3   *Day-to-day operating decisions,* such as how to deal with a specific discipline or production problem. Supervisory or junior managerial staff should be involved because only people of this level have the detailed administrative or technical know-how needed to deal with the problem.

When people from relatively low levels are given high-level problems to solve, Parkinson's law of triviality tends to operate : time spent in making the decision is inversely proportional to its importance. I've heard of £50,000 being voted for a new project after ten minutes' brisk opinion-giving – and of a meeting which decided where to site a new coffee machine only after ninety minutes' solemn discussion.

Generally, the *number* of decisions made varies with the level of the leader. At top level, for instance, the leader's contribution to the organisation may turn on the two or three critical strategic decisions that he takes during the year – whether or not to move into a new market, say, or produce a new range of products. Mere speed and frequency in reaching decisions may have little relevance at this level. But leaders at lower levels in the hierarchy generally have to be adept at taking many quick decisions on inadequate information.

High-quality information

High-quality information is the essential raw material from which good decisions emerge. High-quality information is accurate, timely, clear and relevant to the problem. The quality of information available depends partly on the efficiency of the management information system, partly on the decision-maker himself : does he know the kind of information that is needed and where to obtain it? When assembling information it is important to ask the right questions and to go to the people who can answer them – to the appropriate level and to the right experts. The knack required is to pinpoint the problem by asking the right questions so that you get exactly the facts you require.

Many leaders learn from experience which information sources are reliable and use these sources more than others. Roosevelt, for instance, checked and balanced information from official sources against information from a number of unofficial sources. 'He would call you in', one of his aides has said, 'and he'd ask you to get the story on some complicated business, and you'd come back after a couple of days of hard labour and present the juicy morsel you'd uncovered under a stone somewhere, and *then* you'd find out he knew all about it along with something else you *didn't* know. Where he got this information from he wouldn't mention' [11.2].

If the information needed for decisions is unreliable or taking too long to come in, it might make sense to consider re-styling the reporting system – for instance, more exception-reports and fewer regular, routine reports. Alternatively, why not transfer the responsibility for information gathering to another section or individual?

One executive makes a practice of setting several subordinates to work independently of each other – and unknown to each other – to collect the same body of information. The results are then carefully compared. 'In this way I get an all-round look at the problem and can immediately see any contradictions or inconsistencies'. Such methods sound somewhat devious, but at least they ensure that wide-ranging, reliable information is available for problem-solving.

How much information is enough?

When information available is inadequate – when the problem has been insufficiently researched – decisions tend to be made in very broad, general terms. On the other hand, too many undigested facts can change the decision-maker into a Hamlet paralysed by indecision. In any case, it is hardly ever possible to assemble enough information to remove *all* doubts about a decision. The moral is clear: don't force the decision-makers to read themselves to death just to find out what the problem is. Perhaps one of the basic tests of efficiency is *how little* information an executive or committee needs to make good decisions.

Of course, some decision-makers require more information than others – for instance, those dealing with complex technical problems. And some executives are temperamentally more cautious than others and demand more information as a basis for their decisions. High-risk decision-makers make their decisions as soon as they have enough information to indicate a fair chance of correctness. Conservative decision-makers wait until they have enough information to indicate a very good chance of correctness.

A good way of ensuring that members of decision-making committees are getting up-to-date information is to invite an expert to attend the meeting so that he can brief members on the problem and answer their questions. Specialist officers attend local government committee meetings to provide up-to-date information and professional advice.

A survey of 166 senior managers by Heller, reported in *Managerial Decision-making,* shows that the most frequently used method of making decisions is for a manager to consult with subordinates and then to make the decision himself. The survey also reveals that the more important a decision is, the more likely that it will be made by managerial diktat.

Because they are clever enough and careful enough, some autocratic executives manage to rule their empires by 'democratic' leadership methods. For instance, according to Nixon, President Eisenhower used his White House subordinates to work on presidential problems. They did the spadework, put in the long hours of analysis and argument. But once they had drawn up their reports and made their recommendations the President took over and made sure that he alone took the decision [11.3].

Many senior executives operate in this way, using discussion and consultation not in the interests of democracy but in the interests of orderly government. One executive reports: 'Frankly I use meetings as a kind of sounding board for thinking my problems out loud. I never feel bound by their recommendations'. This manager, like many others, uses joint discussion not as a device for power-sharing but as a weapon for attaining his own ends. Some managers see staff discussions as an opportunity to sell proposals, or to justify decisions they have already taken, or to win cooperation in putting those decisions into effect. Important decisions are extremely difficult to carry out properly in the absence of widespread support.

The autocrat may judge the success of meetings by how quickly and easily he was able to sell his proposals to the other participants. And sometimes, if he is clever enough, they may think they are selling his proposals to *him.* Those who out-manoeuvre their colleagues in this way can usually rationalise their tactics to themselves by believing that it is all for the general good and in the interests of the company that their proposals and ideas should win.

Pelz found that optimum performance is associated with:
1   Consulting some colleagues whose orientation differs from one's own – who challenge one's ideas and point out shortcomings.
2   Consulting some colleagues who share one's orientation – who support and develop one's ideas.

The advantage of democratic discussion is that the manager gets the benefit of both kinds of consultation – and the result is better decisions.

Irrational decisions

One divisional head believes that 'effective leaders don't make a lot of decisions. They take the important ones and delegate the rest.' And he adds: 'I try not to get involved in operational decisions. Each of my

subordinates knows the areas in which he's expected to take the decisions
– and the decisions that he's expected to refer to me.'

This kind of working arrangement is admirable. But how many of the decisions that are taken by the leaders themselves are the result of what Sir David Kelly has described as 'casual unreasoning action by ordinary men in positions of extraordinary power?'.

President Kennedy once called a meeting to decide whether or not to veto a measure by Congress to protect domestic sugar producers against foreign competition. The State Department representative explained why he favoured a veto. Then the Secretary of Agriculture said why he supported Congress. Kennedy was undecided, and said he'd like to hear what Hubert Humphrey thought. Humphrey was quickly brought into the meeting by phone. His voice crackled over the wire. Kennedy put the phone down, hesitated a moment, then said, 'I guess I'll let it go through'. It is amazing how many important decisions are taken in this casual way.

Even the kind of problems that get discussed in the first place may be determined by irrational motives. 'Choosing the new plant site', says systems consultant Dill, 'may take precedence over reorganising staff functions, not for logical or strategic reasons but because it is being pushed by the president . . . because a group of executives have decided it is a more interesting project to work one, or because the men who must supply the basic data for the staff reorganisation are already over-committed to other projects'.

Self-interest

Another brake on rational decision-making is self-interest. The departmental or functional representative usually can't afford to exercise his independent judgement. Or he may not be able to help seeing the problem in a coloured, lop-sided way. Perhaps the leader's particular contribution is to ensure that such distortions are neutralised by employing a rational decision-making method.

Sometimes an executive gets a reputation for being indecisive simply because he is unwilling to take what for the organisation would be quite acceptable risks. The unwillingness may have been created by long exposure to corporate control procedures which tend ultimately to bias managers against any decisions which might result in losses. Some executives say that they feel obliged to take decisions which have the effect of minimising risks to corporate investment.

Formal training in decision-making may not be much help to these executives, because trainers tend to deal with decision-making as if it were an entirely rational process and wholly a matter of impersonal methods and 'techniques'. Professor Harry Levinson, of the Harvard Business School, has pointed out that the greatest difficulty people have in making decisions is 'the fact that emotion makes it hard for them to see and deal with their problems objectively'.

Another limitation on the value of training is that in the open situation of real life, principles and correct methods get ignored and decisions are taken on the basis of hunch or precedent or rule of thumb, because there simply isn't time for a systematic approach. Thus many decisions are reached on the basis of inadequate or inconclusive data. Sometimes, of course, a snap decision can be better than a laboured assessment of all the alternatives: speed of decision-making is important in an environment where facts have an unnerving tendency to change their appearance overnight. But when the problem is big enough, time should be *made* available to ensure that a sound decision is taken. It takes time to make decisions in a rational, systematic way. But not as much time as it takes to unravel all the problems that build up as a result of over-hasty decisions.

Epilogue

What is an effective leader? In attempting to answer this seemingly simple question I have talked to scores of successful leaders from a wide range of business organisations; read the biographies of successful business leaders; studied the extensive literature on the subject – some of it, at any rate. Most of all, I have been interested in finding out what business leaders actually *do*, and in what they themselves have to say about leadership in management.

Reviewing the evidence, there seems to be widespread agreement that the successful leader in a business organisation is a manager or supervisor who possesses the personal qualities and skills needed to deal effectively with the major components of his or her job; and that the skills required cover five or six major areas:

1   First, and most important, the ability to weld a number of individuals into a cohesive and effective team.
2   Secondly – and closely connected with the first – the ability to motivate and inspire subordinates to achieve good results.
3   Face-to-face communication skills are considered much more important – especially at senior levels of leadership – than professional or technical competence.
4   The ability to formulate ambitious corporate or departmental goals, and to drive the organisation or unit towards them.
5   The ability to apply firm controls to production, labour and (at senior levels) cash-flow and budgeting.
6   Decision-making ability, which is often based on a correct choice of decision-making method.

Surprisingly, the leaders I met appeared to represent the full range of leadership styles, from autocratic to laissez-faire. Most of the autocratic leaders worked in relatively stable industries (with regard to markets and technology) such as heavy engineering, machine tools and motor manufacture; most of the 'democrats' worked in dynamic, fast-changing industries (notably the computer industry) or in 'creative organisations', e.g. a publishing company or an advertising agency. Clearly, the correct style of leadership for any particular situation depends largely on the nature of the work. For instance, mass production requires tight supervision and control – and a hard-line leadership style – because the job *has* to be done in a certain way.

All the leaders I met turned out to be extremely hard-working individuals who often gave the impression of playing a game that they very much wanted to win. Mostly they were 'proactive' rather than 'reactive' managers: initiators and opportunity-grabbers; more interested in change than in stability; leaders as opposed to administrators.

References

1.1 Charles Burck, 'A group profile of the *Fortune 500* chief executive', *Fortune* (May 1976).

1.2 F. Sturdivant and R. Adler, 'Executive origins', *Harvard Business Review*, p130 (November/December 1976).

1.3 See *Newsweek*, pp56-68 (21 June 1976).

1.4 M. D. Cohen and J. G. March, *Leadership and ambiguity*, McGraw-Hill (1974).

1.5 D. G. Clark, 'The industrial manager', in *Industrial Society* (D. Pym, Editor), pp253-4, Pelican (1968).

1.6 George Copeman, *The chief executive*, Leviathan House (1971).

1.7 Henry Mintzberg, *The nature of managerial work*, Harper (1973).

1.8 Douglas McGregor, *The human side of enterprise*, McGraw Hill (1960).

1.9 J. C. Wofford, 'Factor analysis of managerial behaviour variables', *Journal of Applied Psychology*, Vol. 54, pp169-73 (1970).

1.10 F. E. Fiedler, *A Theory of Leadership Effectiveness*, McGraw-Hill (1967).

1.11 W. Schutz, *FIRO (Fundamental interpersonal relations orientation)*, Rinehart (1958).

1.12 W. Bennis, *The unconscious conspiracy*, AMA (1976).

1.13 C. A. Gibb, in *Leadership: selected readings*, p11, Penguin (1969).

1.14 G. Lippitt, 'What do we know about leaders?', *NEA Journal*, p556 (December 1955).

1.15 D. McClelland and D. Burnham, 'Power is the great motivator', *Harvard Business Review* (March-April 1976).

1.16 J. and D. Rawls, 'Towards better selection and placement of strategic managers', in H. I. Ansoff *et al* (Editors), *From strategic planning to strategic management,* John Wiley (1976).

1.17 Ralph Lewis, 'Choosing and using outside directors,' *Harvard Business Review* (July-August 1974).

1.18 See Joseph Bailey, 'Clues for success in the president's job', *ibid.* (May-June 1967).

1.19 D. Clifford, 'Thriving in a recession', *ibid.* (July-August 1977).

1.20 See M. Maccoby, *The gamesman: the new corporate leaders,* Simon & Schuster (1977).

1.21 Paul Brouwer, 'The power to see ourselves' in E. Bursk and T. Blodgett (Editors), *Developing executive leaders,* Harvard University Press (1971).

1.22 C. Gosselin, 'Why girls go for men at the top', *Chief Executive,* p32 (November 1977).

1.23 See Peter Cohen, *The gospel according to the Harvard Business School,* Doubleday (1973).

1.24 See J. and J. Veroff, 'Reconsideration of a measure of power motivation', *Psychological Bulletin,* Vol. 78, pp279-91 (1972).

1.25 J. A. C. Brown, *The social psychology of industry,* p239, Penguin (1954).

1.26 J. R. P. French and B. Raven, 'The bases of social power', in D. Cartwright and A. Zander (Editors), *Group Dynamics: research and theory,* Harper (1968).

2.1 A. M. Schlesinger, *The coming of the new deal,* p157, Houghton Mifflin (1959).

2.2 A. Porter, 'Books and the bramble bush', *Advanced Management,* pp20-1 (December 1962).

2.3 R. M. Belbin, B. R. Aston and R. D. Motram, 'Building effective management teams', *Journal of General Management,* p23 (Spring 1976).

2.4 Bruce Harriman, 'Up and down the communications ladder', *Harvard Business Review,* p148 (September/October 1975).

2.5 See V. H. Vroom, *Some personality determinants of the effects of participation,* Prentice-Hall (1960).

2.6 Harry Levinson, 'Who is to blame for maladaptive managers?', in E. Bursk and T. Blodgett (Editors), *op. cit.*

2.7 A. Zaleznik, *Human dilemmas of leadership,* Harper (1966).

2.8 H. Guetzkow and R. Stogdill, *Studies in naval leadership,* Carnegie Press (1964).

2.9 J. J. Morse and J. W. Lorsch, 'Beyond Theory X', *Harvard Business Review,* pp61-8 (May-June 1970).

2.10 C. Argyris, *Interpersonal competence and organisational effectiveness,* p81, Irwin-Dorsey (1962).

3.1 H. I. Ansoff, 'The concept of strategic management', *Journal of Business Policy,* Vol. 2(4), p2 (1972).

3.2 Bryan Wilson, *The noble savages,* Quantum Books (1975).
3.3 Chester Barnard, *Organisation and management,* pp240-1, Harvard University Press (1956).
3.4 See A. Zaleznik, 'Managerial behaviour and interpersonal competence', *Behavioural Science,* pp156-66 (April 1964).
3.5 M. D. Cohen and J. G. March, *op. cit.,* p148.
3.6 P. Selznick, *Leadership in administration,* Harper (1957).
3.7 M. Hanan, 'Venturing corporations – think small to stay strong', *Harvard Business Review* (May-June 1976).
3.8 See A. D. Chandler, *Strategy and structure,* MIT Press (1962).
3.9 C. Wright Mills, *White Collar,* p260, Oxford University Press (1951).
3.10 William Whyte, *The organisation man,* p152, Simon and Schuster (1956).
3.11 Donald Schol, 'Champions for radical new inventions', *Harvard Business Review* (March-April 1963).
3.12 W. Bennis, *op. cit.,* p26-7.
3.13 H. Boettinger, 'Is management really an art?' *Harvard Business Review,* p55 (January-February 1976).
3.14 David McClelland, *The inner experience,* Irvington Publishers (1975).
3.15 C. A. Gibb in *Leadership: selected readings,* p10, Penguin (1969).
3.16 A. K. Rice, *Learning for leadership,* Tavistock (1965).
3.17 C. Bonington, *Everest the hard way,* p30-1, Random (1977).
3.18 See 'A dollop of good, gutsy Maine business sense', *Fortune,* p27 (July 1976).
3.19 See J. Eastlach and P. McDonald, 'CEO's role in corporate growth', *Harvard Business Review* (May-June 1970).
3.20 F. Fiedler, *Theory of leadership effectiveness,* McGraw-Hill (1967).
3.21 V. A. Nazarevsky, 'A Soviet economist looks at US business', *Harvard Business Review,* p53 (May-June 1974).
3.22 *Third Report from the Select Committee on Science and Technology,* HMSO (1976).
3.23 H. Mintzberg, 'The manager's job: fact and folklore', *Harvard Business Review,* p51 (July-August 1975).
3.24 See C. Jones, 'The money value of time', *Harvard Business Review,* p29 (July-August 1968).

4.1 P. Selznick, *op. cit.,* p107.
4.2 Arthur M. Louis, 'An awesome mind was Fletcher Byrom's secret weapon', *Fortune,* p188 (July 1976).
4.3 A. Bavelas, 'Leadership: man and function', *Administrative Science Quarterly,* No. 4, pp491-8 (March 1960).
4.4 Donald Clifford, *op. cit.,* p63.
4.5 F. Wittnebert, 'Big equals less profitable', *Harvard Business Review,* p20 (March-April 1975).

226   4.6   G. Ingham, *Size of industrial organisation and worker participation*, p79, Cambridge University Press (1970).

5.1   R. House, 'A path goal theory of leadership effectiveness', *Administrative Science Quarterly*, Vol. 16 (December 1971).

5.2   K. C. F. Lathrope, 'Behavioural implications of management training' in J. Humble (Editor), *Improving the performance of the experienced manager*, McGraw-Hill (1973).

5.3   H. Hague, *Executive self-development*, Macmillan (1974).

5.4   R. Revans, *Developing effective managers*, Longman (1971).

5.5   For a fuller account of the management performance system, see M. Beer and R. Ruh, 'Employee growth through performance management', *Harvard Business Review*, pp59-66 (July-August 1976).

5.6   F. Fiedler, *op. cit.*, p254.

5.7   J. Adair, *Action-centred leadership*, McGraw-Hill (1973).

5.8   Robert Schrank, 'Two women, three men on a raft', *Harvard Business Review*, p101, May-June 1977.

5.9   A. Zaleznik, 'Managers and leaders: are they different?', *ibid.*, p76 (May-June 1977).

6.1   A. Zander, 'Team spirit v. the individual achiever', *Psychology Today*, p67 (November 1974).

6.2   R. R. Blake and J. S. Mouton, *The Managerial Grid*, Gulf Publishing (1964).

7.1   M. Anshen, 'The management of ideas' in E. Bursk and T. Blodgett, *op. cit.*, p45.

7.2   Kenneth Michel, 'Design of an intrafirm management development programme for strategic management' in H. I. Ansoff, *op. cit.*, p247.

7.3   Robert Heller, *The once and future manager*, p75, Associated Business Programmes (1976).

7.4   Antony Jay, *Corporation Man*, p129, Jonathan Cape (1972).

7.5   Graham Tarr, *The management of problem-solving*, Macmillan (1973).

7.6   Harry Levinson, *The exceptional executive*, p116, Harvard University Press (1968).

7.7   D. Norburn and P. Grinyer, 'Directors without direction', *Journal of General Management*, Vol. 1(2), pp37-48 (1974).

7.8   W. Brown, *The earnings conflict*, p46, Heinemann, (1973).

7.9   See *A study of the UK nationalised industries: their role in the economy and control in the future*, HMSO (1976).

8.1   J. H. Carter, 'Military leadership', *Military Review*, Vol. 32, pp14-18 (1952).

8.2   R. Blauner, *Alienation and freedom*, pp15-23, University of Chicago Press (1964).

8.3   See, for instance, E. E. Lawler and L. W. Porter, 'Perceptions
regarding management compensation', *Industrial Relations,* pp 41-9 (October 1963).

8.4   L. Martin, 'What happened at NCR after the boss declared martial law', *Fortune,* p103 (September 1975).

9.1   Saul Gellerman, 'Supervision : substance and style', *Harvard Business Review,* p97-8 (March-April 1976).

9.2   Antony Jay, *Management and Machiavelli,* p215, Holt, Rinehart and Winston (1968).

10.1   For a full account of the method, see C. Riviere, (The six winners of the PA-Vision management awards', *Vision,* p53 (September 1975).

10.2   John Hacket, 'Ideas for action', *Harvard Business Review,* pp6-7 (January-February 1974).

11.1   R. F. Bales, 'In conference', *ibid.,* p44 (March-April 1954).

11.2   Richard Neustadt, *Presidential power,* p157, John Wiley (1960).

11.3   Richard Nixon, *Six Crises,* p140, W. H. Allen (1962).

Index

As far as possible business people are identified by a reference to the firm they are or have been connected with. The firms themselves are shown by the symbol (f) after the name. Other names give first names or initials — or in a few cases a year — where these are known, and these people together with names where no identification has been possible can generally be taken to be expert researchers. Where the page reference is followed by figures in square brackets the user should look for this on the page concerned and not the name which can be ascertained by reference to pp 223-7.